MAKING KIWIS

GREATEST HITS

of 20th Century New Zealand History

Graeme Ball

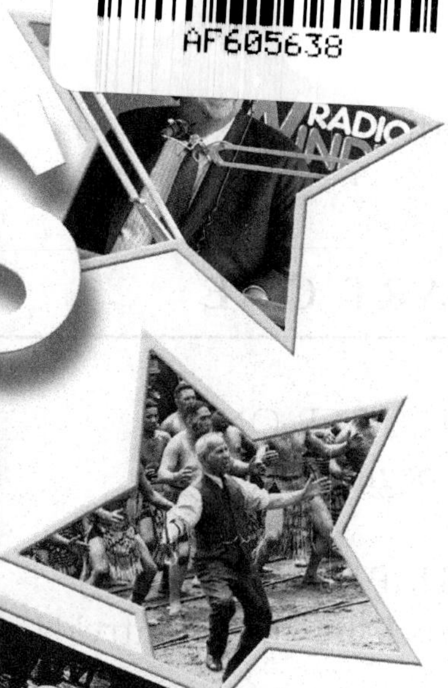

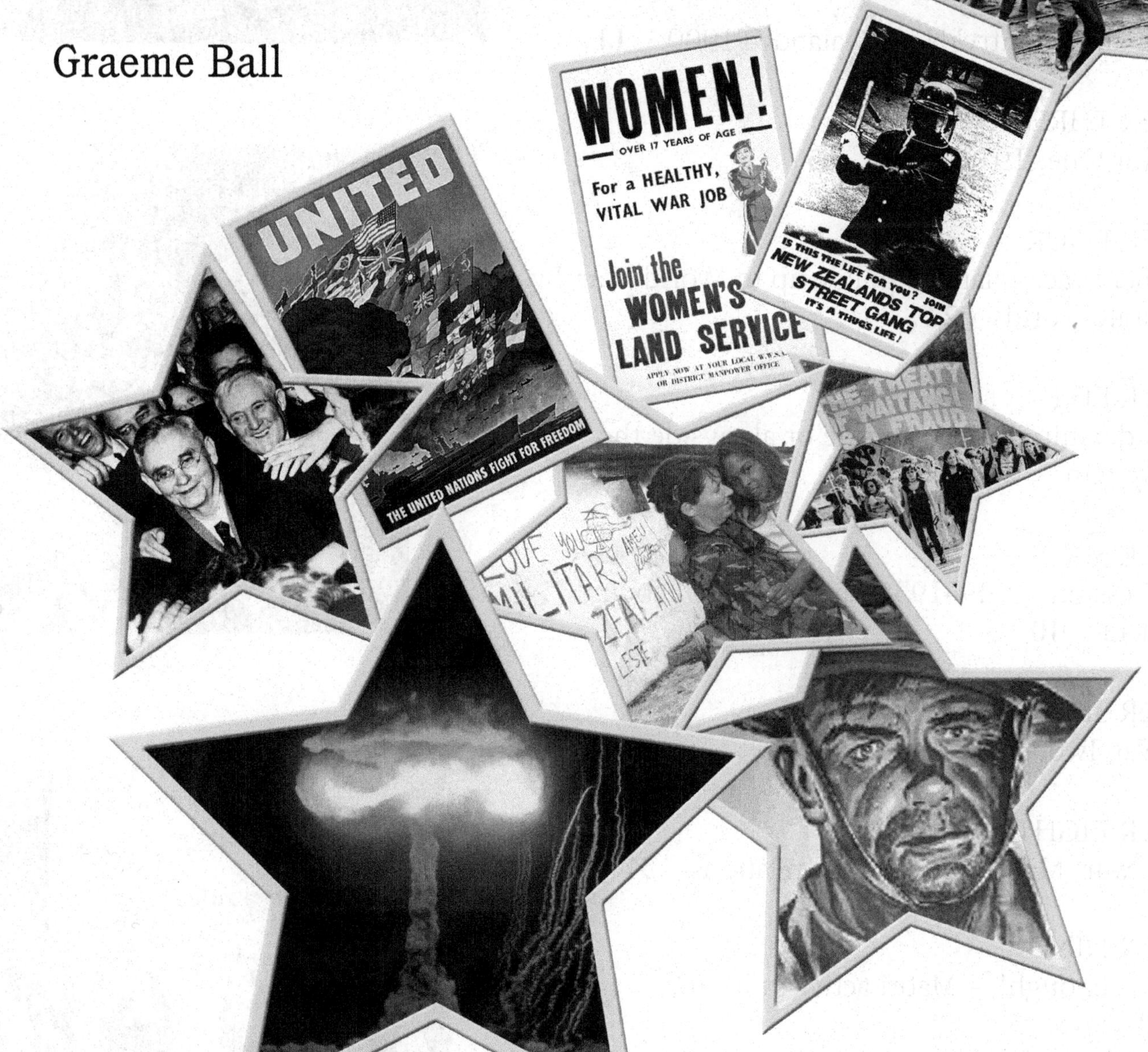

NELSON CENGAGE Learning

Australia • Brazil • Japan • Korea • Mexico • Singapore • Spain • United Kingdom • United States

CONTENTS

PART TWO

OUR COUNTRY
WEAPONS FREE

TODAY WITH
RADIO WINDY 890
THE BEST”
RADIO

CHEW THESE FOODS
for CLEAN TEETH
WOMEN!
OVER 17 YEARS OF AGE
For a HEALTHY, VITAL WAR JOB
Join the WOMEN'S LAND SERVICE
APPLY NOW AT YOUR LOCAL W.W.S.A. OR DISTRICT MANPOWER OFFICE
THE FUN OF THE FAIR

INTRODUCTORY NOTES

This textbook is intended for those schools that may have decided to drop AS1.6 (the shaping of New Zealand identity), but would still like to do a meaningful study of New Zealand in the 20th century. For this purpose, the most important parts of the following themes have been used, in an effort to give an overview of some of the most significant developments. In some cases the text has gone beyond the outdated prescription (as it stood at the time of writing).

- Maori–Pakeha Race Relations (1900–2000)
- New Zealand Search for Security (1945–2000)
- The Place of Te Tiriti o Waitangi in New Zealand Society (Waitangi Tribunal)
- Effect of Population Movement on Maori Society (urbanisation)
- Social Welfare (The Depression; 'Rogernomics' and 'Ruthenasia')
- Social Change: the role of women (1900–2000)

IDEAS FOR USING THIS TEXT

This is a large textbook for a Year 11 class. It has attempted to strike a balance between depth and breadth, without unduly sacrificing either. The teacher can approach the material here in several ways:

1 Devote enough time to a New Zealand unit to cover the whole book in class time.
2 Select only the parts most relevant to the chosen course, and use the remaining sections as 'Extension Reading' for the more able.
3 Select core parts that the class will do together. Identify other parts that can be done as seminars by groups.

Because of these options, there has been no effort made to differentiate the text (the other two texts in this series have some parts identified as 'Extension Reading').

ASSESSMENT

Using any of the above approaches, the internal component of the Year 11 course can be based on this book. Focusing questions for AS1.1 could be derived from the AS1.4 and AS1.5 practice tasks at the end of each section, or from the New House website. (Exemplars for AS1.1/AS1.2 are available on the TKI website.)

ACHIEVEMENT STANDARDS – SKILLS

This book has been written to mesh in with the requirements of Achievement Standards as far as possible. As well as general activities, other activities have been written to reflect the skill requirements of most of the Achievement Standards, whether Internal or External. Some of the AS1.3 (interpretation of historical resources) activities are contextualised with regard to this topic, but the skills are the same.

AS1.1
- Select relevant evidence.

AS1.2
- Identify relevant key ideas and support each with a piece of evidence.

AS1.3
- Identify historical facts, ideas, and points of view. Make judgements about the usefulness/reliability of evidence. Identify simple relationships such as cause and effect, specific and general, continuity and change. Distinguish fact from opinion; recognise bias and propaganda; be aware of the limitations of basing views on a single piece of evidence.

AS1.4
- Describe and explain perspectives and related actions of people in an historical setting.

AS1.5
- Describe the causes/course/consequences of an historical development. On the inside back cover instructions are given on how to plan and write an essay. Each section has one or two AS1.5 style essay questions (with some content guidance).

AS1.6
- Although this text has been written specifically for those schools that are not doing AS1.6, the issue of New Zealand identity is an important one. At appropriate points in the text, the preceding events are analysed in terms of their impact on the shaping of New Zealand identity.

HYPERLINKS

Words in the text that appear like this are hyperlinked to websites. To access these, students and teachers need only log onto New House's website (www.newhouse.co.nz). Once in, click onto the site for this textbook. The hyperlinked words will appear in the same order as they are in the text, with reference page numbers and a brief explanation of the link.

DICTIONARY OF NEW ZEALAND BIOGRAPHY

The Dictionary of New Zealand Biography is a great on-line source suited to more able students. Biographies and images of all the main figures (unless still alive in the 1990s) can be found at this site.

MIND-MAPPING

It is worth spending a lesson on teaching students how to create effective mind-maps. For a practice one, do something simple like characters in their favourite TV programme (*The Simpsons* is an 'oldie but a goody'). For other information on how to do mind mapping, see *Top Tools for Social Sciences Teachers*, p.44.

In brief, each main idea is represented by a different-coloured thick branch. The branches spread out from a strong central image that represents the sub-topic. Each branch has a number of twigs which represent supporting detail/evidence. Use CAPITALS for each of the 2–3 key words in each branch. Each twig should have 2–3 key words, plus a pictorial.

REVIEW OF DATES ...

Students sometimes get confused about dates. The ones we will be talking about mostly are in the 19th and 20th centuries. (Quibble, if you will, over the start dates for new centuries!)

- 19th century = 1800–1899
- 20th century = 1900–1999

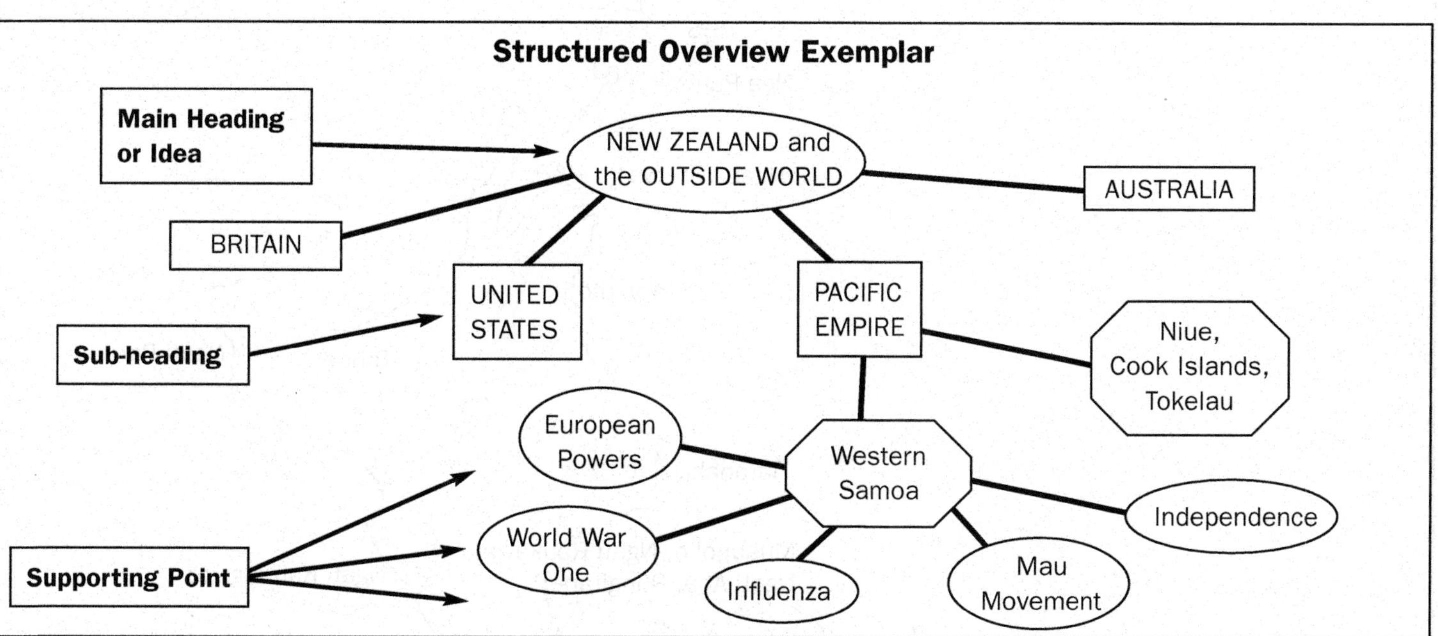

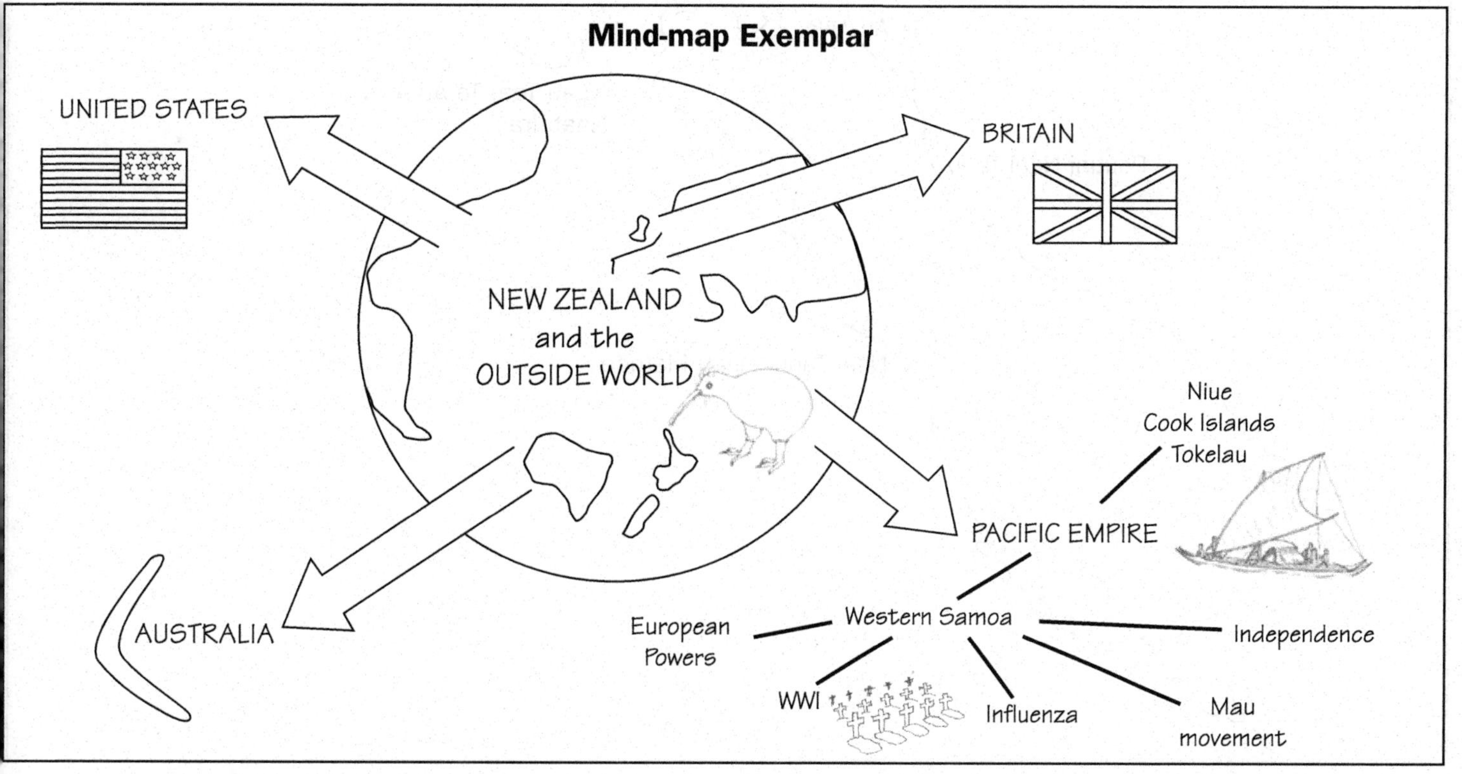

PART ONE

CHAPTER ONE

IT BEGINS ...

The Early Polynesian ancestors of the Maori people are believed to have discovered and begun settling New Zealand from somewhere between 800 and 1250AD. In 1642 the Dutch explorer Abel Tasman was the first known European to sight New Zealand. By this time Maori had settled most of New Zealand and tribal boundaries were beginning to be established. The main settlements and population were in the North Island.

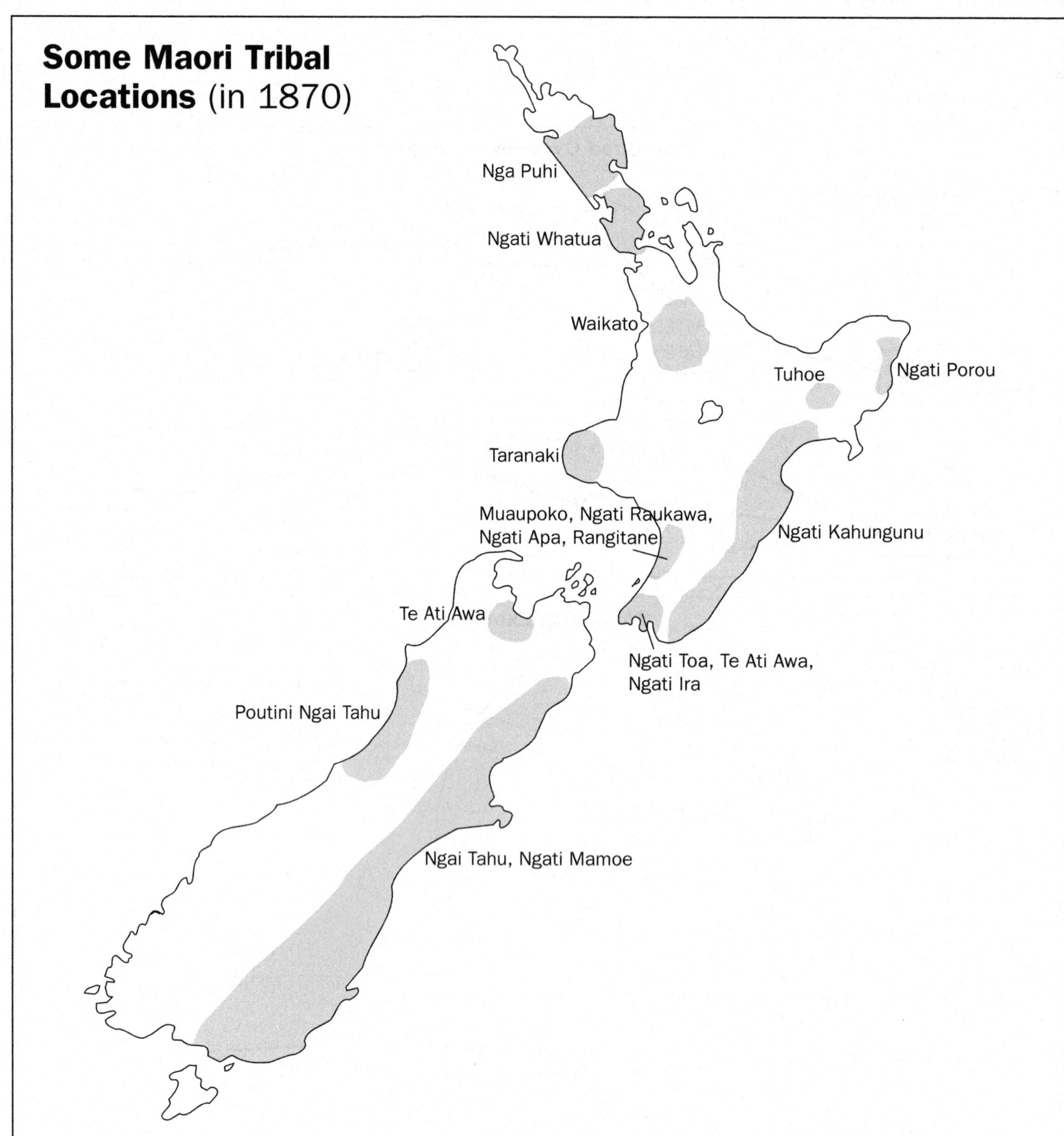

The next European explorer known to have reached New Zealand was the Englishman, Captain James Cook, in 1769 aboard the *Endeavour*. Cook and others like him were part of a continuing process of European exploration and expansion into the little-known world of the Pacific. Cook's reports on his discoveries were published upon his return to England. This attracted the next group of Europeans to New Zealand. These people were intent on harvesting the natural resources that Cook had described, such as flax, whales, seals and timber. The Maori people were willing to help do this, for they received benefits too. These benefits were European trading goods, such as axes, nails, spades, blankets, and muskets.

Captain James Cook (1728–1779). Cook and others like him were part of a continuing process of European exploration and expansion into the little-known world of the Pacific.

MAORI ADAPTS TO PAKEHA

When any two cultures meet for the first time there are several ways in which they can interact. Here are the main ones. All of these methods were tried by different Maori groups at some time in the 19th (and/or 20th) centuries.

Separation/Segregation People from each culture get on with their own lives without interacting at all. Little or no exchange of ideas, trade goods, or ways of living takes place.
Integration The two cultures intermingle, each sampling the other's ways, taking on some aspects that they like. With enough time, the two cultures *could* intermingle so much that they produce a single new culture.
Assimilation One culture is taken over and completely absorbed by another more dominant culture. Little or nothing is left of the absorbed culture's original ways.
Confrontation Interaction of any sort breaks down or one culture resists change caused by another. This may or may not be violent.

ACTIVITIES

- Use a full page. Divide it into four boxes.
- In the boxes put one of the headings ('Separation/Segregation', 'Integration' and so on). Put at the top the title "Ways Maori and Pakeha Could Have Responded To Each Other".
- Draw a pictorial that sums up the key idea about each form of interaction.

ACTIVITIES

1 Use the map on page 6 as a guide only to draw a full-page *free-hand* sketch of New Zealand. Locate and label the following places:

- Whangarei
- Auckland
- Wellington
- Christchurch
- Dunedin
- Hamilton
- Stewart Island
- New Plymouth
- Wanganui
- Hawke Bay
- Gisborne
- Napier
- Bay of Plenty
- Lake Taupo
- Waikato River
- Southern Alps

2 Trace the map of tribal areas on page 6. Shade in and label any further iwi/hapu locations that are of importance to you and/or your local area.

3 **Extension**
Again, using the map on page 6 as a guide only, draw another full-page *free-hand* sketch of New Zealand.

a Use an atlas and the information below to locate and label the main places where Captain James Cook landed in NZ during his first exploration here in 1769–70.

b Draw lines around the coast between the places to show Cook's path and direction of travel.

- Poverty Bay: 6th–11th October, 1769
- Tolaga Bay: 23rd–29th October, 1769
- Mercury Bay: 3rd–15th November, 1769
- Hauraki Gulf: 19th–21st November, 1769
- Bay of Islands: 29th Nov–5th Dec, 1769 (then south back down the East Coast to …)
- Queen Charlotte Sound, 15th Jan –31st March 1770.

Cook returned to New Zealand twice more, in 1773 and 1777. He was killed by natives in Hawaii in 1779.

THE TREATY OF WAITANGI

As Europeans arrived from the late 1700s on, Maori and Pakeha generally got on well, because both peoples were very keen to trade. Violence would have interrupted trade, so was not very common. However, as the number of Europeans grew, crimes and other problems between Maori and Pakeha increased. From Britain's point of view, the main concern was a need to legally extend its law to cover the Pakeha trouble-makers. Britain definitely did NOT want to make New Zealand part of its Empire. This was because colonies were always expensive to run. It felt, however, that it had to step in and control the Europeans. Maori did not want to solve disputes with Europeans by force, even though they certainly could have. There were about 100,000 Maori in 1840, many of them battle-trained and musket-armed. There were only about 2000 Pakeha, spread around the country. Many Maori were willing to see Britain extend its power into New Zealand to govern its own people.

On February 6th, 1840, a Treaty (legal contract) was signed by those assembled at Waitangi. Governor Hobson represented the British Crown (government). About 45 Maori chiefs were present on that day to sign. Throughout the following months copies of this Treaty were taken around the country and many other chiefs also signed. Some significant tribes, however, refused to. So, what was the Treaty all about?

The Articles of the Treaty: the '3Ps'

There are three parts, or Articles, in the Treaty of Waitangi and this, in a nutshell, is what they were about at the time:

Article 1: Power: who was to rule over New Zealand.

The English version clearly stated that Britain would be given sovereignty (the right to make the laws and enforce them). The Maori-language version stated that Maori would give Britain the right to 'govern' the country – probably understood by Maori as a sharing of power.

Article 2: Property: who owned what.

In both versions, Maori were guaranteed possession of their land and other treasures (the English version specifically mentioned forests and fisheries), unless they wished to sell them. Chiefs were also guaranteed that they would not lose control over their lands and other possessions.

Article 3: People: rights.

In both versions Maori were guaranteed the same rights as British citizens.

ACTIVITIES

1 What feature of Maori-Pakeha relations before 1840 (and beyond) led to a relatively peaceful interaction?

2 Explain why both Britain and some Maori were willing to enter into a Treaty together.

3 You have been asked to produce a pictorial representation of the Treaty of Waitangi for use in Intermediate schools. Divide a full page up into four boxes (two for Article One). Use only a few key words in each box.

Refer to Source A

4 What country is represented by the flag draped across the table?

5 Identify two features each that show both Maori and Pakeha cultures.

6 Explain why the historian would be very careful about using this Source.

A modern reconstruction (1938) of the signing of the Treaty of Waitangi, showing Tamati Waka Nene signing the Treaty in front of James Busby, Captain William Hobson, and other British officials and witnesses. Some Maori signatories are assembled on left.

"WHO'S THE BOSS?": THE NEW ZEALAND WARS, 1845–1872

Both the British and Maori had different understandings of what the 1840 Treaty said. Put simply, both sides had gone away after the signing thinking that they had authority in New Zealand. At first this did not cause major problems. Maori got on with their own lives as they always had. Although the British believed that they were in charge, there were too few to really assert their authority. However, as more and more settlers arrived and their demands for access to Maori-owned land grew, tension increased. The New Zealand Wars thus broke out over two main issues: LAW (who would make it) and LAND (who would own it).

Northern Wars, 1845

When the Nga Puhi chief Hone Heke cut down the British flagpole at Kororareka (Russell, Bay of Islands) for the fourth time in 1845, war broke out. Heke was angry because the benefits he believed the Treaty would bring were not appearing. After several battles a peace deal was negotiated.

The Taranaki and Waikato Wars (1860–64)

By the late 1850s the government had acquired an enormous amount of Maori-owned land, by various means. For the most part this was by legal but sometimes unscrupulous ('dodgy') methods. Much of the South Island had been purchased. There were, however, still large areas of the North Island (where most Maori lived) still in Maori hands. Some tribes, based around the Waikato, were increasingly alarmed by the rapid loss of land. They decided in 1858 to set up their own Maori King – the Kingitanga or King Movement. This was so that they could rule over themselves and stop the selling of their lands. The government saw the Kingitanga as a rebellious movement and as a challenge to its own authority.

War broke out in Taranaki in 1860 over a disputed land sale. Neither side achieved a clear advantage in the fighting,

Above

Hone Heke (centre), with his wife Harriet and ally Kawiti.

SOURCE D

Above right

Taranaki 1863. Fighting here broke out briefly in 1863, but it sparked an even greater conflict in the Waikato. In all, some 18000 British and local troops (including many Maori) fought against a peak of about 4000 Kingitanga supporters.

SOURCE C

The attack on Hone Heke's Pa, Okaihau, 1845. The painting was by Lance-Sergeant John Williams.

BEING 'MAORI'

Pakeha referred to the native people of New Zealand collectively as Maori. The fact was that 'Maori' thought of themselves not as one people, but as individual tribes. This was much the same way as Europeans of the time thought of themselves as French, or German or Spanish and so on. There certainly had been dramatic changes to the lifestyles of the various tribes in New Zealand that made working together more necessary, however tribalism – complete with its rivalries – was still strong. It would remain so at least up until World War Two. Thereafter, tribalism became much less important for those Maori who made their way to the cities – or were born there. For many of those who remained in the countryside, tribalism remained an important part of identity.

and it ended in a negotiated settlement. The government then set out to break the power of the Kingitanga. It brought in British troops and had a total of up to 18,000 soldiers to take on a maximum of about 4000 Maori warriors. Some tribes that were traditional rivals of Waikato, such as Nga Puhi and Te Arawa, also fought with the government troops. They were called kupapa or 'friendlies' by the government. The main battles in the central North Island were over by 1864. The Waikato Maori and their allies were defeated. A few smaller-scale but significant battles continued up until 1872.

In terms of the relative population size, the invasion of the Waikato by British and other troops in the 1860s would be the equivalent of an army of about one million invading New Zealand today.

After the Wars: the Law is Mightier than the Sword

In 1863, the government passed laws confiscating millions of hectares of 'rebel' land. Further laws were passed that made it even more difficult for Maori anywhere to resist pressure to sell their land. By the end of the 1800s, Maori land holdings were down to a little over three million hectares. They had owned all of New Zealand's 26.4 million hectares at the start of the 1800s. To make matters worse, the Maori population had fallen dramatically. At the same time there was a dramatic increase in the number of settlers arriving in New Zealand.

After the Wars settlers wanted more land to clear for new farms.

ACTIVITIES

1 Use the information and dates on pages 8–10 to create a timeline. Begin in 1840 and end in 1900. Go up in increments of ten years on the horizontal axis. Don't forget a heading!

2 How accurate is it to call the wars in New Zealand the 'Maori-Pakeha Wars'? Explain your answer.

3 Refer to Source B, page 9. What evidence is there of a European influence in this picture?

4 Refer to Sources C and D, page 9. Explain how useful these are to the historian and indicate what limitations they may have.

CHAPTER TWO

'FOR KING AND COUNTRY': NEW ZEALAND @ 1900

In 1840 New Zealand was still very much a Maori country. There were an estimated 100,000 Maori and only about 2000 Pakeha. Within 60 years, however, New Zealand had been transformed into a mostly Pakeha country. By 1900 there were about one million people, many of them of British origin. The Maori population was slowly recovering from a low of about 42,000. For most of the new arrivals in New Zealand during the 19th century, Britain was still thought of as 'Home'. For this reason, many new New Zealanders felt intensely loyal towards the place of their birth (or their parents' birth). Some even believed that, in the years to come, New Zealand would become even greater than the 'Mother Country', Britain. Some commentators predicted that the New Zealand population would eventually grow to 40–50 million people.

New Zealand had adopted British customs, beliefs, education, and political and legal systems, as well as British values. New Zealanders were prepared to defend these values, anywhere that Britain's Empire came under threat. An example of this was New Zealand's participation in Britain's war against the Boers in South Africa. When the South African War broke out in 1899, New Zealand was the first colony to offer to send troops. Few questioned whether the war was right or wrong. To question Britain was to be disloyal. Furthermore, New Zealanders could not believe that the Boers were fighting to be free of Britain's Empire. To New Zealanders, Britain ruled the 'greatest and most benevolent [caring] empire the world has ever known.'

A key element to this close relationship with Britain was the economic dependence of New Zealand on the 'Mother Country'. This had come about through a major technological development in the 1880s: refrigerated shipping. This new technology shaped the course of New Zealand's history for the next 100 years. In 1882, the first shipment of frozen meat left New Zealand, bound for Britain. This marked the beginning of an explosive growth in the New Zealand economy. By the early 20th century virtually the whole of New Zealand's export economy depended upon the sale of its farm produce to Britain alone.

One effect of this was that Pakeha settlers demanded more land. This land would have to come from Maori. Another significant effect of the boom was a further strengthening and tightening of the bond many New Zealanders felt towards Britain. It became important to be very loyal to Britain, so that it would continue to take New Zealand's exports, rather than those of the many competitors. Loyalty to Britain was thus reinforced as a feature of New Zealand's culture.

New Zealand soldiers with a Cohorn mortar, near Ladysmith, Natal, South Africa.

SOURCE B

Frozen New Zealand meat on sale in London, around 1900.

Britain

In many Pakeha New Zealanders' eyes, Britain almost *was* the world. In January 1901 Queen Victoria announced that her grandson, Prince George Duke of Cornwall, was to tour New Zealand later that year. This caused tremendous excitement. When Queen Victoria died shortly after this announcement, New Zealand went into mourning. The sadness, however, was offset by the anticipation of the coming Royal Tour. The towns and cities on the Royal route went wild, each attempting to outdo the others in their expressions of patriotism. British flags and the colours red, white and blue appeared everywhere.

Victoria, Queen of Britain and its Empire (including New Zealand) 1837–1901.

Many Maori were also involved. Five thousand gathered at Rotorua to welcome the Royal couple. This was the largest hui in living memory at that time. Even the Waikato tribes were prepared to put aside their grievances resulting from the land confiscations of the New Zealand Wars. However, when it became known that the Royal couple would not attend a welcome in the Waikato, the Maori King Mahuta refused to go to Rotorua. He believed that he should have the opportunity to welcome the Royal couple onto his own territory.

ACTIVITIES

1 For each statement below, find an appropriate piece of supporting evidence from the text on page 11. Evidence may be a quote, statistic or fact.

- **a** By 1900 Pakeha well outnumbered Maori.
- **b** Immigrants to New Zealand transplanted many of their ways of living from their home country.
- **c** Pakeha New Zealanders were very loyal to Britain.
- **d** Technological developments had a significant impact upon New Zealand.
- **e** Technological developments had a significant impact upon Maori.
- **f** New Zealand's close relationship with Britain was also based on self-interest.

Refer to Sources A and B (page 11)

2 What image of New Zealanders is portrayed in Source A? Provide evidence to support your answer.

3 What feature of this photograph would make the historian cautious about using it to learn more about actual fighting conditions during the Boer War?

4 What key idea from the text does Source B support?

5 How might the activity shown in Source A have contributed to the event shown in Source B?

6 Are these primary or secondary sources? Explain your answer.

A visit of a different sort from the 'Mother Country' also captured the imagination of New Zealanders. In 1910 Field Marshall Lord Kitchener, the British Army's commander, arrived. He had come to advise the government on the country's defences. Kitchener recommended that New Zealand form its own army, and this was duly done. As part of this process, New Zealand introduced conscription. Along with Australia, New Zealand thus became the first country to introduce conscription in times of peace. Kitchener visited again in 1911 and was pleased with the progress that had been made. However, despite this apparent progress, when World War One (WWI) broke out in 1914, two-thirds of the recruits did not make the Army's top fitness grade.

> **Conscription**
> The compulsory call-up of men to join the Army.

Most New Zealanders believed that Britain and its Navy would save New Zealand from any threat. To ensure that Britain saw it this way too, the government decided to give Britain a 'present'. A year before Kitchener's visit, Prime Minister Joseph Ward announced the donation to Britain of a £2million warship. It was to be called HMS *New Zealand* and would be built in Britain. This action met with general approval. It showed that New Zealand was making a contribution to its own defence. When the completed vessel visited New Zealand in 1913, patriotic crowds swarmed over its decks.

G. R.

MILITARY TRAINING.

DOMINION OF NEW ZEALAND.

NOTICE AS TO MILITARY TRAINING.

NOTICE IS HEREBY GIVEN that every male inhabitant of New Zealand who, on the 1st day of March, 1911, had attained the age of fourteen years or upwards, but had not attained the age of twenty-one years, and who is a British subject and has resided in New Zealand for at least six months, IS HEREBY REQUIRED before 7 p.m. on the 2nd day of June, 1911, to fill in a prescribed form of registration in respect of military training under the Defence Acts, and to post or deliver the same to the Area Sergeant-Major of the territorial area in which the applicant for registration resides.

Forms of registration may be obtained at any Post Office or Police Station. No postage is required where the form is posted as aforesaid.

Any person to whom this notice applies who fails to take any step necessary to secure his registration as aforesaid is liable to a fine of FIVE POUNDS, and shall not be eligible for employment in any branch of the Government Service.

Dated at Wellington, this 10th day of April, 1911.

GEO. FOWLDS,
Acting Minister of Defence.

United States of America

Britain was not the only country to send its military here. In 1908, Aucklanders welcomed with great enthusiasm the visit of 16 warships of the American Pacific fleet. The ships were painted white and this gave rise to the name the 'Great White Fleet'. Even though this visit was second in importance to any from Britain, it was a *close* second. King Mahuta, commanding the historic *Taheretikitiki* canoe, was amongst those who welcomed the warships. Many saw the fleet as a display of European power, directed as a quiet warning to a rising Japan and to the 'hordes' of China – the so-called 'Yellow Peril'.

Pacific 'Empire'

New Zealand's interests were not only focused on looking up to Britain (or the United States). Under 'King Dick' Seddon, New Zealand wanted its own Pacific Empire. Seddon was Premier (similar to Prime Minister) from 1893 to 1906. He had long argued that New Zealand should expand into the Pacific. In 1901, Britain finally agreed to place the Cook Islands and Niue under New Zealand's control. Like other politicians before him, Seddon wanted more. Calls had already been made for Norfolk Island, Samoa, Fiji, and the Society Islands to become part of New Zealand's Pacific Empire. Seddon had even suggested to the U.S. President that New Zealand should take over Hawaii. In 1923, Britain granted control of the Ross Dependency in Antarctica to New Zealand. In 1925, Tokelau also came under New Zealand control.

Western Samoa

New Zealand had a chance to prove itself as a Pacific Power during and after World War One. The Western Samoa story starts in 1899. In that year tension between Britain, the United States and Germany had very nearly boiled over into war. The conflict arose over which European Power would control the islands of Samoa. An agreement was eventually reached whereby the United States was granted eastern Samoa (which was then renamed American Samoa) and Germany controlled Western Samoa. The Samoan people had no say in the matter. Premier Seddon was outraged. He believed that Britain had abandoned New Zealand's interests in the Pacific to a 'foreign' Power. New Zealand wanted Samoa – preferably all of it.

Revenge came in 1914 with the outbreak of World War One. New Zealand troops were sent to capture Western Samoa. This was the first 'enemy' territory taken in the war. The small German garrison surrendered without a shot being fired. New Zealand then governed Western Samoa, first as an occupying force during the war, then as a League of Nations Mandate.

New Zealand's record in Western Samoa up to World War Two (WWII) was not good. The army administrators appointed to rule had little experience in governing. They had even less experience in governing peoples from another culture. Despite this, there was a belief that New Zealand leaders knew the most about governing 'Natives'.

There were two substantial setbacks in New Zealand's relationship with the Samoan people. The first major calamity happened at the end of WWI. Officials allowed a passenger ship to dock at Apia without the usual procedures of checking for disease. Due to this mistake, an outbreak of the 'flu rapidly spread. Almost a quarter of Western Samoa's population died. The death rate of nearly 230 for every 1000 people was one of the highest in the world. Assistance was offered by officials in American Samoa but was rejected by the New Zealand administrators. Samoans in the west were angered by this seeming lack of concern for their welfare. During the 1920s tension grew further. A Samoan opposition movement – the *Mau* – was formed and began to resist the orders issued by the administrators. Things came to a head on 'Black Saturday', December 28th 1929. Eleven Mau supporters were shot dead by New Zealand police during a protest march. Other Mau members fled into the bush. A New Zealand air force plane was called in to assist the police in tracking them down. The Mau was declared to be an illegal movement.

The Mau, however, remained strong. Women now took the leading role in passively resisting what were seen as unjust policies. When the Labour government came to power in 1935 the proclamation that had declared the Mau an unlawful organisation was cancelled. The first real steps towards independence for Western Samoa were taken in 1947 with the passing of the Samoa Amendment Act. Full independence came in 1962.

Australia

Relations with New Zealand's closest neighbour, Australia, became less important in the 20th century than they had been in the 19th. In earlier years, New Zealand, New South Wales and the state of Victoria were called the 'Big Three' of Australasia. However, by the 20th century Australia had become more of a competitor than a partner. This was because its farmers also exported their products to Britain. New Zealand had been invited to become part of Australia in 1901, but rejected the offer. Relations between New Zealand and Australia became closer during and after WWII. In 1944 the two countries signed the Canberra pact, in which defence and Pacific matters were addressed. For New Zealand, this was the first security agreement that it had signed by itself with another country. In 1966, the NZ-Australia Free Trade Agreement came into effect. This brought the two countries together economically. In 1982 another trade agreement called Closer Economic Relations (CER) was signed. Both countries also worked closely on defence arrangements with the United States and Britain up until the 1980s. In 1999 the two ANZAC countries again worked together in a peacekeeping mission in East Timor.

Mau prisoners being taken away. With the men arrested, women took over leadership roles in the Mau.

ACTIVITIES

1 Which country was most important to New Zealand in 1900? (You may wish to look back further in the text.) Explain your answer.

2 Of the relationships with other countries described in this section, which ONE is different to all of the others? Explain your answer.

Refer to the text in this section

3 Use the title and headings from this section to create a mind-map OR structured overview diagram (see page 5) that shows the key points about New Zealand's relationship with the outside world @1900.

- For the mind-map you will need a strong central image that communicates the key idea about the relationship as a whole.
- Provide information on Britain, the United States, the Pacific, Western Samoa, and Australia. You will first need to identify 3–5 key ideas for each of these.

CHAPTER THREE

WORLD WAR ONE, 1914–1918

BACKGROUND

Tension between the main European powers had been growing since the late 19th century. In August 1914 this tension erupted into war. On one side were Britain and its Empire, plus France and Russia. These countries were known as the Allied forces. On the other side were Germany, Turkey and Austria-Hungary. They were called the Central Powers. Both sides believed that the war would be won quickly – that it would be 'over by Christmas'. Four years on it was finally grinding to an end after the loss of more than ten million lives. This was World War One (WWI) or, as it was known at the time, the Great War.

When Britain declared war on Germany on August 4th 1914, New Zealand was quick to offer its support. Many New Zealand men were enthusiastic to 'do their bit for King and Country' – over 70% of those who went to war signed up to go voluntarily. They unquestioningly shared the belief that Britain was right and Germany wrong. In addition, few New Zealanders had travelled overseas, so this was an opportunity for adventure. About 10% of New Zealand's total population of one million went away to fight. In terms of the number of men who were of fighting age (19-45 years) the figure is much higher – 42%, or more than four out of every ten men. To get an idea of just how big an effort this represented, an equivalent proportion of United States' men at that time would have produced an army of ten million.

Of the more than 100,000 New Zealanders who went to fight, nearly 17,000 were killed. A further 41,000 were wounded, making a total casualty rate of 58%. Nearly half the casualties occurred against the Germans between 1916 and 1918 on the Western Front in France. Over 500 women also served in the war as nurses. They were stationed at Western Samoa, Egypt, England and France. Eleven drowned when a hospital ship was torpedoed in 1915.

The issue of whether or not Maori should be required to fight in WWI caused some problems. At first the British government did not like the idea of 'coloured people' of any country fighting against and killing whites, even if they were German whites. This situation challenged the deeply-held racial views of the time. Some Maori leaders, however, demanded that Maori be allowed to prove their loyalty. As the battlefield losses grew, the New Zealand government finally agreed to Maori serving in combat roles. A Pioneer Battalion was formed in which 2227 Maori served, as well as some Cook Islanders and Niueans. Pioneer Battalion casualties were 336 killed and 734 wounded, a casualty rate of 48%. Maori fought exceedingly well and were said by the historian James Cowan to have 'proved superior to many of the white troops ...'

ACTIVITIES

Use a full page. Draw SEVEN rows of stick figures of people, each row having ten figures. Leave room (3–4 lines) between each row to add labels.

- On the first row draw in speech bubbles from seven of the figures saying something like "Me! Me! I'll go!"
- On the second row colour or shade one of the ten figures.
- On the third row colour or shade four (plus only the *feet* of a fifth).
- On the fourth row put big crosses (X) through one and a half figures and draw in crutches for four more figures.
- On the fifth row put big crosses through one and a half figures and draw in crutches for three more.
- Leave the sixth and seventh rows for now. They will be used later.

Now, refer to the three paragraphs of information on the number of New Zealanders who served and the number of casualties (including the Maori Battalion). Choose the appropriate label for each row from those given below. ONE is irrelevant – do not use it.

a Casualty rate (killed and wounded).

b Proportion of New Zealand's *total* population that went to fight.

c Maori Battalion casualty rate (killed and wounded).

d Proportion of women who served overseas.

e Proportion of soldiers who fought who had *volunteered*.

f Proportion of men of fighting age (19–45) who fought.

ACTIVITIES

Refer to Source A

Imagine that you are in the crowd seeing off the soldiers to WWI. You might be:

- Maori or Pakeha
- The wife, daughter or sister of someone going
- The son or brother of someone going

1 Write down what you can SEE, HEAR, SMELL, FEEL, and TASTE. Use your imagination; try to be realistic.

2 Write down also what emotions you are feeling (don't talk about modern views of war).

A typical scene as troops left New Zealand to join the fight.

OFF TO THE FIGHT

New Zealand's first active campaign was in August 1914 with the taking of Western Samoa. The Germans captured there were taken to Motuihe Island in the Hauraki Gulf in Auckland. They were imprisoned along with German and Austrian civilians who had been in New Zealand when the war broke out. The first New Zealand troops left for the European war in October 1914. They sailed to their headquarters in Alexandra in Egypt where they were joined by an Australian contingent. In February 1915, the New Zealanders saw their first action when they resisted an attack across the Suez Canal by Germany's ally, Turkey.

The ANZACs at Gallipoli

The next major engagement was in April 1915. The ANZACs (Australia, New Zealand Army Corp) were sent along with French, Indian and British troops to take the Turkish-controlled Gallipoli Peninsula. The Turks' coastal guns stationed on this peninsula prevented Allied vessels from passing through the narrow waterway called the Dardanelles. If the attack on Gallipoli was successful, it would remove this threat to shipping. It would also allow an attack on the Turkish capital of Constantinople (now called Istanbul). The objective of such an attack would be to knock the Turks out of the war. With the Turks out, more Allied pressure could be applied to Germany. That was the plan. It failed utterly.

The Gallipoli campaign began on April 25, 1915 with the landing of troops at ANZAC Cove. This was a day that New Zealanders and Australians would remember in the future as ANZAC Day. The Australians were first ashore, followed by the New Zealanders. (British and French troops landed at a different location.) Strong sea currents had swept the ANZACs' boats some two kilometres away from the intended landing place. Instead of a gently sloping beach the ANZACs faced steep cliffs. Atop those cliffs the Turks had an easy line of fire.

Landing at Anzac Cove, Gallipoli.

Evacuation of the wounded from ANZAC Cove in Gallipoli by boat.

Despite this, the Allies managed to make some headway. Both sides settled in to a cycle of attack and counter-attack from entrenched positions. Rats, flies, sickness, Turkish snipers and a lack of medicine, water and good food made life in the Allied trenches terrible. In a little over three weeks after the first troop landings, the casualties on both sides had risen dramatically. A one-day truce was called in May so that the bodies, rotting in the fierce heat, could be buried. At the end of that day the fighting started again.

Life in the trenches at Gallipoli.

In August 1915 New Zealand troops took the highest point, Chunuk Bair, after vicious fighting. In the distance they could see for the first time their goal, the guns that protected the waters of the Dardanelles. However, because of the chaos of the different battles going on at the time, no other troops were sent to reinforce the New Zealanders. They were eventually driven back by a Turkish counter-attack.

The Gallipoli campaign ended eight months after it began, having achieved nothing. Ironically, one of the most successful operations was the secret evacuation of Allied troops, with few casualties. In terms of its contribution to the war effort, the Gallipoli campaign has been called a 'sideshow' to the main struggle that was occurring on the Western Front. It was a costly 'sideshow'. Of the 8,556 New Zealanders who served in Gallipoli, 2721 died and 4752 were wounded, a total casualty rate of 87%. In other words, of every ten men who went to Gallipoli, nearly nine were killed or wounded. Almost 300 of the deaths were caused by disease.

ACTIVITIES

1. What was the goal of the Gallipoli campaign?
2. What was the first major problem faced by the ANZAC troops?
3. What was one of the 'successes' of the whole campaign?
4. Refer back to the activity on page 15. On the sixth row of figures put crosses (X) through three and crutches on six others. Add this caption: 'Casualty rate (killed and wounded) at Gallipoli'.

Refer to Sources B to D

5. What is the likely relationship between Sources B and C?
6. What key idea in the text about the ANZAC landing does Source B support?
7. What key idea in the text about the nature of the fighting at Gallipoli does Source D support?
8. What evidence is there in Source B that the Turks are in a position to fire down onto the ANZAC troops?
9. What do the photographs in Sources B to D show about the nature of the warfare at Gallipoli?

Refer to all of the sources and the text

10. You are a soldier or nurse at Gallipoli. Write a one-page letter OR create a postcard (half-page pictorial plus 6–8 lines of writing) to send home to your parents. Describe the conditions that you have experienced.

The Western Front

New Zealanders also fought against the Germans in northern France. In April 1916, the 20,000 strong New Zealand Division – now commanded by a New Zealander – arrived at the Western Front. The first major action occurred in July in the Battle of the **Somme**. This was one of the most disastrous Allied attacks on the German positions of the whole war. In 23 days of constant fighting 1560 New Zealanders were killed and 5440 were wounded.

Another major battle took place in June 1917 at **Messines**. This was more successful, with the NZ Division achieving its initial aims. New Zealanders also fought in another of the most significant battles in October 1917, at a place called **Ypres**. In April 1918 New Zealand troops came under their worst artillery bombardment of the war as they struggled to stop a major German breakthrough near **Amiens**. In August 1918 New Zealanders helped capture **Bapaume**. After this time German troops were in a continual fighting retreat.

Bernard Freyberg commanded a British Brigade. Here he describes an attack against the well-defended German 'Hindenburg Line' in 1917. (Freyberg was in command of the New Zealand troops during WWII.)

"During the fighting, attacking companies waded knee-deep, and often up to their waists in mud before gaining their objectives, while, in many cases, whole waves [of men] disappeared, or were held captive in the mud within speaking distance of the British line, until they either died from exposure or were blown to pieces by artillery fire. It was a most wicked battle and the night after the attack, men with ladders and ropes worked away in the most appalling danger, trying to save those who were bogged. [During advances] ... packhorses carried forward eight rounds [of artillery ammunition] at a time, and the slaughter of these animals ... threatened to cause a horse shortage."

In the Battle of the Somme New Zealand soldiers each carried:

- two gas masks
- a rifle with bayonet
- 200 bullets
- two bombs
- two empty sandbags (to build defences)
- a waterproof sheet
- water bottle and pack, containing rations for one day.

Every second man would also carry a shovel or pick for digging trenches, and between the platoon (about ten men) would be carried extra smoke bombs and flares.

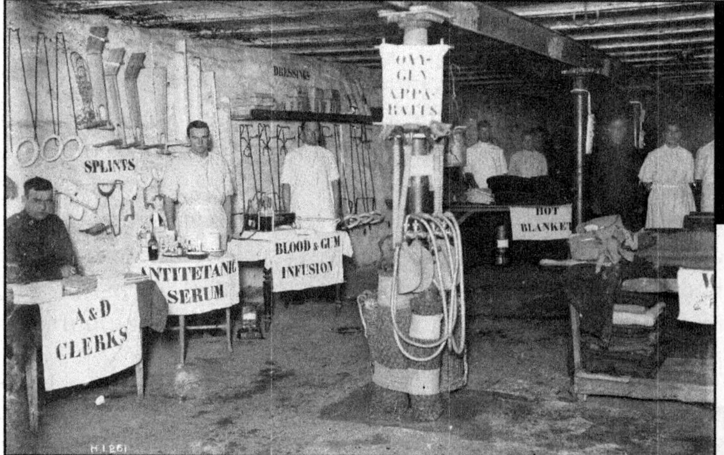

A typical WWI field hospital.

SOURCE E

A typical battlefield on the Western Front.

The last major battle for New Zealand troops was the capture of **Le Quesnoy** in early November 1918. Recognising that the war was lost, the Germans agreed to an armistice (cease-fire). This came into effect on November 11th 1918 at 11am – "the eleventh hour of the eleventh day of the eleventh month" of 1918. New Zealanders were then stationed in the German city of **Cologne** for several months as part of the Allied Army of Occupation.

Accurate casualty figures are difficult to find. It seems that of the 58,000 who served on the Western Front, nearly 12,500 men were killed and 34,000 wounded.

Middle East – Sinai and Palestine*

ANZAC troops also fought in the Middle East. The New Zealand Mounted Rifles (NZMR) did deep patrols into the Turkish-controlled **Sinai Desert** for two and a half years from 1916. A successful battle in July 1916 at **Romani** against a Turkish force of 18,000 prevented the Turks from capturing the **Suez Canal**. If this attack had been successful it would

**Modern-day Israel and Jordan cover much of the territory of Palestine.*

have allowed the Turks to take the whole of Egypt. Control of the Suez Canal would have severely limited Allied shipping.

In early 1917 ANZAC troops pushed across the Egyptian-Turkish border at **Rafah**. From there they eventually defeated the Turkish force, thus capturing the last Turkish-controlled part of the Sinai. **Gaza** fell after heavy fighting in March 1917. The coastal town of **Jaffa** surrendered to the New Zealanders in November 1917. **Jerusalem**, **Bethlehem** and **Jericho** quickly followed. In March 1918 New Zealand troops crossed the **River Jordan** and in September took **Amman**. The Turks surrendered on October 31st 1918; Palestine had fallen.

Of the nearly 18,000 who served in Palestine 640 were killed and 1146 wounded.

SOURCE H

A camel convoy is loaded with frozen mutton in Palestine (1917) for transport to the front line.

ACTIVITIES

1 On maps of France and the Middle East show as many of the places as you can where New Zealanders fought overseas in WWI. Include the place name, date and a brief description of the battle or significant place.

2 Refer back to the activity on page 15. On the seventh row put crosses through two figures and draw crutches on six more. Add this caption: 'Casualty rate (killed and wounded) on the Western Front'.

Refer to Sources E–H

3 Describe the technology shown in Sources E and H. What might be the advantages and disadvantages of each?

4 What is the likely link between Source E and Source G?

5 Make TWO links between Source E and Source F.

6 From Source F, provide a quote of no more than three words that is an opinion.

7 What key idea about war do Sources E and G provide evidence for?

8 What is ONE limitation of Source G for the historian who wants to know about battlefield medical treatment?

Refer to Source I

9 Which country spent most on the war?

10 How much did the Central Powers (refer to the start of this chapter) spend on the war?

11 Which country sent the most troops to war?

12 Why must the historian be careful when using the figure for the number of troops that Britain sent to war?

13 Compare and comment on the figures shown here for New Zealand and Belgium. (The Western Front was partially on Belgian territory.)

14 Which country had the lowest death rate (compared to the number of troops sent)?

15 What ONE other statistic would an historian want to see in order to understand the level of contribution made by each country?

SOURCE I

World War One Statistics

The Cost of the War

Country	US$ millions	Men Sent to War	Deaths
Australia	1,423	300,000	59,330
Austria-Hungary	20,623	7,800,000	1,200,000
Belgium	1,154	267,000	13,716
Britain	35,334	8,904,467*	750,000
France	24,266	8,410,000	1,357,800
Germany	37,775	11,000,000	1,773,700
New Zealand	379	100,000	17,000
Russia	22,294	12,000,000	1,700,000
Turkey	1,430	2,850,000	325,000
United States	22,625	4,355,000	126,000

*This figure includes *all* of the British Empire

PROFILE

Ettie Rout

Not all of the fighting in WWI was against enemy soldiers. Ettie Rout (in the middle of the photo without a hat) was a nurse during the war, although not the usual sort. She was a woman who, in her own words, was 'born too soon'. By this she meant that her ideas and actions were too radical for the times. 'Respectable' people at the time did not talk openly about sex. Even fewer wanted to admit that New Zealand's fighting men would even think of visiting prostitutes. Ettie Rout, however, believed that soldiers *would* visit prostitutes. She understood that peacetime moral values did not always apply during the stresses of war.

In 1916 Rout travelled to Egypt. Once there she criticised the Army's Medical Corps for refusing to acknowledge and deal with the problem of sexually transmitted diseases. She also argued that the Army should provide hygienic brothels for the men to visit. Rout took up the same issues with leaders in London, but with little success. Because no one else would take responsibility, Rout again decided that she would have to act. She developed a kit to issue to soldiers to help protect them from disease. When she moved to Paris in April 1918 she persuaded a Madame Yvonne to run her brothel in a hygienic manner. Rout would then direct the New Zealand soldiers who arrived on leave to Madame Yvonne's establishment. For her efforts Rout earned both praise and condemnation. A French doctor called her a 'guardian angel', but a British Bishop condemned her as 'the most wicked woman in Britain.' Her work was not publicised in New Zealand during the war. Indeed, in order to keep up the myth of the 'purity' of New Zealand's young men, it was made a wartime offence to publish news of her actions.

At Home with the War: Passive Resistance

While many New Zealand men were keen to fight, some believed that it was wrong. This was usually because of religious or moral objections to war. When called up to fight, passive resisters refused to go. Men from some workers' organisations also refused to fight. They claimed that the wealthy were either profiting from the war, or were getting special treatment. There certainly were instances of this. Two businessmen got out of going to the war because of 'their importance to the commercial life of Auckland.' Most ordinary people were not so lucky. Few exemptions were granted.

Whatever the reason for not wanting to fight, the wider community and the government had little patience or sympathy. Resisters often faced a hostile and violent reaction. Those who had sons, fathers or brothers fighting overseas saw resisters as cowards who were leaving others to do the hard work. After conscription was introduced for the war in 1916, resisters were either imprisoned with hard labour or forcibly sent to the frontlines. Despite this, resistance to going to fight grew as news of the terrible casualties began to trickle in.

One person who resisted going to the war was Archibald Baxter, father of the poet and author James K. Baxter. He was imprisoned in Wellington before being forcibly sent to the front lines in France. When he still refused to fight he was given 'Number One Field Punishment' (called 'the crucifixion') in the winter weather for two hours each of 28 days. Here he describes his first day.

'I stood with my back [to the pole] and he [the guard] tied me to it by the ankles, knees and wrists. He was an expert at the job, and he knew how to pull and strain the ropes till they cut into the flesh and completely stopped circulation. When I was taken off my hands were always black with congested blood.... Most knots slacken after a time. His never did.... I was strained so tightly against the post that I was unable to move body or limbs a fraction of an inch.... The pain grew steadily worse until by the end of half an hour it seemed absolutely unendurable. Between my teeth I said: "Oh, God, this is too much. I can't bear it." The mental effect was almost as frightful as the physical. I felt as though I was going mad. That I should be stuck up on a pole suffering the frightful torture ... seemed part of some impossible nightmare that could not possibly continue.'

ACTIVITIES

1. What was the moral issue that Ettie Rout addressed during WWI?
2. Apart from medical reasons, under what circumstances could some people get out of going to the war?

Refer to Source J

3. What key idea from the second paragraph on 'Passive Resistance' does Baxter's account of his treatment support?
4. How reliable is Source J for the historian who is looking into the treatment of conscientious objectors? Explain your answer.
5. Do you think that this sort of punishment was justified, given that other men fought in the war? Give reasons for your answers.
6. Provide a quote of no more than ten words that suggests that Baxter's punishment also had a psychological effect.

At Home with the War: 'Enemy Aliens'

Anti-German hysteria and propaganda increased as the war continued. There was a fear that 'enemy aliens' in New Zealand would sabotage the war effort. The fear was largely irrational, but that didn't stop scare stories in the newspapers. According to one, Germans were more sexually perverted than the British. Also, according to the report, they were more likely to go insane and commit suicide. The same paper objected to kindergartens on the basis that they were a German idea.

To escape public persecution, some businesses changed their German-sounding names to more patriotic ones. This was often a well-advised move. In Wanganui, a butcher's shop owned by a German-born New Zealander had its windows smashed by a crowd of up to 3000. The neighbouring piano shop and a Hallenstein's clothing store received the same treatment. A well-respected German-born university professor in Wellington was hounded out of his job by an outraged public. This was despite the University Council defending his position. Even Coburg Street in Auckland had its name changed to Kitchener Ave. (Coburg was the name of the German husband of Britain's Queen Victoria. He had died in 1861.)

ACTIVITIES

1. Use the information above to create either a poster or a letter to the editor of a newspaper that shows both your patriotism towards Britain and your anti-German feelings.
2. Write a letter to the editor of a local newspaper. Explain why you feel it is wrong to be part of the 'mob mentality' that would persecute someone just because they have a German-sounding name.

WORLD WAR ONE AND NEW ZEALAND IDENTITY

Traditional histories of WWI tell us that a strong sense of New Zealand identity was 'forged in the field of fire', especially at Gallipoli. This may well have been true for the ordinary soldier. One New Zealander, Ormond Burton, wrote that: 'Somewhere between the landing at Anzac [Cove] and the end of the Battle of the Somme [in France] New Zealand very definitely became a nation.' For the first time, New Zealanders were interacting with large numbers of men from different parts of the world. They discovered that they spoke, thought and acted differently. This was true even when compared to men from Britain and Australia.

New Zealanders developed their own nicknames for themselves. These included 'Kiwis', 'Diggers' (from digging trenches), and even 'Pig Islanders'. Others called them 'Maorilanders' or 'Fernleaves' (because of the badges on their uniforms).

While the ordinary soldier may have found a new sense of New Zealand identity, the country's politicians were more cautious. The historian James Belich tells us that New Zealand's leaders wanted to maintain the British link. Belich argues that it was important to make Britain feel that it owed New Zealand something, after we had sacrificed so much in the war. Britain's debt to New Zealand would be repaid by continuing to take as much as possible of New Zealand's farm produce. This in turn would ensure New Zealand's economic security. Belich and other historians see the experiences of WWI as a continuation of the *tightening* of New Zealand's relationship with Britain.

One way in which this 'tightening' was encouraged was by commemorating the war. Memorials were put up in many towns throughout New Zealand, acknowledging the sacrifice made for the Empire. In 1929 the magnificent Auckland War Memorial Museum was opened. In Wellington a National War Memorial was completed in 1932. The first ANZAC Day ceremony took place in 1916, one year after the landing of New Zealand troops at Gallipoli. From 1920 a law made ANZAC Day a public holiday.

For some Maori, their involvement in WWI seemed to offer the chance to prove themselves the equal of Pakeha. In this way they hoped to be accepted after the war as full members of New Zealand society. This hope was rather too optimistic. It would take another world war before Maori were accepted more on their own terms.

ACTIVITIES

Make your own brief notes under the section heading on this page, using the following key ideas as a guide:

- Differences
- Belich and 'tightening'
- Commemoration.

AS1.4 REVIEW ACTIVITY

In paragraphs of about 100 words for each, describe the perspectives (views), and actions (with an accompanying explanation) on WWI for the following people:

- **A typical New Zealand soldier or nurse**
- **Ettie Rout**
- **Archibald Baxter (or any other passive resister)**
- **A patriotic New Zealander at home.**

CHAPTER FOUR

GOVERNMENT RACE RELATIONS POLICY UP TO WORLD WAR TWO: TWO SEPARATE WORLDS

GOVERNMENT 'SOCIAL POLICY' UP TO WORLD WAR TWO (WWII)

For most of the period up to the outbreak of war in 1939, race relations in New Zealand could be described as 'benign segregation'. What this means was that Maori lived within their own tribal areas and were essentially 'out of sight, out of mind'. As long as land continued to move freely from Maori to Pakeha ownership, governments mostly allowed Maori to live their own lives free from interference. Official policy towards Maori was still one of assimilation. Under this policy it was intended that Maori would lose their 'savage' ways, such as language, customs, beliefs and lifestyle. They would become, in effect, 'brown Pakeha'. Little of the old Maori ways would survive, except in museums. William Herries, Minister of Native Affairs from 1912–1921 said: *'I look forward for the next hundred years or so, to a time when we shall have no Maoris at all, but a white race with a slight dash of the finest coloured race in the world.'*

Assimilation
One culture is taken over and completely absorbed by another, leaving little or nothing of its original ways.

SOURCE A

A Maori village in the early 20th century.

In theory, Maori were supposed to assimilate and become fully part of the Pakeha world. The reality was that by the start of the 20th century most Maori remained marginalised on the outside of Pakeha society. Landless Maori were usually employed in low-paying seasonal jobs such as shearing, drain-digging or fruit-picking on Pakeha-owned land. Because of poverty, Maori health and housing conditions were generally poor. Disease continued to take a heavy toll on the people. (Despite this, resistance to diseases was increasing and the population had begun to recover by the early 20th century.) Most Maori – about 90% in the years up to 1926 – lived in rural areas. Here they were 'out-of-sight, out-of-mind'.

Marginalised
To be left outside of the normal way of life, unable to share in the benefits that others receive.

ACTIVITIES

Refer to the text on this page.

1. Explain in your own words the term 'assimilation'.
2. What sort of cultural things were Maori expected to lose by becoming 'brown Pakeha' (assimilating)?
3. Provide evidence (a quote, statistic or other fact) that the government's policy *was* one of assimilation.
4. Give examples of the ways in which Maori were marginalised by the early 20th century.
5. Provide a fact that proves that Maori were mostly rural dwellers at the beginning of the 20th century.
6. Why might the historian be willing to accept William Herries' statement on its own as a reliable indication of government policy?
7. What key ideas in the text does Source A provide evidence for?.

PAKEHA-MAORI ATTITUDES

Many Pakeha appreciated the ceremonial aspects of Maori culture, especially during events like Royal Tours. The rest of the time, however, the Pakeha attitude towards Maori was generally negative. Pakeha thought that the communal nature of tribal life was immoral. Maori were also said to be lazy, wasteful, dirty and too care-free, because they wouldn't think of the future or work on the land that they did own. Pakeha (and some Maori) had sayings that put Maori down. For example, 'Maori time' meant being late. What critics did not understand was that Maori had lost much of their land. They had also had their whole lifestyle disrupted during and after the New Zealand Wars of the 1860s. Adjustment to the Pakeha world was often difficult, especially as little assistance was given.

The historian Michael King says that Maori, on the other hand, viewed the 'typical' Pakeha as 'self-centred, materialist, acquisitive [greedy], unfeeling about his extended family and callous [uncaring] about treatment of the dead'.

Another Viewpoint

Maori in New Zealand were certainly marginalised, and they missed out on the same benefits and assistance as Pakeha. They also faced outright discrimination. However, they were treated better than other 'native races' in places like the United States, Canada, Australia and South Africa. Maori were made full citizens in 1840 when the Treaty was signed. They were granted representation in parliament in 1867. In contrast, American Indians were not made citizens (with voting rights) until the 1920s, and Aborigines only in the 1960s. Maori were represented in the 'top ten' positions in parliament in all of the years between 1892 and 1934 (and then at later dates, too). Two were for brief periods Acting Prime Minister. In New Zealand, there was no systematic campaign to exterminate the Maori as there had been against the Australian Aborigines and some Indian tribes in the United States. When some US servicemen refused during World War Two to drink in a bar with 'nigger Maoris' a riot broke out, with Pakeha fighting alongside Maori. While it is true that in New Zealand assimilation was government policy, this was not taken to the same extent as in Australia. There, 'half-caste' (mixed Aborigine-European) children were taken from their 'Native' parents to be brought up as white Australians.

ACTIVITIES

1 Stereotypes usually tell us more about what is important to the people making the statements. From the text, state what you think was important to Pakeha with regard to a 'proper lifestyle'.

2 Now use the quote from Michael King on how Maori viewed Pakeha to explain what was important to Maori.

PAKEHA VIEWS ON 'MAORI WAYS'

"It is almost miraculous that any of them live pure [moral] lives. The surroundings of a Maori village are demoralising in the extreme ..." *Maori feasts were also condemned:* "... the beer is placed where everyone, even the tiny child, can get as much as he wants. Imagine the sight that meets the eye. The most saddening, most disgusting spectacle is that of an intoxicated [drunk] Maori woman who knows no shame."

New Zealand Illustrated Magazine, c.1910

Refer to Source B

3 Identify the facts in Source B.

4 What key ideas in the text *Pakeha Attitudes Towards Maori* does this evidence support?

5 In what way does Source A seem to support the views given in Source B?

6 Why might an historian be cautious about relying on this piece of evidence to describe Maori lifestyles?

GOVERNMENT LAND POLICY

For much of the 20th century, owning and farming land was one of the main means of creating wealth in New Zealand. In terms of developing the country economically, the government's policies were focused on getting more land for Pakeha settlers. By 1900 only about 12% (3.2 million hectares) of New Zealand remained in Maori ownership. Much of this was of low quality for farming, or was scattered in small, uneconomic plots. Thus, most Maori missed out on the wealth created by the farming boom of the early 20th century. By the 1920s the government realised that if it kept acquiring land from Maori they would soon have none at all. The rate of land loss was slowed.

Those Maori who *did* want to develop their land found it difficult for several reasons. In some cases, a number of individuals owned a single block of land. Getting agreement on what should be done with it was not always easy. In other cases, one individual might own very small plots scattered in a number of different areas. Both these situations made getting loans to buy goods such as grass seed, or equipment such as tractors, difficult. Banks readily provided loans to Pakeha farmers who owned land themselves – the farm could be used as security for the loan. This was much more difficult where Maori owned land tribally, or owned too little to be security for a loan.

Not all tribes were affected in the same ways. One of the tribes that fared best was Ngati Porou in the East Cape region of the North Island. They had not sold much of their land. Nor had they had any land confiscated. This was because they had supported the settler government in the wars of the 19th century. However, with no road or rail to move goods in or out, it was still difficult for Ngati Porou to do well.

CHAPTER FIVE

MAORI LEADERSHIP: INSIDE, OUTSIDE OR ALONGSIDE THE PAKEHA SYSTEM?

Faced with a Pakeha government that neglected their concerns, Maori leaders had three main choices. Some became part of the Pakeha system. They did this by being elected to parliament in one of the four Maori seats. From there they worked *inside* the Pakeha government to try to change things. A second option, taken up eventually by some traditional tribal leaders, was to work *alongside* the Pakeha system. At first, governments paid little attention to these tribal leaders. Soon, however, officials came to realise that tribal leaders provided an effective link to Maori communities. A third option, taken up by one notable Maori leader in the 20th century, was to build a separate community, *outside* direct Pakeha influence. The government did not like separatist movements and, as with earlier cases, responded with armed force.

INSIDE THE PAKEHA SYSTEM: THE 'YOUNG MAORI PARTY'

James Carroll, 'father' of the Young Maori Party.

Peter Buck.

Maui Pomare.

Some important Maori leaders of the early 20th century served *inside* the New Zealand political system. The most well-known leaders are James Carroll (Timi Kara), Apirana Ngata, Maui Pomare and Peter Buck (Te Rangi Hiroa). They each were elected to one of the four Maori seats. Although these leaders actually represented different political parties, they were nicknamed the 'Young Maori Party' (YMP). Between them they worked to make gains for Maori. To be accepted inside the Pakeha parliament they had to excel at 'being Pakeha'. Yet this was not enough, for they had only four votes between them in a 76-seat parliament. Furthermore, those who entered parliament were not usually traditional Maori leaders. Because of this they had to struggle to earn the respect of even their own tribes. This was even more difficult outside their own tribal area, for tribal rivalries and jealousies remained strong. Despite the efforts of the YMP, many Maori still saw them as merely the contact point between the Maori and Pakeha worlds.

The Maori leaders who came to be known as the 'Young Maori Party' all had several features in common. They had been educated in both Maori ways and in the Pakeha system (at Te Aute College in Hawke's Bay). They believed that Maori needed to assimilate – adopt Pakeha ways – in order to do well in the Pakeha world. Some, like Maui Pomare and Peter Buck, were firmly assimilationist. They both believed that tribalism held Maori individuals back from doing well. James Carroll, known as the 'father' of the 'Young Maori Party', was assimilationist too. However, he also believed that Maori should retain those parts of their culture that weren't unsuited to Pakeha ways. Apirana Ngata was also an assimilationist, but became much less so in his later years. All YMP members also rejected separatism as a way forward for Maori.

The influence of the Young Maori Party began to decline by the late 1910s. During the 1920s Carroll died and Buck left New Zealand to go overseas. The leadership of the remaining YMP members was being challenged by the emergence of new Maori leaders, such as the prophet Wiremu Ratana and the traditional tribal leader Te Puea Herangi. In 1930 Pomare died. Ngata continued to work amongst Maori and in parliament during the 1930s. He lost his parliamentary seat in 1943.

Maori Health

One issue in particular that all YMP members were greatly concerned about was the state of Maori health. Maori life expectancy in 1905 was only about 33 years, and infant mortality (death-rate) was high. Carroll, Ngata, Buck and Pomare all believed that Maori would need to learn Pakeha ways to beat Pakeha disease. This was because traditional remedies offered little protection against diseases such as tuberculosis, typhoid and dysentery.

Between them, they all took actions to improve Maori

health. Carroll was responsible for having the Maori Councils Act (1900) passed in parliament. Maori from villages were elected to newly-created Councils, which were overseen by Maui Pomare and Peter Buck. Both men travelled widely amongst Maori communities, instructing the elected councillors. They gave help to the sick, advised on sanitary disposal of rubbish and sewage, and inspected water supplies. During their visits to villages they would sometimes show microscope slides of the harmful bacteria present in the water supply. In a three-year period they burned over 1000 sub-standard whare (houses) because of the health risks they posed. Nearly 1200 new whare were built, as well as 839 toilets. The vaccination programme undertaken by Buck and Pomare was responsible for eventually stopping a 1913 smallpox epidemic. In addition, their reports gave the government its first accurate information on Maori health. Although there was an increase in Maori life expectancy to 46 years by 1925, this was in fact little to do with the efforts of the Maori Councils. The real reason was that the Maori population was finally building a natural resistance to disease. The Councils ceased to exist when, in 1930, Maori health was brought under the control of the government's Health Department.

ACTIVITY

1. Identify from the text the key ideas about the 'typical' features of a Young Maori Party member. Identify also two difficulties that they faced.
2. Draw an outline figure (or stick figure) to represent a 'typical' YMP member. Draw in labels pointing to appropriate parts of the figure's body to highlight the 'typical' features (and difficulties faced). For example, you might have a label saying 'Link between the Pakeha and Maori worlds' with an arrow pointing to the hands.

AS1.2 SKILL: PROVIDING SUPPORTING EVIDENCE FOR KEY IDEAS

1. Below in the 'Evidence' column are some of the Maori Council Health Regulations from 1900. Read the Key Ideas about Maori health contained in the left-hand column. Match one or more pieces of supporting evidence from the right-hand column to the appropriate Key Idea. Pieces of evidence can be used more than once.

Key Ideas	Evidence: Maori Council Health Regulations
1 Some Maori houses were not kept in a hygienic state.	a Houses should be built with wooden floors at least six inches [15cm] above ground …
2 Drunkenness was a problem in some Maori communities.	b If there is no chimney, no fire should be lit inside …
3 Some Maori houses were stuffy or damp.	c Houses should have provision for ventilation to allow stale air to flow out and fresh air to flow in …
4 People could become sick from water-borne diseases.	d The lying-in-state for corpses should not exceed four days before burial; there should be one burial place for each village.
5 A common Maori custom was to honour the dead in the family's house.	e The Inspector would have the power to order a person to wash and tidy up his house …
6 Some Maori houses did not have proper fireplaces.	f No alcohol would be permitted within the perimeter of a pa at Maori gatherings.
	g No refuse [rubbish] should be left in a pa.
	h Water supplies must be protected from contamination.
	i All pa should be fenced to keep animals out.

2. What was the main purpose behind the sort of Health Regulations shown in the table above?
3. What ONE key idea from the first paragraph in this section of the text do these Health Regulations support?
4. What were the successes of the Young Maori Party with regard to Maori health?
5. You are Maui Pomare (or Peter Buck). Use the information in the main text above, and the Health Regulations, to write a 100–200 word speech to give upon your arrival in a Maori village.

PROFILE

Apirana Ngata

Apirana Ngata is probably the greatest Maori leader of the 20th century, in terms of achievements for his people. He was from the Ngati Porou tribe, being born at Te Araroa on the East Coast in 1874. He was the first Maori graduate from a New Zealand university (1897) and the first Maori lawyer. This was a source of great mana, although it took some time for tribal leaders to overcome their suspicion of his Pakeha ways. In 1905 Ngata was elected to parliament in the Eastern Maori seat. His three university degrees made him the most qualified man in parliament, Maori or Pakeha. He worked closely with James Carroll and eventually became a Cabinet Minister (a top position in government).

Ngata was an effective leader because, although a member of the Liberal Party, he was able to work closely with the Reform government too. In this way he put his concerns for the Maori people above his own personal political ambitions. He also involved himself fully in Maori cultural and social activities. His views on land issues and his interest in seeing the Maori culture survive made him increasingly unpopular with many Pakeha. He was, however, knighted in 1927 for his tireless work for the Maori people.

In 1928 Ngata was active in seeing the creation of a Maori Anglican bishop. That same year his Liberal party won the election, and Ngata became Native Minister (he was Acting Prime Minister briefly in 1930). This position enabled him to promote Maori land development schemes all over the country. So quickly did these expand that financial accountability was soon lost and accusations of corruption began to emerge. A government inquiry found little to blame directly on Ngata, although he may have favoured his own tribe. Evidence was found, however, of wrongdoing by some employees under him. Ngata took responsibility and resigned from Cabinet. The whole affair created great distrust amongst Maori. They saw Ngata as the victim of Pakeha efforts to undermine his successes. Ngata remained in parliament until he lost his seat in 1943. Despite this, he remained an influential adviser, particularly to Labour's Peter Fraser. Ngata died in 1950.

ACTIVITIES

1. Refer back to the first paragraph under the heading 'Inside the Pakeha System: The 'Young Maori Party' and the profile of Apirana Ngata. What key idea about how the YMP members had to earn the respect of their Pakeha colleagues does Ngata's university achievements support?
2. Why was Ngata so effective in promoting Maori interests in parliament?
3. What sort of things was Ngata able to do once he became Native Minister?
4. Write a short speech outlining Ngata's achievements, to be delivered at his funeral in 1950.

Maori Land Alienation

With the exception of Maui Pomare, the continuing alienation of Maori land was another issue that concerned the Young Maori Party. Pomare believed that the pressure of land sales would force Maori to become more business-like in their approach to their resources. The other YMP members feared that Maori would never do well in the Pakeha world if they lost their economic base. James Carroll, supported by Apirana Ngata, was responsible for introducing into parliament in 1900 a law that gave more control to Maori landowners. Maori were encouraged to lease, rather than sell, their land. This policy of taihoa (slow down) was so successful in reducing the sale of land that settlers and Pakeha parliamentarians were annoyed. In 1905 a new law was passed that again gave Pakeha greater control. Immediately the rate of land alienation increased. A further one million hectares was sold between 1911 and 1920. This left Maori with less than two million hectares.

Alienation
The loss of land, whether willingly through sales, or by government action such as confiscation.

Land Confiscations

Ngata in particular was also very active in trying to have the unjust land confiscations of the past compensated. These confiscations had occurred after the wars in the Waikato and Taranaki in the 1860s. For over ten years Ngata made little progress. Things changed in 1926 when Prime Minister Gordon Coates established the Sim Commission to look into land confiscations. Ngata had a close personal relationship with Coates, who had become Native Minister in 1921 and Prime Minister in 1925. Coates was the first Pakeha politician in the 20th century who showed a real understanding of Maori concerns. In 1931 the

Gordon Coates

Maori Land at 1910 (North Island)

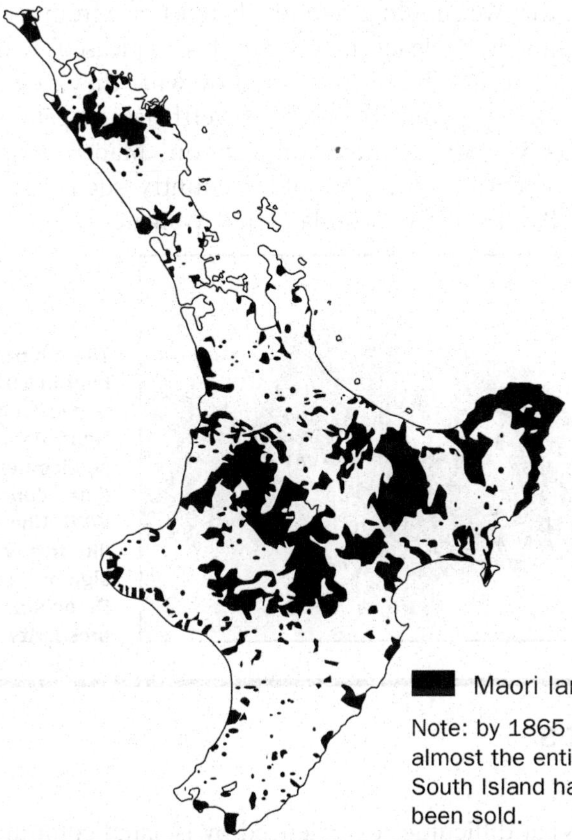

Maori land

Note: by 1865 almost the entire South Island had been sold.

THE STOUT-NGATA REPORT

"The necessity of assisting the Maori to settle his own lands was never properly recognised.... The spectacle is presented to us of a people starving in the midst of plenty. If it is difficult for the European settler to acquire Maori land ... it is more difficult for the individual Maori owner to acquire his own land, [even if he be] ... ever so ambitious and capable of using it."

ACTIVITIES

1. Refer to Source A. What key idea from the 'Maori Land Alienation' section does this map seem to support?
2. Refer to an atlas. What are the main areas where Maori still own much of the land? What is the general nature of this land (e.g. farmland, mountains etc.)?
3. What is the key problem facing Maori, according to Source B?
4. Who do you think the writers of the Report would like to see providing assistance for Maori?

. Taranaki tribes accepted as compensation an annual payment of £5,000; Waikato – led by Te Puea Herangi – negotiated until 1947 before accepting the same amount.

Cultural revival

From the 1920s Ngata looked to record and revive Maori culture in New Zealand, before it was lost forever. He also looked for ways to blend aspects of traditional Maori culture with Pakeha ways. In this way, Ngata was going beyond even an integrationist approach to race relations. His views were now more in line with the bi-culturalism of the 1970s, where it was recognised that there were two distinct cultures in New Zealand.

ACTIVITIES

Ngata writes to Peter Buck about his changing views on assimilation

"I rather think that ... you and I must acknowledge that our hearts are not with this policy of imposing Pakeha culture forms on our people. Our recent activities would indicate a contrary [opposite] determination to preserve the old culture forms as the foundations on which to reconstruct Maori life and hopes."

1. Provide a quote from Ngata's letter of no more than seven words where Ngata gives his own definition of 'assimilation'.
2. Identify one word in the letter that shows that Ngata believes that Maori society has in the past been damaged.

Land Development – Co-operatives and Consolidation

Ngata believed that Maori needed to develop their land along Pakeha lines. This would include the use of Pakeha farming techniques in order for Maori to become more economically self-sufficient. He was also aware of the government's view on Maori land that was not being cultivated. The government saw it as land that should be available for use by Pakeha farmers. To ensure 'productive' use of land, Ngata established the Waiapu Farmers' Co-operative Company on the East Coast in 1912. By being part of the Co-operative Company Maori farmers could combine their purchasing strength to get goods cheaper. In addition, they could combine to sell their produce at higher prices, rather than competing with each other. Banks also felt more secure lending to the Co-operative Company rather than to economically weak individuals. The process of forming these co-operatives was called **incorporation**.

Ngata also encouraged a process called **consolidation**. In many cases, Maori owned scattered bits of uneconomic land. Through consolidation owners could swap or sell these pieces so that each individual ended up with one larger block of land. This could then be farmed much more economically.

Under Ngata's schemes of co-operatives and consolidation Ngati Porou did well. They established dairy, sheep and beef farms, as well as forestry schemes. By 1916 the tribe owned 156 flocks totalling nearly 181,000 sheep, as well as mechanical shearing machines and their own company for making dairy products. Income was reinvested in the farms and also in building community facilities, such as churches and marae. Ngata used the traditional rivalry that had always characterised inter-hapu relations to encourage other tribes to adopt his schemes.

Ngata's winning formula began to spread. Seeing the sort of prosperity that Ngati Porou enjoyed, other leaders wanted their tribes to share in it, too. Te Puea Herangi of Waikato and Whina Cooper of the Hokianga are two notable examples. By 1936 Ngata had been able to extract from a penny-pinching government £1.5million to fund his schemes. As he said in a letter to Peter Buck: 'Did you ever expect that we should get so much assistance from the State [government]?' Ngata may have been pleased with his success, but Pakeha were angered by what they saw as too much money going to Maori. Nevertheless, Ngata's work eventually had a huge impact on Maori economic development in some areas of the country, such as the East Coast, Bay of Plenty, Northland and Waikato.

This Church was built in 1924 as a memorial to Ngati Porou servicemen killed during WWI. Churches like this were a sign of Ngati Porou's growing prosperity.

ACTIVITIES

1 What was the Pakeha government's view on uncultivated Maori land? How did this affect Ngata's view on how Maori should use their land?

2 Draw diagram(s) that show the benefits that came from incorporations (co-operatives) for the individual Maori farmers who belonged to them.

3 Draw diagram(s) that show how the process of consolidation created farms that could be run economically by their Maori owners.

4 Do a 'before and after' pictorial to show how Ngati Porou benefited from Ngata's land schemes.

Refer to Source C

5 Describe the technology used on the Winiata farm.

6 Provide evidence that would support the claim that this farm has not yet been fully developed.

7 Explain how Ngata's Co-operatives could have benefited the Maori farmers at Winiata.

Refer to Source D

8 How *might* an historian use this photograph to support the claim that Ngata's land development schemes were successful in the East Coast area?

9 What difficulties experienced by isolated communities are evident in this photograph?

10 What other evidence might an historian want to see in order to get a full understanding of the success of Ngata's land schemes in the Gisborne area?

Refer to Source E

11 Using the map and your own knowledge, name the tribe that is located in the area north of Gisborne.

12 What do the dots represent?

13 Identify four regions in the North Island where there were a significant number of Ngata's land development schemes. You may need to use an atlas.

14 Identify three regions in the North Island where it appears that there were no land development schemes. Why might this be?

15 "Maori land was not well-developed for farming before Apirana Ngata introduced his development schemes." How could an historian use the map to provide evidence to support this statement?

Refer to Source F

16 List as many features as you can that identify the meeting house as being specifically Maori.

Maori farmers at Winiata.

Mustering sheep for sale, Gisborne.

Raukawa meeting house at Otaki. The third reconstruction of this historic meeting house involved contributions from the School of Maori Art that Ngata helped establish.

North Island Land Development Schemes

SOURCE E

MAORI PARTICIPATION IN WWI

All members of the YMP supported Maori participation in WWI. This was out of a desire to have Maori prove their loyalty to the Crown through their sacrifice in war. This in turn would prove that Maori were worthy of being treated as equals to Pakeha. Another reason was to expose Maori to military organisation to demonstrate the effectiveness of Pakeha ways. Peter Buck put his beliefs into action by enlisting in the Army in 1914. James Carroll was 56 years of age and Apirana Ngata 40 when the war broke out; both were too old to fight.

Both Ngata and Pomare were active in encouraging Maori to sign up to serve in WWI. Ngata in particular argued successfully that Maori should be grouped into their own Battalion. This, he said, was where they would function best, rather than serving in unfamiliar Pakeha units. For his part, Pomare joined a committee to encourage Maori enlistment. When conscription for Pakeha was introduced in 1916, he urged that Maori be conscripted on the same terms as Pakeha. In June 1917 Maori were included in conscription laws.

Tribes such as Nga Puhi (Northland), Te Arawa (Bay of Plenty), Nagti Porou (East Coast) and Ngai Tahu (South Island) were keen to join up. Pomare could take much of the credit for this. However, Maori in the Waikato resisted Pomare's calls to enlist. This was because the government had done little by 1914 to settle their land grievances. Pomare's calls for Maori conscription also drew a bitter response from Waikato. When he visited the area in an effort to encourage enlistment, Pomare was offered a grave insult – a whakapohane (haka in which the men bare their backsides).

SOURCE G

Members of the Maori Pioneer Battalion taking a break from trench improvement work, near Gommecourt, France.

Pomare's view on Maori participation, prior to the outbreak of WWI

"If ever this country was threatened, we would stand side by side with you [Pakeha] to the last man and woman – stand in defence of the country where it has been our happy lot to co-mingle man to man."

Ngata's views on Maori participation in WWI

"We could not maintain our self-respect and ask the Government of New Zealand during this war, which is being fought for the safety of the Empire everywhere, that we Maoris should stay at home while the Pakehas went. We would lose our self-respect. It was to maintain the self-respect of the people we represent that we ... [told] ... the Government that it was objectionable from our standpoint if the Bill [law] said straight out that Maoris were to be excluded. It would be regarded as a [bad] reflection on a warrior race."

ACTIVITIES

Refer to Sources G–I

1. Read the first six words of Pomare's speech (Source H), and the first sentence of Ngata's speech (Source I). How has the situation facing New Zealand changed?
2. Give quotes of no more than eight words each from both Pomare's and Ngata's speeches that show that there is danger to Britain and/or its friends.
3. Give a quote of no more than eight words that could be used to show that Pomare supports assimilation.
4. Give a fact from Ngata's speech (you don't have to quote; just summarise it).
5. Give a quote of two words that shows that Ngata believes Maori are well suited to participating in WWI.
6. With regard to WWI, in what way does Ngata believe that Maori want to demonstrate continuity with their past traditions?
7. In the speech, what reason does Ngata give for wanting Maori to fight in WWI?
8. Why *might* an historian be happy to use these two pieces of evidence on their own to prove that the Young Maori Party supported Maori participation in WWI? Why might someone else argue that, on their own, the speeches are not good enough evidence?
9. Describe the link between the views expressed in Sources H and I, and the scene shown in Source G.
10. Give TWO pieces of evidence from Source G that suggest that the soldiers are not currently under threat.

OUTSIDE THE PAKEHA SYSTEM: RUA KENANA

There were some Maori leaders who did not support Britain's war. One of these was the prophet-leader Rua Kenana. In 1907 Rua had chosen to separate himself and his Tuhoe followers and operate *outside* the Pakeha system. He did this by building a community in the isolated Urewera mountains, at a place called Maungapohatu.

Wooden circular temple built in 1908 by Rua Kenana in the village of Maungapohatu. The temple was a completely circular building. The upper storey was set apart for the prophet, his wives and two chiefs. This level could be entered only by an outside staircase, upon which Rua also built a round platform, where he used to speak to the people and commune with the Holy Ghost. The building was brightly painted, the background white with diamonds of yellow and clubs of blue.

ACTIVITIES

1 Study the photograph above carefully. What aspects of Rua's temple show a Maori influence? What aspects show a Pakeha influence?

2 Compare the photograph to the description of Rua's community in the profile. In what ways does the photograph support the description?

3 Rua Kenana has given you the photograph (above) and his profile as a brief outline of the early history of his community. He has asked you to identify THREE key ideas and then turn them into postage stamps for use at Maungapohatu. He has asked you to produce these in sketch-form on a single page for his inspection. Each stamp needs to include:

- The name of his community
- A strong central image with no more than three key words per stamp
- A different price for each (in pence).

PROFILE

RUA KENANA

Rua Kenana had been brought up with stories of the 19th century prophet-leader Te Kooti. Kenana believed that he was 'The One' that Te Kooti had prophesised would return to lead Maori in their struggle to regain their lands. At Maungapohatu, Rua intended to use the best that the Pakeha world had to offer, while keeping Maori traditions alive. He called his establishment the New Jerusalem and the City of God, with himself as Messiah. Within a year crops were planted, cattle were being grazed and houses built. Rua also established a water supply and a communal bank. A parliament modelled on the old Muslim temple in Jerusalem, the *Dome of the Rock*, was also built. Rua would not allow his followers' children to receive a Pakeha education. Although his community faced difficulties, it provided stability for its 1400 members. Maori at this time were struggling to adjust to the major changes brought about by increasing Pakeha settlement.

Participation in World War One

Kenana believed that Maori and Pakeha should be treated equally. The government and most Pakeha rejected this. The common view was that Maori were not yet 'civilised' enough to come under the same laws as Pakeha. Rua's motto, however was 'One law for two people.' For this reason, Rua was opposed to Tuhoe Maori signing up to fight in WWI. He believed that until Maori were treated equally with Pakeha they should not do anything to help the war effort. He even claimed that he favoured a German victory. Such outspoken statements finally led to a decision by the government to arrest him. An old charge of 'sly-grogging' – the illegal sale of alcohol – provided the necessary reason.

SOURCE J

Rua Kenana's defiant statement to the police

"I have 1400 men here. I am not going to let any of them enlist or go to the war. You have no King now. The King of England is no good. He is beaten. The Germans will win. Any money I have I will give to the Germans. The English are no good. They have two laws, one for the Maori and one for the Pakeha. When the Germans win I am going to be king here. I will be King of the Pakeha and King of the Maori."

The arrest of Rua resulted in the worst Maori-Pakeha clash of the 20th century. It also revealed to Maori – as well as to Pakeha – the extent to which the government was prepared to go to ensure that its authority was not challenged. A party of seventy police was sent to arrest Kenana, arriving on April 2nd, 1916. In the resulting shoot-out two Maori were killed and a policeman seriously wounded. Rua was arrested and taken to Auckland. He was sentenced to serve one year of hard labour, followed by 18 months' imprisonment. When Rua was released, he returned to his community. During his absence it had struggled, particularly as it had had to pay the costs incurred by the police during Rua's arrest. By the early 1930s Maungapohatu had failed economically and the people were forced to leave. In 1937 Rua died, aged 68. He had predicted that he would rise from the grave three days after his death. Eventually his followers gave up the wait and sealed his body alongside his house in a concrete coffin that Rua himself had built.

Judge Chapman's verdict

'Now you learn that the law has a long arm, and that it can reach you however far back into the recesses of the forest you travel, and that in every corner of the great Empire to which we belong the King's law can reach anyone who offends against it. That is the lesson which you and your people should learn from this trial.'

Rua Kenana is handcuffed, third from the left, beside his son Whatu Rua. Constable Fahey, with the wounded arm, is next to Whatu.

Police commissioner John Cullen, on horseback, leading prisoners from Maungapohatu, on Wednesday 5 April 1916. Rua is alongside the horse.

ACTIVITIES

Refer to Source J

1. Provide a quote of no more than TWELVE words that shows that Rua does not necessarily wish to expel Pakeha from New Zealand.
2. What specifically is Rua Kenana's main reason for not being happy with the English/New Zealand government?
3. How did Rua's statement in Source J lead to Judge Chapman's verdict in Source K?

Refer to Source K

4. Provide a quote that is a fact.
5. Provide a quote that is an opinion.
6. Provide a quote of no more than twelve words that shows that Judge Chapman wants to make an example of Rua Kenana to warn other Maori against actions such as his.

Refer to Sources L–M

7. How do the photographs support the statement made by Judge Chapman in Source K?
8. Provide evidence that suggests that the Sources L and M are photographs of Maungapohatu.
9. Give THREE ways that the scene shown in Sources L and M would support the claim that the police action against Rua Kenana is over.

Refer to Sources N and O

10. What aspect(s) of these photograph(s) suggest that they were taken after Rua's release from jail?
11. Provide evidence from either photograph that would support the claim that Rua had abandoned separatism after being released from jail.

SOURCE N

SOURCE O

ALONGSIDE THE PAKEHA SYSTEM: TE PUEA HERANGI

PROFILE

Te Puea Herangi

One other significant Maori leader that rejected participation in WWI was Te Puea Herangi of the Waikato. Te Puea Herangi belonged to the Kahui Ariki (Maori Royal Family). Although known to Pakeha as 'Princess' Te Puea, this was a name she did not herself use. In her early life she was rather spoilt and had become a concern to her family. By the time she was in her twenties, she was living a somewhat wild life in Auckland with a Pakeha. In 1910 she returned to the Waikato at age 27. She had to work hard to overcome the suspicions of some who still saw her as a 'wild child'. However, she soon proved her intelligence, determination and leadership abilities. The government soon recognised the value of working with such leaders. Te Puea responded by agreeing to work *alongside* the Pakeha system to aid her people.

Te Puea died in 1952 and over 10,000 people attended her tangi, including many Pakeha. For Maori, it was the largest inter-tribal gathering up to that time. Over her lifetime Te Puea had worked alongside three Maori Kings to settle grievances with the government, and to improve conditions for her people. Although some of her own people felt that she became *too* close to the government, she is still considered by many to be the most influential woman in New Zealand's political history. More than most other Maori leaders, Te Puea understood how to bring about changes in Maori society. She did this by making it seem as though the changes were in line with traditional ways of dealing with situations. She knew that her people felt more comfortable with changes that were linked to the known past. Te Puea thus helped reinforce the tribal identity of the Waikato people.

The Maori Royal Family Tree

Potatau I (Te Wherowhero)
- 1858–1860

Potatau II (Tawhiao)
- (Te Puea's grandfather)
- 1860–1894

Mahuta
- (Te Puea's uncle)
- 1894–1912

Te Rata
- 1912–1933

Koroki
- 1933–1966

Te Atairangikaahu
- (first Maori Queen)
- 1966–

Te Puea Herangi on Waikato Involvement in WWI

When WWI broke out in 1914, Te Puea Herangi argued that Waikato Maori should not fight. She felt this way for two reasons. Te Puea's grandfather, Tawhiao, had been the Maori King during the Waikato wars of the 1860s. When they came to an end, he declared that Waikato should never again fight. Te Puea intended to follow that instruction. She also saw no reason why her people should fight and die for a British King and a New Zealand government that had taken their lands. During WWI, Te Puea was called 'the German woman' by some. This was because she was the grand-daughter of William Searancke, who was (wrongly) thought to be a German. Her views and actions, and a widespread belief that she was a German sympathiser, angered many Pakeha.

When the Young Maori Party and the government began to pressure Waikato Maori to sign up to fight, Te Puea led the resistance. This included opposition to conscription when it was introduced for Maori in 1917. Waikato and Maniapoto Maori in particular were targeted by the government. In 1918, Te Puea gathered together at Mangatawhiri those who had been balloted (called up to fight) and led the passive resistance when they were arrested. Because of her stand, Te Puea became a well-known figure in New Zealand.

Waikato's anti-conscription campaign begins

Tumokai Katipa, who later became Te Puea Herangi's husband, recalls in the 1980s the beginning of Waikato's anti-conscription campaign at Mangatawhiri.

"It was getting dark in there. We only had two kerosene lamps hanging from the roof in the centre, so that the light flickered on some people's faces and others were in shadow. We were all uncertain, frightened, not knowing what was going to happen to us. Then Te Puea stood by the door and said it was time to begin. "But first" she said, "we must karakia [pray]. Is there somebody here who will lead?" She expected a parson [priest] to stand up. But do you know there wasn't [any]? There was absolute silence. All the Christian churches had deserted us because they thought we were breaking the law. They didn't want to get caught with us or go to prison with us."

ACTIVITIES

1. Give two reasons why Te Puea Herangi was opposed to Waikato participation in WWI.
2. For what two reasons were many Pakeha suspicious of Te Puea Herangi?

Refer to Source P

3. Why was there no parson (priest) at Mangatawhiri to lead the karakia?
4. Provide evidence that supports the claim that the anti-conscription campaign was an illegal action.
5. Provide evidence to show that the Waikato people understood that the government might take action due to their anti-conscription campaign.
6. In a quote of no more than twelve words identify an opinion.
7. Give TWO reasons why an historian would be cautious about using this source alone to understand the Waikato anti-conscription campaign.

The 1918 'Flu Pandemic

Like the Young Maori Party, Te Puea was concerned in particular about the welfare and health of her people. A smallpox epidemic in 1913 had been bad enough, but worse was to come. As the rest of New Zealand celebrated the end of the war, a killer virus had already begun to spread. When the soldiers came back to New Zealand from WWI they were told that they were coming home to a country fit for heroes. This bright future was shattered before the war had even ended. An influenza pandemic began in November 1918 and was spread rapidly around the world by soldiers returning from the war. At least 25million people died in the outbreak, far more than the 10million killed during WWI. It was the worst 'plague' since the Black Death of the 14th century. The official death toll for New Zealand was 6600, but estimates of the real toll are as high as 8600.

Pandemic
An outbreak of a disease that affects the whole country or world. (An epidemic is localised.)

Because of the inadequate housing and conditions that most Maori lived in, they made up about 80% of the victims. For every 1000 Maori, on average 23 were killed. Many were from the same villages, as the disease spread rapidly in unhygienic conditions. The 'flu was a major setback for the recovery of the Maori population. In both Maori and Pakeha communities, great gaps were left by those who had died. Combined with the losses during the war, many children were left as orphans.

SOURCE Q

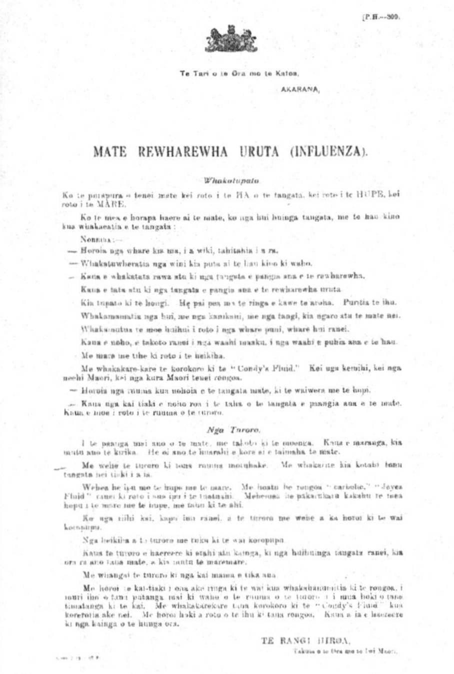

[P.H.—300.

Te Tari o te Ora mo te Katoa,

AKARANA,

MATE REWHAREWHA URUTA (INFLUENZA).

Whakatupato.

Ko te purapura o tenei mate kei roto i te HA o te tangata, kei roto i te HUPE, kei roto i te MARE.

Ko te mea e horapa haere ai te mate, ko nga hui huinga tangata, me te hau kino kua whakaeatia e te tangata :

Nonoua :—

— Horoia nga whare kia ma, i a wiki, tahitahia i a ra.

— Whakatuwheratia nga wini kia puta ai te hau kino ki waho.

— Kaua e whakatata rawa atu ki nga tangata e pangia ana e te rewharewha.

Kaua e tata atu ki nga tangata e pangia ana e te rewharewha uruta.

Kia tupato ki te hongi. He pai pea mo te ringa e kawe te aroha. Puritia te ihu.

Whakamutua nga hui, me nga kanikani, me nga tangi, kia ngaro atu te mate nei.

Whakamutua te moe huihui i roto i nga whare puni, whare hui ranei.

Kaua e noho, e takoto ranei i nga waahi maaku, i nga waahi e puhia ana e te hau.

Me mau me tihe ki roto i te heikiha.

Me whakakare-kare te korokoro ki te "Condy's Fluid." Kei nga kemihi, kei nga neehi Maori, kei nga kura Maori tenei rongoa.

— Horoia nga ruuma kua nohoia e te tangata mate, ki te waiwera me te hopi.

— Kaua nga kai tiaki e noho roa i te taha o te tangata e pangia ana e te mate. Kaua e moe i roto i te ruuma o te turoro.

Nga Turoro.

I te paunga mai ano o te mate, me takoto ki te moenga. Kaua e maranga, kia mutu ano te kirika. He ai ano te huarahi e kore ai e taimaha te mate.

Me wehe te turoro ki tona ruuma motuhake. Me whakarite kia kotahi tonu tangata hei tiaki i a ia.

Wehea he ipu mo te hupe me te mare. Me hoatu he rongoa "carbolic," "Jeyes Fluid" ranei ki roto i aua ipu i te tuatahi. Mehemea he pakaru kakahu te taea hopu i te mare me te hupe, me tahu ki te ahi.

Ko nga rihi kai, kapu inu ranei, a te turoro me wehe a ka horoi ki te wai koropupu.

Nga heikiha a te turoro me tuku ki te wai koropupu.

Kaua te turoro e haerere ki etahi atu kainga, ki nga huihuinga tangata ranei, kia ora ra ano tana mate, a kia mutu te maremare.

Me whangai te turoro ki nga kai mama e tika ana.

Me horoi te kai-tiaki i ona ake ringa ki te wai kua whakahanumitia ki te rongoa, i muri iho o tana putanga mai ki waho o te ruuma o te turoro, i mua hoki o tana timatanga ki te kai. Me whakakarekare tana korokoro ki te "Condy's Fluid" kua korerotia ake nei. Me horoi hoki a roto o te ihu ki tana rongoa. Kaua a ia e haerere ki nga kainga o te hunga ora.

TE RANGI HIROA,
Takuta o te Ora mo te Iwi Maori.

Influenza notice, in Maori

SOURCE R

The Waikato Experience

Tumokai Katipa, who later became Te Puea Herangi's husband, ferried the bodies of victims of the 'flu pandemic to a burial place at Taupiri Mountain.

"We'd get to Taupiri, unload the bodies, bury them in a wide grave, and then return ... Sometimes we had to turn around and go straight back with some more [bodies]. Each time we got there – hello, somebody else dead. This went on for two weeks.... There was no time for relatives to mourn. Most of them couldn't anyway [they were too ill or too weak]."

SOURCE S

Dr Doris Gordon recalls the arrival of the influenza pandemic in Stratford in 1918, at the same time as people were crowding the streets to celebrate the end of WWI.

At 9pm I was in the home of a master painter whose only two children had earlier both got out of bed and walked two blocks to witness the celebrations. I verified that the elder son was dead, went into the kitchen to sign the certificate, and was startled to find the undertaker there, [measuring] tape in hand; and I literally shivered when he suggested I also sign the death certificate for the other lad, who was undoubtedly just about to die. It seemed ghoulish to sign while there was still a flickering pulse, but the undertaker was as hard pressed as I was.

ACTIVITIES

Refer to Source Q

1. Provide evidence that the influenza notice is an official government publication.
2. How effective do you think such a notice would be in warning Maori about the dangers of influenza? Explain your answer. What might this suggest about the government's ability to deal with the influenza crisis amongst Maori?
3. What other sources would an historian want to use to test whether your response is accurate?

Refer to Source R

4. What is the link between Source Q and Source R?
5. Identify one opinion in Katipa's statement.
6. Identify any key idea(s) in the main text on the 1918 'flu pandemic for which Katipa's statement would provide good supporting evidence.
7. Why does Katipa's statement on its own not provide the historian with sufficient evidence about the effect of the 1918 'flu pandemic on Maori communities?

Refer to Source S

8. Provide a quote of TWO words that means that Dr Gordon was extremely busy.
9. What key idea about the impact of the influenza outbreak can be found in both Source R and Source S (use your own words)?
10. Provide a quote of no more than FIVE words where Dr Gordon is expressing an opinion.

Other Issues: A Waikato 'Home'

Te Puea believed that the Waikato people needed to have a spiritual home. In addition, she saw a need for an economic base from which the tribe could develop. This, she believed, was the only way of restoring hope and well-being to a scattered and demoralised people. In 1921 Te Puea moved her people to Ngaruawahia. Here she began to rebuild what had once been the centre of Waikato power. The building of Turangawaewae Marae was a massive undertaking that would take five years. It was also an expensive job. Te Puea raised additional funds by creating and then touring a concert party (*Te Pou o Mangatawhiri*). The concert party was named after the boundary-stream that British troops had crossed when they attacked Waikato in the 1860s. 'I am going to keep reminding the Pakeha of these things', Te Puea said, 'until we get compensation for what was stolen.'

The concert party had the side-effect of reviving forgotten action songs and haka. On a tour in 1928 Te Puea met Apirana Ngata and he introduced her to the Prime Minister, Gordon Coates. When Ngata showed her his land development schemes (see pages 27–28) she was soon an enthusiastic supporter of them. Land in the Waikato was quickly sub-divided and converted into dairy farms. This provided the Waikato people with a sense of self-worth and economic independence. Turangawaewae had become the spiritual and economic centre of the Waikato people, just as Te Puea had hoped.

ACTIVITIES

Refer to Sources T–U

1 Provide one piece of evidence from Source U that would support the claim that the establishment of Turangawaewae was not an act of 'disloyalty' to the Crown.

2 What does this source suggest about inter-tribal relations at the time? Why, *on its own*, is this photograph not sufficient evidence to support your answer?

3 Explain how Ngata could use such gatherings to spread his ideas about Maori land development schemes.

4 What key idea in the *first* paragraph of the text 'Other Issues: a Waikato 'Home'' does Poutapu's statement in Source T support?

5 Refer to the main text and Sources U and T. It is 1921 and you have just arrived at Ngaruawahia along with Poutapu and the rest of the community from Mangatawhiri.

- Make one sketch that shows the scene that Poutapu describes. Do another using the information in the second paragraph of the text and Source U, showing how Ngaruawahia was developed.
- Provide a brief note with the sketches that explains the effort required.

SOURCE T

Turangawaewae (standing place)

Poutapu records the huge job ahead of the new arrivals at Ngaruawahia.

"On the flat where we landed, below a steep bank, it was swampy, water-laden. And covered with gorse and blackberry and all the kinds of scrub you can imagine. That's what we had to live amongst. Then there was the bank behind, also covered in scrub, and then the piece at the top where the marae itself was to be. That too was a tangle of scrub. There were high gum trees where we wanted to put the main buildings and a great hole where Te Puea said the courtyard of the marae was to go."

AS1.4 REVIEW ACTIVITY

In paragraphs of about 100 words for each, describe the perspectives (views) and actions (with an accompanying explanation) for the following:

- Rua Kenana on participation in WWI (see page 31–32)
- Te Puea Herangi on participation in WWI
- Te Puea Herangi on the well-being of her Waikato people.

Ngati Porou group, including Apirana Ngata, at the opening of Mahina-a-rangi meeting house, Turangawaewae Marae, Ngaruawhahia. Iwi from other areas also attended the ceremonies.

PROFILE

Wiremu Ratana

Ratana was born in 1873 of Ngati Apa and Nga Rauru descent. Originally a Wanganui ploughman, he was known as a wild and moody fellow who drank too much. One close relative even thought that he was insane. After claiming to have received a vision from God, he became a faith healer who started a religious movement. In later years he became a political leader who entered into a fruitful alliance with the Labour party. He was the last prominent Maori prophet-leader in a line of prophets extending back to the New Zealand Wars' period.

In 1918 Ratana had a vision and spoke to his family: 'May peace be upon you; I am the Holy Spirit who is speaking to you; wash yourselves clean, make yourselves ready.' In this way Ratana became known as the mangai, or 'mouthpiece' of God. Throughout the following weeks his family thought that he had gone mad. He put the clothes of some of his whanau in piles, claiming that they were the clothes of the dead. They all died in the influenza pandemic then sweeping through the country. Those who had obeyed his advice to leave their homes survived.

Ratana became the head of a religious movement whose followers were called the morehu ('survivors' or 'ordinary people'). Many Maori soldiers from WWI joined his ranks. These were men from areas where tribal leadership was weak. They were disillusioned with the inability of Maori leaders, including the Young Maori Party, to make any gains for them in the Pakeha world. As stories of Ratana's miraculous abilities spread, crowds of those seeking to be healed gathered. So many Maori (and Pakeha) were trying to get to Ratana's pa near Wanganui that a new railway stop had to be created. Piles of abandoned walking sticks, crutches and wheelchairs grew at his pa, evidence of his success. He became known as the 'Maori Miracle Man'. A temple was built as the spiritual centre of his movement.

INSIDE THE PAKEHA SYSTEM: TAHUPOTIKI WIREMU RATANA

Ratana's approach to Maori-Pakeha relations was different to that of the Young Maori Party, Rua Kenana and Te Puea Herangi. He began as a spiritual leader *outside* the Pakeha system, but then later worked *inside* it when he turned to politics. He also promoted a healthy lifestyle for Maori, and the value of gaining a good education. Ratana was 41 when WWI broke out and was over the fighting age. It is not clear what his views on the war were.

Political Activity

Although Ratana had rejected any political involvement in the early years, his movement had been joined by many younger Maori. They wanted more control for Maori over their own affairs. In 1922 Ratana announced his political goals. These included recognition by the government of the Treaty of Waitangi, compensation for land confiscation, and equality between Maori and Pakeha. In 1928 he finally announced that he aimed to win all four of the Maori seats (the 'Four Quarters').

The Ratana movement's strength continued to grow, including inside parliament. Eruera Tirikatene won the first seat for Ratana's party in 1932. By 1934 Ratana had an astounding 40,000 followers, around half the Maori population. In 1936 Ratana formally entered into a long-lasting alliance with Labour, which was the government at the time. A Ratana candidate won the last Maori seat in 1943, with the defeat of Apirana Ngata. Tahupotiki Wiremu Ratana did not live to see the fulfilment of his prophecy that his party would win all four Maori seats, for he died in 1939. His belief, however, in a unified political movement working for the benefit of the morehu continued after his death. Although politically the Ratana movement had lost its influence by the end of the 20th century, the church still had a following of some 37,000 people.

ACTIVITIES

Below is the tenth article from the creed (statement of faith) of the Ratana religion.

"10. I believe that Tahupotiki Wiremu Ratana is a MOUTHPIECE of JEHOVAH, spreading abroad new light as the above truths concerning the salvation of the Spirit and the vitalising of the body."

1 What word in Maori means 'mouthpiece [of Jehovah]'?

2 Provide a quote of no more than four words from the creed that suggests that Ratana's religion is different from all other previous Maori prophet movements.

3 Explain how this article of the creed would make it difficult for anyone within the movement to challenge Ratana's authority and right to lead.

AS1.4 REVIEW ACTIVITY

In paragraphs of about 100 words for each, describe the perspectives (views) and actions (with an accompanying explanation) of:

- Wiremu Ratana on Maori leadership
- Apirana Ngata on the development of Maori land (see pages 26–28).

Maori Customs and Leadership

Ratana believed that Maori superstition needed to be overcome and replaced with a belief in God. This, he said, had been revealed to him in a vision. He believed that superstitions such as maketu and tapu – with their accompanying fear of the morepork and of spirits contained in sticks and clothing – were holding Maori back. He also wanted to overcome the influence of the tohunga (Maori priest/healer), which remained powerful in more remote areas. Ratana also rejected traditional Maori practices, including chiefly authority and tribalism. He believed that these were ineffective and divisive. He discouraged his followers from carving, from learning and reciting whakapapa (genealogy), and from using traditional karakia. When he began building churches, they did not include Maori carvings. He also formed his own brass band and a Maori Ladies' Orchestra. Hymns were written in order to replace traditional waiata.

Ratana's views and actions displeased other leaders. The Waikato's Kingitanga felt threatened by the huge support that Ratana's movement received. Ratana also caused concern amongst parliamentary leaders such as Ngata when he claimed that their successes were too few. Nor did he think that separatism was the answer, noting that Rua Kenana's attempts at it had failed. Ratana thus believed that Maori should put aside their divisions and differences in order to focus on gaining improvements.

SOURCE V

The Ratana temple at Ratana Pa.

SOURCE W

A Ratana youth band, Wanganui.

ACTIVITIES

Refer to Sources V and W, and the photograph on page 38

1. What statement in the text about Ratana's churches does the photograph in Source V support?
2. What statement in the text about Ratana's views on Maori culture does the photograph of the youth band in Source W support?
3. Where did the Ratana Movement start? Provide evidence from the photograph on page 38 that could be used to support the claim that the Ratana movement spread to other parts of New Zealand.
4. Provide evidence from each of the photographs that *could* be used to support the claim that the Ratana Movement was not traditionalist.
5. Find evidence in at least one of the photographs that shows that the Ratana Movement was not a 'disloyal' or separatist movement.

AS1.5 ESSAY PRACTICE

Follow the steps on the inside back cover to write the following essay.

Describe actions taken by the 'Young Maori Party' and Wiremu Ratana to achieve gains for Maori by working inside the Pakeha system. What other methods were used by different Maori leaders to make gains for Maori?

- Land issues (including consolidation and incorporation); health; World War One
- 'Outside': Rua Kenana's separatism; 'Alongside': Waikato and WWI; Waikato and Maori welfare

OR

In what campaigns did New Zealanders fight during WWI? What was the response of groups other than soldiers to WWI?

- Gallipoli, Western Front; Sinai and Palestine
- Ettie Rout; passive resistance (and official/public response to it); response to 'enemy aliens'

PART ONE

CHAPTER SIX

THE DEPRESSION (1929–1935) AND THE FIRST LABOUR GOVERNMENT

In October 1929 the value of shares on the New York Stock Exchange suddenly crashed. This marked the beginning of what came to be called the Great Depression. America's dramatic economic slump soon affected most of the world. The worst years were between 1931 and 1933. Businesses closed, unemployment increased and hardship became widespread. In a time of limited social welfare, many ordinary people suffered terribly. There seemed to be nothing that they could do about economic forces which they did not understand, and which were beyond their control. Those with a safe job or who were well-off did not suffer – some even prospered. Many of these people believed that the poor had only themselves to blame for their situation.

By the end of 1932 the official unemployment figure in New Zealand was 70,000. The real figure is higher, because women, Maori and men under 20 years of age were not counted. It was believed that Maori could rely on their tribes for assistance. Also, it was thought that Maori needed fewer things in life than Pakeha. Maori unemployment was estimated at 40%, while the Pakeha rate was about 12%. Women were supposed to be supported by either their fathers or husbands. Estimates thus put the real level of unemployment nearer 100,000 or 17% of the population of just over 1.5million. For the first time in the 20th century, unemployment even reached into the professional classes. Doctors, lawyers, accountants and teachers were also affected, although not as widely as unskilled or semi-skilled workers.

A meagre unemployment 'dole' was introduced for men in 1932 (funded from an extra tax), but it was not paid unless they did some sort of work. Public work schemes were established, such as road and tunnel building, or planting of forests. Other public work was as pointless as digging holes and then filling them in again. Those receiving any form of relief payments had to prove that they were not lazy or wasteful. Inspectors would often go to houses to confirm that this was so. In one case, a man was denied relief payments until he got rid of his canary, because it was said to be an unnecessary extra cost. Another was told to plant a garden, even though the only tool he had was a pocketknife – and outside his rental home was all asphalt!

SOURCE A

Hallelujah, I'm a bum
Hallelujah, bum again
Hallelujah, give me a handout
To revive us again
Why don't you work like other men?
How the hell can we work
When there's no work to do?

SOURCE B

Men from one of the unemployed men's camps excavate a hillside to improve the Akatarawa Road, as part of a relief work scheme.

George Forbes, leader of the Depression-era Coalition government. His colleague, Keith Holyoake (Prime Minister 1960–72) once said of Forbes that the only reason that he graduated from primary school was because it burnt down. Forbes was the wrong man, in the wrong place, at the wrong time in terms of dealing with the problems of the Depression.

What made matters worse for New Zealand was the fact that its overseas debt, per head of population, was one of the highest in the world. In 1933, a huge 40% of the government's income went on paying only the interest on its debt. To attempt to live within its means, the government cut back on expenditure. This reduced further the amount of money in the economy. Exports continued to fall, and so did people's incomes and living standards – by a total of 20%. The seeming inability of the government of the time to do anything saw frustration boil over. Protests grew, and in April 1932 riots broke out in Dunedin, Auckland and Wellington. Special police were immediately recruited and given wide powers under the hastily passed Public Safety Conservation Act. The surprising point about the riots is not that they happened, but that they hadn't happened sooner, or been more violent. Revolutionary ideas, such as communism or German-style fascism, appealed to only a few. Most people just wanted to be able to work and earn a decent living.

Rioting unemployed workers in Cuba Street, Wellington, are dispersed by mounted and foot police.

ACTIVITIES

Refer to the text

1 Draw three pie graphs, one to represent the total (real) unemployment figure, and a second and third to represent Maori and Pakeha unemployment figures. Label each clearly. Why do you think the Maori unemployment rate is an *estimated* figure?

2 Match the terms from Column B with the correct term from Column A. Then write a brief sentence using each of the matched pairs to develop their key idea. (The terms in Column A are in order.)

Column A	Column B
• Economic slump	• Public Safety Conservation Act
• Official unemployment figure	• 'A decent living'
• Dole	• Real unemployment figure
• Overseas debt	• Expenditure reduced
• Frustration	• Limited social welfare
• Revolutionary ideas	• Public work schemes

Refer to Sources A, B and C

3 Irony is when authors may say the opposite of what they really mean, in order to make their point. What point is being made in Source A?

4 What key idea from the main text do Sources B and C support?

5 Describe the sort of technology that the men are using to do their work. Why did the government consider this an economic way of doing this work?

6 How did the situation in Source A lead to the scenes shown in Sources B and C?

Refer to Source D

7 What key idea from the main text does this source support?

8 Provide evidence that supports the claim that the protesters are not intent on violence.

9 As well as this source, what other information would an historian want to find in order to determine just how widespread disturbances were during the Depression?

10 Use all of the sources to explain the causes and effects of frustration that occurred during the Depression.

LABOUR AND THE WELFARE STATE

Before Labour came to power, the government's policy to deal with the Depression was to sit tight and wait until things improved. According to standard economic theory of the time, governments were not supposed to interfere in the natural economic cycle. The Labour Party promised a more active approach. It pointed with disgust to the fact that people were hungry in the cities while farmers were being forced to let their crops rot, all in the name of standard economic practice. The riots in 1932, although totalling only six days, were a turning point. People wanted action from the government. Labour convincingly won the 1935 election by 55 seats to 25. The popular Michael Joseph Savage became Prime Minister. Labour set out to restore to New Zealanders their pride and dignity, by ensuring work for all. A Christmas bonus was immediately granted to all workers. This simple gesture won over many. Other steps were taken, including re-opening teacher training colleges and lowering the school starting age again to five. Free milk was introduced into schools to help deal with malnutrition. But more far-reaching steps were to come.

Labour was returned to power in 1938 with an increased percentage of the vote. It then began introducing its promised comprehensive welfare system. This was intended to provide social security for all New Zealanders, 'from the cradle to the grave'. Labour would, it said, help the poor by putting an end to uncertainty and reliance on charity. This was not a new idea, for there had been a slowly increasing number of benefits available since the late 19th century. What was new was the scale; nowhere else in the world was there such a comprehensive scheme. Provision was made for all people in old age to receive an income (a mixture of pensions and superannuation). Benefits for sickness, unemployment and other misfortunes created a 'safety net' for those at risk. Medical care was to be made free for all, including hospitals, doctors' visits, prescriptions and maternity care. A building programme (State houses) was begun in order to deal with the severe housing shortage. Free education was to be provided for all children. Other measures also gave the government more hands-on control of the economy.

SOURCE E

LABOUR
is making them
the NATION'S PRIDE
SAFEGUARD
Their future!
VOTE LABOUR

A Labour Party election poster, 1938. While Pakeha supported the Labour Party directly, Maori voted for the Ratana MPs, who were in alliance with Labour.

Prime Minister Michael Joseph Savage is greeted by an enthusiastic crowd during the 1938 election.

In 1936 Labour agreed to an alliance with the Ratana MPs. Although this put pressure on the government to look into Maori issues, Labour was already committed to doing so. Discrimination in the allocation of benefits was removed. However, Apirana Ngata in particular opposed Labour's plans. He was concerned that Maori would become dependent on government 'hand-outs'. Labour and the Ratana MPs rejected this view. They believed that *all* New Zealanders deserved a guaranteed minimum standard of living. Extra funding was also provided for Maori housing, as well as for Ngata's land development schemes. By 1940, over 1500 houses had been provided, over 3000 farm-worker jobs were created and 1900 more Maori were farming their own land.

Some historians have called the 1938 Social Security Act the most important law in New Zealand's history. Along with countries in Scandinavia, New Zealand was again leading the way in terms of social policy. Other western nations soon modelled their own welfare policies along similar lines. Critics such as former Prime Minister George Forbes opposed Labour's plan. Forbes believed that Social Security would bankrupt New Zealand. Despite these dire warnings, the economy flourished. By 1939 New Zealand had the third highest living standard in the world. Labour, however, cannot take all the credit for this. New Zealand was (and still is) a small country dependent upon the health of the wider world economy. By 1935, when Labour first came to power, the world economy had already begun to improve.

Furthermore, the tight economic policy of the previous government had seen the build-up of a healthy cash surplus. Labour was able to use it. Along with the cost, the other main criticism of the Welfare State was that people would become dependent on government handouts. These two concerns lay behind the major reforms that came in the 1980s (see page 116).

Old age pensioners collecting social security at a Post Office.

ACTIVITIES

1. Why did the Labour government reject 'standard economic theory'?
2. What were the two views on providing State welfare for Maori?
3. What was so different about the welfare system that Labour introduced? Provide a quote from the text that Labour used to describe their scheme.
4. In broad terms, what sort of benefits did Labour's welfare scheme provide?
5. 'New Zealand's standard of living was raised to third in the world by the policies of the Labour government.' Explain why you agree or disagree with this statement.

Refer to Sources E to G

6. Who, according to Source E, would receive the main benefits under a Labour government?
7. How useful is this source to the historian studying this period? Explain your answer.
8. Why is Source F on its own not sufficient proof that Labour was popular in 1938? Provide a fact from the main text that would be proof.
9. Describe the link between Sources E, F and G.

NEW ZEALAND IDENTITY: BETWEEN THE WARS

As the war clouds again gathered in Europe in the late 1930s, most Pakeha New Zealanders still felt that they were British. Many Maori also felt part of the British Empire, to greater or lesser degrees. The experiences of WWI made many New Zealanders feel not so much that they had developed a separate identity, but that they had proved themselves to be 'better British'. Smaller groups, such as the relatively few Chinese, Indians, Lebanese and Dalmatians in the country, did their best to be part of this identity. If not, they at least tried to be inconspicuous in terms of their own cultural values.

One of the 'threats' to New Zealand's sense of 'better British' identity came from the impact of American cultural influences. From the early 1920s, concern was being raised about the American presence in the media. In 1927, 350 out of the 400 films shown in New Zealand were from the United States. This led to the introduction of a law in 1928 for quotas of British films. By the 1930s, the proportion of British films being shown had increased to 50%.

SOURCE H

SOURCE I

Our Union Jack, on Empire Day
Floats proudly in the breeze;
Not here alone, but far away
In lands across the seas.

Wherever British children dwell
Or British folk may be,
On Empire Day our flag shall tell
That we are Britons free ...

'Tis thus it speaks, our Union Jack
Its message from the mast
To follow in the noble track
Of heroes in the past

Empire Day – Queen Victoria's birthday (May 24th) – was a commemoration of Victoria's long and splendid reign, as loyalists saw it. New Zealand continued to recognise this day up until 1958, when its name was changed to Commonwealth Day. This is a poem from a 1922 School Journal.

When American radio serials began to be broadcast in the early 1930s, there was further criticism of them being 'un-British'. One critic noted that New Zealanders were imitating Americans by saying 'Okay, baby'. Apart from a brief period during WWII, American radio serials were banned until the 1960s. Australian radio serials were deemed to be more acceptable, and they became popular.

Debate on a law to limit non-British films, 1928

"I say nothing against the American nation, but we ought to remember that we are British and as such we have a duty to encourage the production of films which depict the life of Britishers rather than Americans."

A more specifically New Zealand identity began to emerge with the election of the first Labour government in 1935, but the outbreak of war four years later curbed this. However, New Zealanders' view of themselves as ground-breaking seemed to be confirmed with the policies of the Labour government. Labour took State welfare to an extent not seen anywhere else in the world. As one Labour Minister said: 'This policy was made in New Zealand, by New Zealand citizens who know New Zealand conditions.' When National came to power in 1949 it did not dramatically change Labour's welfare policies. State welfare had become an important part of New Zealand identity – for both Maori and Pakeha. It was based on a sense of egalitarianism (equal treatment for all).

SOURCE J

The poet Eileen Duggan wrote despairingly in 1924 of New Zealand's failure to build on the sense of separate national identity that seemed to have come out of WWI.

'Five years ago New Zealand was a healthy, rosy child peeping out from behind mother's apron. Now it is a simpering debutante [shy maiden], paying calls, and echoing Mother's phrases ... At present the cry is Empire. The children have it week in, week out ... I feel as if I want to stop every child in the street and say – 'this is your country – You can see it – touch it – love it. What do you know of Empire?'

Maori Identity

Up until WWII, iwi links (tribalism) remained the single strongest influence on identity for many Maori. Most settlements were still rural and communal, with little room for Pakeha ideas of individualism. Most were still poor, isolated and marginalised outside the Pakeha mainstream. Tribal leaders such as the Waikato's Te Puea Herangi reinforced the place of the tribe in Waikato identity. Even in areas where tribalism was not strong, one of the other alternatives – assimilation – had failed to take hold. The Young Maori Party (YMP) had been unsuccessful in their efforts to persuade Maori to adopt Pakeha ways. Few Maori saw the YMP as more than the contact point between their world and the Pakeha world. Assimilation, then, had not appealed to Maori. Nor had separatism. Even at its height, Rua Kenana's separatist community in Maungapohatu had remained relatively small. However, Kenana's influence, even if limited, does show that some Maori were still willing to look to a prophet to help them deal with the world.

A different prophet who drew a far larger gathering than Kenana was Wiremu Ratana. Ratana was different to all of the other Maori leaders in the period up to WWII. He rejected entirely the tribal identity that the Kingitanga depended upon. He also rejected both Rua Kenana's separatism and the Young Maori Party's efforts in parliament. He claimed that both were ineffective and had done nothing for the ordinary Maori. While he encouraged Maori to take on Pakeha ways, he still saw Maori as a separate but equal partner to Pakeha, as guaranteed by the Treaty of Waitangi. At its height, some 40,000 Maori – about half the population – claimed to follow Ratana's teachings. This suggests that Ratana provided many Maori with a sense of identity that had previously been unfulfilled.

ACTIVITIES

1 Why would film in particular be seen as such a great threat to the 'Britishness' of New Zealand?

Refer to Sources H to J (pages 43–44)

2 What does the person in Source H represent? Why is it considered so important to be patriotic at this particular time?

3 Quote the line in Source I that states clearly that New Zealanders consider themselves to be British.

4 Quote the line from Source I which seems to indicate that this poem is meant for use in schools.

5 What evidence in Source J supports the claim that New Zealanders saw themselves as British?

6 What does the poet Eileen Duggan mean by the first line in Source J? To what event is she referring?

7 Who is the 'Mother' that Duggan refers to in Source J?

AS1.5 ESSAY PRACTICE

Follow the steps on the inside back cover to write the following essay.

Describe main features of the relationship between New Zealand and Britain between 1900 and 1939 (the start of WWII). In what ways did Maori share this sense of belonging to the British Empire?

- War (Boer and WWI); economic; patriotism (schooling, culture)
- Young Maori Party; Pioneer Battalion; Waikato (Te Puea Herangi) and Tuhoe (Rua Kenana).

CHAPTER SEVEN

WORLD WAR TWO, 1939–1945

OVERVIEW

When Germany invaded neighbouring Poland on September 1st 1939, it sparked a brutal war that would last six years. Some twenty years earlier, the 'Great War' had cost ten million lives – WWII would take more than fifty million, the majority of them civilians.

> "None of us have any hatred of the German people. We are fighting a doctrine that springs from contempt of human nature ... To destroy it, but not the great nation which it has so cruelly cheated, is the task of those who have taken up arms against Nazism."
>
> Prime Minister Michael Joseph Savage, 1939.

According to one version of events, for twelve hours on September 3rd 1939, New Zealand stood alone against the might of the German military. This was not intentional. New Zealand had accidentally declared war before Britain did, because of the time difference between the two countries. Whatever the real story, this time around there was not the same unquestioning enthusiasm as there had been in 1914. New Zealanders knew of the horrors and terrible cost of war. There was, however, no doubt that they would participate. Even so, the Prime Minister, Labour's Michael Joseph Savage, had to be persuaded to make his famous speech about joining the war. Finally he agreed, saying: 'Where Britain goes, we go; where Britain stands, we stand.'

Within the first week of the declaration of war, 12,000 men had volunteered to fight. By 1940, even though 60,000 had signed up, the numbers had slowed. Conscription was introduced. The same Labour politicians who had gone to prison during WWI for their opposition to conscription were now the ones introducing it. In the five years in which conscription was in place, 306,000 New Zealanders were called up to serve in either the military or the work force. This time around, Maori were not conscripted to fight. Many joined up voluntarily anyway.

WWII involved more of the population in a more direct way than had WWI. As well as the army, there were over 12,000 pilots and other flight crew in the RNZAF. They mostly fought as part of Britain's airforce. Around 400 New Zealanders served as aircrew in Malaya and Singapore before both fell to Japan. Over 100 New Zealand pilots flew in the crucial Battle of Britain in 1940. A New Zealander, Sir Keith Park, was in charge of defending London and southern England from German bombing raids. Once this battle was over, about 1200 New Zealanders joined Bomber Command as aircrew. They were involved in some of the most dangerous missions of the war into enemy territory. In another area, over 9000 men also served in the Navy and many of them saw action. HMNZS *Achilles* helped defeat the German pocket battleship *Graf Spee* at the Battle of River Plate. Even the men not fit for active war service were involved. They were part of the Home Guard, an organisation whose job it was to defend New Zealand against invasion. Furthermore, everyone at 'home' was affected by the rationing of foods, fuel and other resources necessary for the war effort.

An RNZAF recruitment poster.

Maori were also more fully involved in the war effort. Leaders like Te Puea Herangi dropped their opposition to fighting. This was because the government had made some progress on issues concerning Maori. Unlike the Pioneer Battalion in WWI, Maori now did not have to fight under Pakeha commanders. Maori were also immediately used as frontline fighting troops. This was because the racial concerns about non-whites fighting whites were no longer as relevant. Some 17,000 Maori signed up voluntarily out of a population of 95,000. A further 11,500 took jobs in essential war industries.

Women were also much more involved. They entered the Armed Forces (as non-combatants) and war industries in New Zealand. All up, 640 women joined the Army's Nursing Service. An additional 5000 served in the Women's Auxiliary Army Corps as drivers, mechanics and as gunners

Three German views of New Zealand troops: the first is at the start of the war and the second from near the end.

"It is just as well that the New Zealand soldiers are, as it were, just poor country lads, who don't know what it [the war] is all about, otherwise the whole Continent [Europe] would be rocking with laughter... Their bones will bleach on the desert and moulder on the steppes and bogs."

Report in a Berlin newspaper upon the arrival of New Zealand troops in Egypt.

"The New Zealanders ... are dangerous opponents. They are specialists in night fighting. They fight over a wide front and their method of attack resembles the German method."

Report in captured documents of the German 278th Division in Italy.

After capturing supplies intended for the Maori Battalion the Germans were surprised to find salted mutton-bird. Not knowing what it was, they used the find as propaganda, saying that the New Zealanders were reduced to eating seagulls.

for anti-aircraft and coastal defences. There was also a section that Maori women could join.

Altogether 194,000 men and 10,000 women out of a population of 1.6 million served in the military. There were over 40,000 casualties, with 11,500 deaths. Nearly 8400 were taken prisoner. Proportionately, these losses were the highest for a Commonwealth country (including Britain). They were bad, but not as terrible as those in WWI.

Maori members of the Women's Army Auxiliary Corp, Wellington wharf.

THE WAR IN NORTH AFRICA AND EUROPE

Most of the ground fighting by New Zealanders took place around the Mediterranean Sea (Greece, North Africa and Italy). The troops who left home early in 1940 were part of the 2nd New Zealand Expeditionary Force (NZEF). The NZEF Headquarters was in Cairo (Egypt), and this was where the first troops were sent for their training. Unlike WWI, they were now commanded by a New Zealander, Major General Bernard Freyberg. Britain, however, still wanted to decide on its own when and where the New Zealand troops should be used. Its leaders still seemed to think that, as in WWI, New Zealand troops were its own to command. This caused some tension between the New Zealand and British governments.

As with WWI, the initial fighting resulted in heavy defeats for the Allies. In March 1941 New Zealanders were sent to help with the defence of Greece. German troops invaded in early April. Within a couple of weeks the Allies had been overcome and the survivors withdrew to Crete.

Bernard Freyberg (left) and Howard Kippenberger, New Zealand military leaders. Note the German-sounding names. This would have been a problem in WWI, but there was not the same level of anti-German hysteria in WWII.

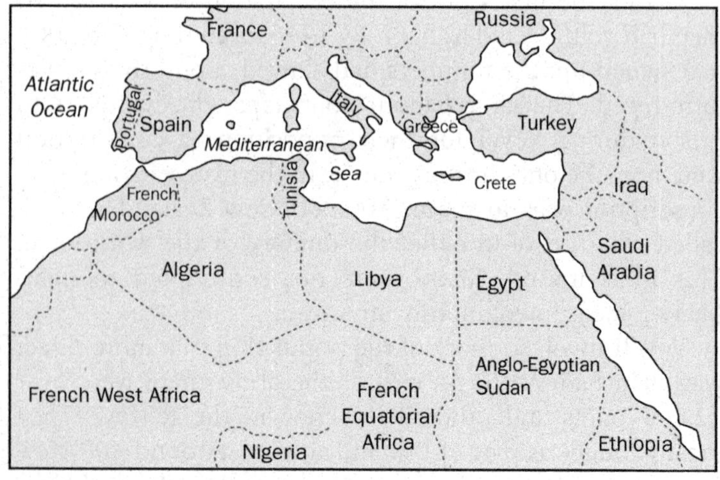

New Zealanders fought mainly in Greece, Crete, North Africa and Italy.

German paratroopers then invaded Crete in May. This was the first ever full airborne invasion. Despite appalling losses, the Germans took Crete within ten days. This was because the defenders had a serious lack of equipment and support – especially air cover – and some bad decisions were made by General Freyburg. Two New Zealanders, A.C. Hulme and Charles Upham, were each awarded a Victoria Cross (VC). This was the highest award for bravery in the British Empire. The failure and losses at Crete meant that it came to be seen by New Zealanders as the 'Gallipoli of WWII'. Ironically, Winston Churchill – British Prime Minister during WWII – oversaw both of these campaigns.

Erwin Rommell, the 'Desert Fox'.

The next action took place in the flatness of the North African desert. It began in late 1941 with a campaign in Libya against the German Afrika Korps. The Afrika Korps was led by the brilliant Field Marshal, Erwin Rommel. The decisive battle came in October 1942 at El Alamein. In it, the New Zealanders helped Britain's General Montgomery finally push the Germans back from Egypt. The important sea route of the Suez Canal, and oil fields in the area, were finally safe. The battles continued through northern Libya and Tunisia before the Germans finally surrendered in May of 1943.

New Zealand troops advancing in the North African desert.

The Maori Battalion

Members of the Maori Battalion in front of a German Messerschmitt fighter plane at Tripolitania. The plane was shot down by the Royal Air Force.

Although Maori had the choice of enlisting in the Army alongside Pakeha, many chose to join the Maori Battalion. Maori men joined up with enthusiasm. During the Battalion's training in New Zealand, Colonel Rennie noted that when the 146 officer recruits were given a long weekend on leave, 170 returned! All were in the correct battledress and the 'extras' had even learned the appropriate drills and commands. On May 1st 1940, the 800 men of the Maori Battalion embarked for Britain.

The Maori Battalion was divided into four companies (about 200 men each). 'A Company' was made up of Northland's Ngapuhi and was nicknamed the 'Gumdiggers'. 'B Company', from Rotorua, Bay of Plenty, Coromandel and Thames Valley was the 'Penny Divers'; 'C Company' from the East Coast was the 'Cowboys'; and 'D Company' – Waikato, Maniapoto, Taranaki, Hawkes Bay, Wellington and all of the South Island – was called 'Ngati Walkabout'.

The Maori Battalion received special praise for its actions during the war. From Crete to Libya, 270 were killed, 815 wounded and a further 20 taken prisoner. Overall, 32 officers and 552 other ranks died. General Freyberg said: 'No infantry Battalion had a more distinguished record or, alas, had such heavy casualties, than the Maori Battalion.' The officers led their men from the front and used non-standard tactics. Because of this, they suffered a high casualty rate. But this approach also won them many victories, and a reputation among both Maori and Pakeha as fine warriors.

Many members of the Maori Battalion were singled out for recognition. One, Arapeta Awatere, was rapidly promoted during these campaigns because of his leadership skills and bravery. In 1944 he became the eleventh commander of the Maori Battalion. He was concerned for the welfare of his men and avoided unnecessary risk. He instructed his men to communicate in Maori while on reconnaissance patrols to avoid eavesdropping by the enemy. On the other hand, he was responsible for the mistreatment of enemy prisoners, and even ordered the execution of wounded German soldiers. This was against the Geneva Convention on the treatment of prisoners. When General Freyberg heard of this, Awatere lost his command and was sent home (but, in recognition of his fighting value, not until *after* the war was over).

Arapeta Awatere

Another who distinguished himself was Lieutenant Te Moana-nui-a-Kiwa Ngarimu. He received a posthumous (after his death) Victoria Cross. Ngarimu's VC was presented to his parents by the Governor General at a hui in Ruatoria in October 1943.

Moana-nui-a-Kiwa Ngarimu

ACTIVITIES

1 Write a short speech that might have been delivered at the Ruatoria hui by the Governor General, Sir Cyril Newall. In it you should briefly:
- identify the reason for the award of Lt Ngarimu's Victoria Cross (for bravery)
- state how his exploits reflect upon the Maori people as a whole
- explain how Lt Ngarimu fulfilled his duty to 'King and country'.

SOURCE A

Maori Battalion Marching Song
By Corporal Anaia Amohau, 1940

CHORUS
Maori Battalion march to victory
Maori Battalion staunch and true
Maori Battalion march to glory
Take the honour of the people with you
We will march, march, march to the enemy
And we'll fight right to the end.
For God! For King! And for Country!
AU – E! Ake, ake, kia kaha e! (Forever be strong!)

Refer to Source A

2 Provide a short quote that shows that the opinions of whanau and other Maori were important to the members of the Maori Battalion.

3 Provide a short quote that shows that the Maori Battalion considered itself part of the British Commonwealth forces.

Refer to the Maori Battalion box on page 47

4 How might being part of the Maori Battalion have *reinforced* tribal identity? How might being part of the Maori Battalion have helped form a *new* sense of identity that went beyond tribalism?

5 Create a full page recruiting poster for the Maori Battalion. Keep it simple and uncluttered, with a strong central image. Choose one or more of the key ideas from the text in any part of this section, such as:
- No organised opposition
- Maori commanders
- Frontline action
- Many Maori have already signed up
- Lt Ngarimu's Victoria Cross
- Continuing the WWI Pioneer Battalion tradition
- The 'earning' of equality.

A member of the New Zealand Expeditionary Force in the Egyptian desert.

Mutiny!
Not everyone was willing to continue putting their lives at risk in order to live up to the reputation that the New Zealanders were earning. After the battles in North Africa, some of the troops were sent home on leave. They were welcomed back as heroes. A movement soon grew opposing their return to the war. Other men who had not yet gone to fight were called on to take their place. The authorities did not accept this view. Over 800 soldiers were court-martialled and convicted for desertion. Another 500 men had all payments due to them withheld. These actions caused a public outcry. In response, the sentences were suspended and all payments were made in full at the end of the war. Out of the 5,500 men who left North Africa on leave in 1943, only 680 returned to the war.

THE WAR IN ITALY

After North Africa, the focus for New Zealand turned to Italy. The first troops arrived in **Taranto** in October 1943. (Sicily was under Allied control, and Italy had already surrendered by this time. The German troops, however, continued the fight.) Most expected that Italy would be relatively easy after battling the Germans and Italians in North Africa. The change to farmland and olive groves was also welcome after the sand and heat of the desert, although there were now more places for the enemy to hide. In addition, the mountainous countryside meant that there were many rivers to cross. Like Gallipoli during WWI, the Allied leaders considered the Italian campaign to be a side-show to the main conflict. That would come with the invasion of German-occupied France in 1944.

The first major battle against the German troops in Italy took place across the **Sangro River**. The New Zealanders were encouraged by the relatively easy victory. This battle, however, was followed by a bitter and costly attack on a well-defended mountain town called **Orsogna**. The New Zealanders' suddenly realised that there was still much to do before defeating the enemy. Probably the most infamous and difficult battle occurred at the medieval town of **Monte Cassino**. Indian and New Zealand troops – with the Maori Battalion as a spearhead – were used as shock-troops, in an effort to storm the ancient monastery. The Germans, however, were well-armed and dug in. The attack resulted in enormous losses, and the morale of the New Zealanders plummeted. In addition, the cold and wet, disease and lack of sleep made it all seem hopeless. Despite one of the most intensive aerial bombing campaigns of the whole war, the Germans still put up stiff resistance. It seemed impossible to budge them.

A German cartoon showing British Prime Minister Winston Churchill and US President Roosevelt.

Eventually, after the loss of 350 men, the attempt to take Cassino was abandoned. The German commander in Italy, Field Marshall Kesselring, was happy: 'I am very pleased that the New Zealanders have had a smack on the nose.' The dispirited Kiwi troops moved around the town and continued up the coast. They went past **Rome** to the **Arno River**, near Florence, where there was vicious hand-to-hand fighting. In April 1945 the New Zealanders took **Bologna** and then moved on to **Venice** and **Trieste**. On the 8th of May the war in Europe came to an end. Germany surrendered after its capital Berlin was occupied by Russian troops – Hitler had committed suicide on April 30th. The New Zealanders still had a couple of tense months to serve as they prevented Yugoslavia's communist troops from seizing control of Trieste.

ACTIVITY

Use a stamp map or download a map of Italy. Locate and label as many of the places as you can that are in bold in the text (pages 48–49).

HOW WELL DID THE NEW ZEALANDERS DO?

Altogether over 1800 New Zealanders were killed and more than 6600 wounded in Italy. High praise came from British leaders such as Prime Minister Winston Churchill and Foreign Minister Anthony Eden. Bernard Montgomery, the Field Marshal in charge of the Allied troops in North Africa, noted how well the New Zealanders had fought. Even Erwin Rommel, the German Afrika Korps Field Marshal, singled out the New Zealanders for praise. The Australian troops, too, said that in fighting ability the Australians were 'second only to the New Zealanders' – high praise indeed. The Maori Battalion was even more successful than the Pioneer Battalion of World War One. Its achievements helped persuade the government to treat Maori as the equal of Pakeha.

THE PACIFIC WAR

For most New Zealanders at home, the war at first seemed far away. This all changed in December 1941. The Japanese attacked the American naval base at Pearl Harbour (**Hawaii**), and the British forces in **Malaya**. The **Philippines**, **Hong Kong** and **Singapore** fell quickly in early 1942. New Zealanders were stunned. The large British naval base at Singapore was supposed to be able to withstand any attack.

New Zealand sent about 20,000 troops to help the American war effort in the Pacific. They were involved in the difficult and costly task of clearing the Japanese out of the many Pacific Islands that they still occupied. One place where New Zealanders fought was the **Solomon Islands**. Disease and the ever-present heat made the job doubly unpleasant. Troops were also stationed at **Norfolk Island**, **Tonga** and **New Caledonia**.

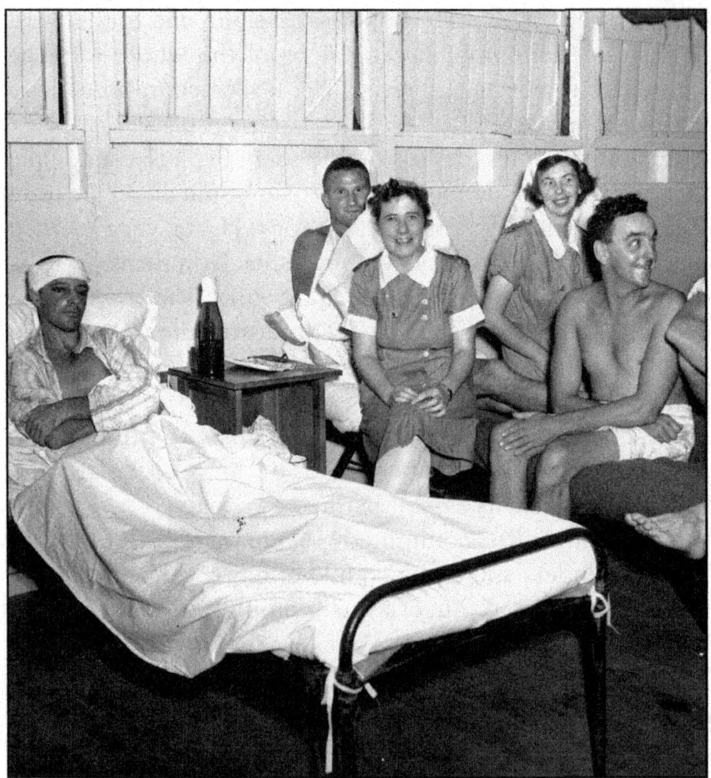

Nurses and wounded soldiers of the 2nd New Zealand Expeditionary Force in the Pacific at the 4th New Zealand General Hospital in New Caledonia.

Members of the 2nd New Zealand Expeditionary Force (in the Pacific) at a burial, Vella Lavella Island, Solomon Islands.

A Japanese soldier called Shoichi Yokoi was discovered on the Pacific Island of Guam in 1972. He had spent 28 years hiding in the jungle, believing that WWII was still in progress.

The Japanese swept down through South East Asia to **Indonesia** and the north coast of **New Guinea**. They looked to have Australia and then New Zealand firmly in their sights. Both countries were alone except for one important ally, the United States. It was the American victories in the crucial naval battles of the **Coral Sea** and **Midway Island** in May and June 1942 that began to turn the Japanese back. The Japanese, however, had come close. They had bombed northern Australia and sent reconnaissance flights and a submarine to New Zealand.

In March 1944 New Zealand's active combat troops were withdrawn from the Pacific. In August 1945 the war with Japan came to an end with the dropping of the two atomic bombs on Hiroshima and Nagasaki. The number of New Zealanders killed and wounded in the Pacific was relatively low (2200 killed and 3000 wounded). Of the 26 who were taken prisoner by the Japanese, only seven survived the harsh treatment.

ACTIVITIES

Use a stamp map or download a map of South East Asia. Locate and label as many of the places as you can that are in bold in the text (page 50). Also show arrows spreading out from Japan to mark the progress of Japanese forces.

INSIDE NEW ZEALAND: THE HOME FRONT

More so than in WWI, the people of New Zealand were involved in WWII. Many were overseas doing the fighting. Others were engaged in the Home Guard providing defence for New Zealand in the event of an invasion. Large numbers worked in factories producing war materials, or on farms to keep the economy going. Men and women, the young and the old, Maori and Pakeha – all played their part. In addition, the rationing of scarce resources affected everybody.

SOURCE D

Rationing continued after WWII had ended. Resentment at this was one factor that contributed to the fall of the Labour government in 1949.

ACTIVITIES

Refer to Sources B and C

1. Who are these posters targeted at?
2. What enemy countries are represented in Source B?
3. What do these posters want people to do? What effect does Source B suggest this will have on the enemy? Explain your answer.
4. What method does Source C use to appeal for support?

Refer to Source D

5. Which country does this poster want people to help out?
6. How does the imagery used suggest that each worker's contribution is important?
7. What group of workers appears to be ignored by this poster, despite their contribution?
8. What key idea from the text do Sources B–D provide evidence for?
9. Who is likely to have produced Sources B–D?

'Enemies' Within

Those who didn't want to be involved in the war effort were imprisoned with hard labour. Eight hundred conscientious objectors received this punishment. Some people weren't *allowed* to be involved in the war effort. They were the 'enemy aliens' – especially Germans or Italians. Over 200 were imprisoned on Somes Island in Wellington harbour. In a few cases, in both New Zealand and Western Samoa, they had in fact been trying to organise Nazi-style movements amongst themselves.

Prisoners of War on Somes Island, Wellington.

After WWI, a significant anti-war sentiment developed. When WWII broke out, few maintained their pacifist beliefs. Robert Semple was a staunch opponent of conscription in WWI (he was jailed for it). By the time of WWII he (and other WWI anti-conscriptionists) was part of the Labour government that introduced conscription.

Home Guard

The Home Guard was established in 1940 with the aim of protecting New Zealand from invasion. Men who were too old or too young to fight were called on to form units and train. At its peak 100,000 men served. At first, sporting rifles and wooden guns were used and the men were taught how to make bombs out of things such as jam tins. Eventually the Home Defence Force consisted of some coastal guns, aerial surveillance of the seas and a few tanks. In some areas public air raid shelters were constructed, including at Parliament House and under Wright's Hill in Wellington, as well as under Albert Park in Auckland. Some people also dug shelters in their back yards. Art treasures and important documents were taken from the nation's galleries, museums and archives to be hidden in the countryside.

One incident that showed the reality of New Zealand's war was the shooting of some Japanese prisoners of war (POWs) in 1943. About 800 captured Japanese had been placed into a camp at Featherstone in 1942. Apparently the prisoners did not understand that international law allowed POWs to be put to (paid) work. They refused when asked to. A riot broke out that led to the deaths of 48 Japanese and one guard.

Christchurch South Home Guard Battalion.

Into the Workforce

Conscription for the armed forces had been introduced in 1940, and in early 1942 the government also 'conscripted' or 'man-powered' the work force. This meant that men and women could be called upon to work in certain industries that were considered to be essential. By the end of the war 176,000 people had been 'man-powered'. Because so many men – about one-third of the workforce – were away overseas, women were called in to do jobs that had previously been 'men's work'. Those who left the cities to work on farms were given the nickname 'Land Girls'. Others worked in factories, drove taxis, buses and trucks, or serviced cars and aeroplanes. In 1939 nearly 25,700 women were employed in manufacturing. This increased to a peak of 37,000 by 1945.

Most women returned to their 'normal' roles as wives and mothers when the men came back from the war. It would not be until the 1960s when young educated women began to challenge their position in society.

ACTIVITIES

1. Choose any of the photographs from pages 52–53. Imagine that you are one of the people in the photograph. Explain the following, with as much detail as you can:
   - What are you doing?
   - When are you doing it?
   - Where are you doing it?
   - Why are you doing it?
   - How are you doing it?
   - What are you thinking/feeling?
2. Use the same photograph (or select another) and explain what happened one week after it was taken. Use your imagination, but be sensible.
3. Explain the terms 'man-powered' and 'land girls'.

Refer to Sources E–H

4. What is the likely relationship between Sources E and F, and between Sources G and H?
5. Make THREE points about the sort of person whom Source F is targeting. Refer to the text and the image.
6. What key idea from the 'Into the Workforce' text does Source G support?
7. What organisation produced the poster in Source H? What does this tell us about how the war affected business life in New Zealand?
8. Imagine that you are one of the women in these photographs. Write a diary entry of about 100–150 words that tells of a typical work day as a 'land girl' or factory worker. Explain how you feel when told that you will no longer have your job after the war.

Land girls': many were from the cities and had never been on farms before.

SOURCE F

Below
Women assembling mortars in a munitions factory.

SOURCE G

SOURCE H

WANTED

200 More Women and Girls for Munitions Work

Our booklet "This is Where We Work" gives you some idea of the all-important work being carried out by the women and girls who are making munitions at the New Zealand Ford Factory; and it shows you the excellent conditions under which they are working.

Today, New Zealand is being called upon for still more supplies for the fighting fronts. We have to step-up munitions production—immediately!

There's a job here for YOU—and 199 other women and girls.

This is YOUR opportunity to back up New Zealand's gallant fighting men

Our own troops, our airmen, our men in the Navy, and those of our Allies, need the munitions—as fast as we can send them. They'll win the war if we all do our part.

Choose this No. I War Job

Apply to Mrs. Stark, Matron, between the hours of 8.30 a.m. and 5.30 p.m. If unable to call, applications for employment can be made by letter, or inquiries can be made by telephone—No. 60-141.

FORD MOTOR COMPANY OF NEW ZEALAND LIMITED
Seaview Road Lower Hutt
Telephone 60-141

The Maori War Effort Organisation

Maori at home were also more fully involved in the Second World War than the First. Paraire Paikea was appointed Minster in charge of the Maori war effort and he established the Maori War Effort Organisation (MWEO). When he died in 1943 Eruera Tirikatene took his place. Tirikatene saw a greater role for the MWEO. He hoped that it would become the basis for greater control of Maori affairs. The government, however, was not sympathetic to this aim. Despite this, the MWEO proved to be an effective way of working, for it was run on a tribal basis. Governments had previously tried to break down tribal bonds, seeing them as a barrier to progress in the Pakeha world. Now, in a time of crisis, these same bonds were to prove their value. The MWEO set up some 400 tribal committees to help recruit soldiers, contribute to the Home Guard and provide food and funds for the Red Cross. It expanded its role into welfare, providing some support for Maori who had migrated to the cities. Around 10,000 Maori men and women were part of the MWEO. Combined with those who served in the military, this makes around 30% of Maori who served 'King and country' between 1939 and 1945. Maori women were also active in the MWEO committees, an experience that would help them take leadership roles in the post-war period.

ACTIVITIES

1 Create a full page recruiting poster for the Maori War Effort Organisation. Keep it simple and uncluttered, with a strong central image. Choose one or more of the key ideas from the above paragraph, such as:

- Organised on a tribal basis
- The MWEO's war role
- The MWEO's welfare role
- Opportunities for women.

2 **A diversion from the War** – 1940 centenary celebrations. Read the text and study the images on pages 54–55.

You have been asked by Radio New Zealand to put together a radio report on the centenary celebrations. Use the main text (and the weblink, if possible) to guide your commentary.

- Include interviews with a variety of people
- Use your imagination, but keep it realistic for the times.

A DIVERSION FROM THE WAR

In 1940, many New Zealanders celebrated the progress made in the one hundred years since the signing of the Treaty of Waitangi. Not everyone was convinced that it was right to celebrate. Some Maori felt that there were still many outstanding grievances to settle. Some Pakeha argued that to spend time and money on the centennial was wrong while the war was on. The Labour government, however, had already made extensive plans for this celebration of nationhood. It also believed that the events might be a boost for the nation's morale.

Apirana Ngata leads the haka at the opening of the Waitangi Meeting House, built for the centennial celebrations.

'The Exhibition is intended to arouse a just pride in our country and its development over the past 100 years. This spirit is of even more importance in a time of great national stress.'

Wellington Mayor and Centennial Exhibition Chairman, T.C. Hislop

Various activities were organised around the country. At Waitangi, a large carved meeting house constructed by Apirana Ngata was opened. In Christchurch a parade that stretched for over three kilometres took place. A government film called *One Hundred Crowded Years* was released. It celebrated Pakeha achievement in the taming of a 'savage' country. Maori images were also prominent. Maori themselves were shown as contented performers of traditional action songs. The role of women in 'taming' the country was shown – as mothers and housewives. Three books were also published. The first looked at Pakeha achievements. The second reported frankly on the injustices Maori had suffered and the achievements that had been made. The third was a school text called *The Making of New Zealand*. But the main event was the six-month long Centennial Exhibition at Wellington.

An enormous Exhibition park was built in Wellington to promote the image of a country that had progressed rapidly in one hundred years. A 52-metre high tower was an appropriate centrepiece and symbol. On either side of the entrance were sculptures of pioneering men and women. The amusement park, Playland, covered four hectares (ten acres) and had a one-kilometre long roller coaster ride. Displays by various government departments told the story of a country where the State looked after the welfare of its people. This was very much in line with the Labour government's beliefs and policies.

New Zealand itself was depicted as young, healthy, naturally beautiful, progressive and inventive. It was also a British country. Lord Willingdon, the British representative in New Zealand, commented shortly before his departure: 'Wherever I have been, I have found New Zealand [to be] as British as ever before.' The displays also presented New Zealand as a country with good race relations. This was a bold claim, especially as the Waikato people, led by the Maori King Koroki and Te Puea Herangi, boycotted the celebrations. They were upset that King Koroki had not been treated appropriately for someone of his position. Nonetheless, there were over 2.6million visitors to the Exhibition between November 1939 and April 1940. This was not a bad turnout considering that there were less than two million people in New Zealand at the time, and few tourists.

New Zealand Centennial Exhibition, special souvenir cover.

The 'American Invasion'

Between 1942 and 1944 100,000 American servicemen arrived in New Zealand. Under pressure, the government had agreed to leave New Zealand troops to fight Britain's war in North Africa. A promise by the U.S President to send troops here sealed the deal. As well as providing protection, the US. troops would also train for the upcoming assault on Japanese-held Pacific islands. The 'American invasion' was an important step towards an increasing dependence on America for security.

For New Zealanders who were isolated at the bottom of the South Pacific, the arrival of the Americans was truly an invasion by an alien culture. One little girl who saw the US troops march down her street ran home calling to her mother that the Germans had arrived. Most of the troops were stationed around Wellington and Auckland in hastily built army camps. Including the crews of ships and other non-fighting military staff, there may actually have been around 150,000 of the 'invaders'. With them they brought new lifestyle items such as Coca-Cola, bubble-gum, nylon stockings, hamburgers and dry-cleaning, as well as a touch of Hollywood-style glamour.

US soldiers with New Zealand girls – a touch of glamour.

The New Zealanders' response to the arrival of the Americans was a mix of gratitude and joy for some, and envy and bitterness for others. Many New Zealand women found the Americans irresistible. New Zealand men in the 1940s were generally unsophisticated and not terribly romantic. The American soldiers, by contrast, had an easy, friendly manner and were generous (with chocolates and stockings) and more romantic. A rather bitter saying of New Zealand men was that the Americans were 'over-paid, over-sexed and over here.' Their bitterness was to a certain extent justified. Up to 2000 New Zealand women married Americans, sometimes because they had become pregnant. More than a few New Zealand men were left broken-hearted. There was also a certain level of anti-American feeling simply because they were not *British*. One factor that caused this dislike to erupt into an all-out brawl was the treatment of Maori by some of the Americans.

The US troops, especially those from the southern states, brought their racial views to New Zealand. They were not welcomed by either Maori or Pakeha. In 1943, what has come to be called the 'Battle of Manners Street' broke out in Wellington. It supposedly began when several US servicemen said that they wouldn't socialise with Maori 'niggers'. Pakeha fought alongside Maori in the brawl that followed. Some reports say that two Americans were killed, but it is difficult to know for sure because the whole affair was hushed up by the government.

ACTIVITIES

For each statement below, indicate whether it is most likely TRUE or FALSE. In either case, provide evidence from the text to support your answer. (Evidence could be a quote, statistic or fact.)

1. New Zealand would have been unable to defend itself from a Japanese invasion.
2. Most parts of New Zealand were affected by the arrival of the American troops.
3. New Zealanders were already used to American culture.
4. Most New Zealand men were glad that the Americans had arrived to defend the country.
5. Many New Zealand women were glad that the Americans had arrived.
6. There was a significant degree of anti-American feeling amongst New Zealanders.

AS1.5 ESSAY PRACTICE

Follow the steps on the inside back cover to write the following essay.

Describe the main theatres of war in which New Zealand troops were involved during WWII. What contribution did those at home in New Zealand make to the war effort?

- Greece and Crete; North Africa; Italy; Maori Battalion
- Home Guard; Maori War Effort Organisation; 'man-powering'; women

CHAPTER EIGHT

AFTER THE WAR: MAORI-PAKEHA RACE RELATIONS

The single biggest issue impacting on race relations after WWII was Maori urbanisation. In the mid-19th century, Maori had had to adapt to a flood of European immigrants, which had a far-reaching impact on their lives. In the mid-20th century, Pakeha had to adapt to a (smaller-scale) flood of Maori migrants into the cities. For those Maori who left their rural homes, the Pakeha world they experienced was at first quite alien. This migration had a far-reaching impact on the lifestyle of those who made the journey, as well as on those who were born into a new generation of urban Maori.

EFFECTS OF AN INCREASING MAORI POPULATION: URBANISATION

The Maori population prior to WWII had been rapidly increasing as Maori health had improved. Disease took fewer lives as changes were made to hygiene, housing and water supplies. By the middle of the 20th century the rate of Maori population increase was over three times that of Pakeha. This contributed to a huge growth in the Maori population to over 100,000 by 1945 (half of whom were 'full-blooded'). This in turn put increased pressure on scarce resources in the countryside, providing a good reason to migrate to the cities. Joining the urban flow were Maori soldiers coming back from WWII. After the excitement of the war, a quiet life in the countryside no longer appealed. The cities offered not only excitement but also work and money. Furthermore, some men already had whanau in the cities. They had been encouraged by the government to move there to work during the early 1940s. By 1945, over 26,000 Maori were living in urban areas. The trend did not slow. By 1981 nearly 80% of Maori lived in cities. By the end of the century around 90% of a Maori population of nearly 526,000 were urban – about 473,000 people. This was a complete reversal from the pre-war period.

Despite over-population in the countryside, urbanisation also had an impact on rural areas. Every year around 1600 mostly young Maori migrated to the cities. This made it difficult to continue to run the land schemes that Apirana Ngata had worked so hard to develop (pages 27–28). As early as 1961, over half of the nearly 300 registered Maori incorporations were inactive.

Maori Urbanisation in Wellington and Auckland

Year	Number of Maori: Wellington	Number of Maori: Auckland
1935	341	1766
1945	No data	4903
1951	1570	7621

The Maori Battalion returns to New Zealand

ACTIVITIES

Read the text and give FULL answers for the following.

1. Why did the Maori population increase so rapidly from the 1930s.
2. Give THREE reasons why many returning Maori soldiers chose to live in the cities.
3. What had changed by the end of the century to be 'a complete reversal from the 1930s'?
4. Provide a FACT that shows that Maori urbanisation had a negative effect on rural areas.

Refer to Source A

5. Between what two consecutive census years did Auckland's Maori population increase the most? Give figures to support your answer. What was the cause of this rapid increase?
6. Why do you think the level of Maori urbanisation was not as great in Wellington? (Refer to the map of tribal locations, page 6.)

MAORI AND PAKEHA MEET: ISSUES IN THE CITIES

With increasing Maori urbanisation Pakeha were, for the first time, coming into contact with Maori in large numbers. Many found the adjustment difficult. Old prejudices persisted and new ones surfaced. One new experience for many rural Maori who had moved to the cities was being on time. Pakeha culture, especially urban Pakeha culture, works to a strict timetable of start and stop times. Traditional Maori culture did not have such rigid expectations. In terms of housing, rents were high in the early post-war years, so Maori would often crowd into houses to save money. Overcrowding led to reluctance on the landlords' part to rent to Maori. Maori complained of the discrimination that they faced. Pakeha landlords complained that Maori did not respect their property. For those Maori who had managed to buy their own homes, there were often difficulties with meeting mortgage repayments. By the late 1960s two-thirds of mortgages handled by the Department of Maori Affairs were behind in payments. Problems with budgeting and alcohol made matters worse.

Personal Identity, Social Breakdown and Crime

Despite the racial problems associated with Maori urbanisation, inter-marriage between Maori and Pakeha increased. Half of all Maori marriages in the 1960s were to Pakeha. While this brought the races closer together, it also created further problems. In many cases the children of mixed marriages ('half castes') were brought up as Pakeha. They lived a Pakeha lifestyle and had Pakeha values. However, because of their skin colour, people – such as teachers – automatically assumed that they were Maori. They were then often treated differently to Pakeha children. This could leave children confused and with no clear sense of identity. This in turn could lead to self-esteem issues, which could cause social and eventually criminal problems.

Many of the Maori migrants to the city in the post-war period were young, and needed strong whanau and tribal support. However, few of the traditional tribal influences such as marae and elders had come from the countryside. *Urbanisation thus achieved the de-tribalisation of Maori much more effectively than any intentional government policy of the previous decades.* A survey revealed that by 1967 nearly 90% of Maori households had changed to a Pakeha-style nuclear family.

The requirements of the urban Pakeha lifestyle further accelerated the process of social breakdown, and the Maori crime rate increased. By the mid-1950s it was over three times that of Pakeha. The sense of alienation felt by many urban Maori, especially the young, translated into anti-social activity. Those who felt that society had no place for them did not feel bound by its rules. In 1950, the Maori imprisonment rate was nearly five times that of Pakeha. By 1985 it was nearly twelve times. In 1997 nearly 45% of the prison population was Maori.

Gangs

For many Pakeha, gangs represented the most frightening face of Maori urbanisation. Detribalisation in the cities had led some Maori to search for a new, tribal-style identity. Some found it in gangs. One thing that members seemed to get from these organisations was a strong sense of belonging. Although by the year 2000 Pakeha and Pacific Islanders were well-represented in gangs, Maori were still most prominent. Police estimated that in 1992 two-thirds of the 6000 gang members in New Zealand were Maori. The mainly Maori gangs included the 'Mongrel Mob', which was formed in the 1960s, and 'Black Power', formed in 1970.

Sir Charles Bennett, former commander of the Maori Battalion, recalls in the 1990s the raised hopes during WWII.

'There was not one incident that I know of where Maori soldiers fought other New Zealanders, though Maori did fight Maori. We thought this is how we are going to be when we go home – firm friends. But that couldn't be preserved back home. The division between the two races created more and more distance between them. But having created that harmonious relationship in war, we knew it could be done. Why can't we create the same relationship on the home front? It's a treasure which we polished to such a fire glow in war, yet it couldn't be preserved in peace.'

SOURCE C

ACTIVITIES

1. Draw a star diagram showing the issues that led to problems as Maori urbanised. (You should be able to identify at least FIVE.) Include a strong central image.
2. Despite some of the negative impacts on race relations of urbanisation, what feature of Maori-Pakeha relations shows that there was actually a high level of interaction? Provide evidence to back up your answer.
3. Graph – or represent pictorially – the figures for Maori versus Pakeha imprisonment rates between the 1950s and 1985. Show the 1997 prison population as a pie graph. Label all your work.
4. Explain the term 'detribalisation'.
5. Refer to Source B. Why do you think the close relationship between Maori and Pakeha *during* the war could not be maintained *after* the war?

LABOUR'S POST-WAR POLICY

After the war, the Labour government made a number of efforts to deal with the issues raised by urbanisation, and to introduce equality for Maori. However, neither Labour nor National governments liked the idea of tribalism, or anything that looked like separatism. They believed that all Maori should be treated as one group. Furthermore, this group should come fully under the same government as Pakeha. Labour's 1945 Maori Social and Economic Advancement Act was the most significant step in the early post-war period. The Act's main focus was on health, education and welfare. Maori Wardens and Tribal Committees were set up. Their job was to implement government policy at a local level.

ACTIVITIES

Refer to Source C

1. From Source C, provide THREE pieces of evidence that show that these health posters are directed at Maori.
2. What health problem are they concerned with?
3. Is this health issue seen as a rural or urban problem? Provide evidence to support your answer.
4. What two methods do these posters suggest for dealing with this health issue?
5. Where do you think it is most likely that these posters would be displayed?

MAORI RESPONSES TO THE PROBLEMS OF URBANISATION, 1940s–1950s

In addition to the problems described in the last section, a further major blow for Maori was the death in the early 1950s of three of the most important Maori leaders – Apirana Ngata, Peter Buck and Te Puea Herangi. This left a leadership gap. Other Maori leaders tried to fill the gap and find solutions to the problems caused by urbanisation. One organisation that was quite successful in this area was led by Maori women.

In 1951 the Maori Women's Welfare League (MWWL) was established with the help of the Maori Affairs Department. The MWWL's aim was to take a leadership role in urban centres in order to improve Maori health and well-being. The MWWL set out to work at both a local and nation-wide level to confront these problems. It also provided a voice for urban Maori who were no longer represented by tribes. In addition, it provided a voice for Maori women, most of whom were not allowed to speak on marae. Within six months of forming, the MWWL had 3000 members and it soon became the leading national Maori organisation.

One of the first main actions of the MWWL was to carry out a housing survey in Auckland. This highlighted the generally poor conditions in which Maori lived. Its findings were reported to the Department of Maori Affairs, and to Auckland City Council. This led to some of the worst houses being demolished and more State-built houses being allocated to Maori. The government came to view the MWWL as a reliable source of information and advice.

Whina Cooper, president of the Maori Women's Welfare League, at its 1953 conference

NATIONAL'S POLICIES IN THE 1950s AND 1960s

National won the 1949 election after 15 years as the Opposition. There were no Maori MPs in its ranks. For the first time in the 20th century there was no Maori representation at all in the government. Despite this, National continued with Labour's policies of equality in areas such as health, education and access to social security and work opportunities. The National government also acted on the country's first comprehensive review of Maori policy. The 1960 *Hunn Report*, as it was called, found that Maori were doing badly in most of the areas that it had reviewed. The *Hunn Report* recommended a policy of integration, even though no one seemed to know just what integration meant in practice. It soon became clear that, at least in the longer term, it still meant assimilation. Hunn believed that as Maori modernised they would willingly take on Pakeha ways. He thus saw no need for Maori to have more control of their lives. Hunn said that by improving education Maori would be able to break out of the 'poverty cycle' and enter more fully into the Pakeha world.

The *Hunn Report* was received favourably by most Pakeha commentators and some Maori. Others, such as the Maori section of the Anglican Church, rejected it. It claimed that the Report's recommendations were nothing more than assimilationist, pointing to the closure of Maori schools and the mainstreaming of Maori pupils as examples. It was also critical that Hunn had spent little time actually consulting with Maori.

> Our future is being decided for us without our hopes and intentions being considered. However well-intentioned such a policy may be, it is in the long run bound to cause more problems than it solves .... Let it be understood that, while we are willing to join with the Pakeha in becoming New Zealanders, we have no desire whatever to become Pakehas.'
>
> Response of the Maori section of the Anglican Church to the *Hunn Report*, 1960

ACTIVITIES

Refer to the text.

1 Match the terms from Column B with the correct term from Column A. Then write a brief sentence using each of the matched pairs to develop their key idea. (The terms in Column A are in order.)

Column A	Column B
• Ngata, Buck, Herangi	• Improve health, provide a voice for urban Maori and women
• MWWL	• Demolition and building
• 3000 members	• Advice and information
• Housing survey	• Leadership gap
• Government	• Leading national Maori organisation

2 What significant change for Maori occurred with the election of a National government in 1949?

3 Why did Hunn recommend no real change in Maori policy?

4 What is the main criticism of the *Hunn Report* itself, as expressed in the statement in Source D?

New Zealand Maori Council

The National government in the 1960s felt that it needed an independent source of advice on Maori views. This was because all the Maori MPs who were in parliament supported Labour. In 1962 the National government created a new organisation, called the New Zealand Maori Council (NZMC). The Maori Council was responsible for advising the government on issues that would improve social and economic conditions for Maori. This included housing, health, employment, education, training, crime and 'personal problems'. The creation of the new Council marked the end of a voice in politics for individual tribes. From the government's point of view, it believed that it had gained a voice that spoke for *all* Maori. During the 1960s, the New Zealand Maori Council replaced the Maori Women's Welfare League as the new political voice for Maori as a whole.

> **NZ Maori Council**
> **Local level:** committees in towns, suburbs or rural areas.
> **District level:** eight districts were established across the whole country.
> **National level:** the NZ Maori Council.

Land Issues

National also looked to deal once and for all with the troublesome issue of Maori land ownership. Much of the remaining Maori land was fragmented into small parcels, which could not be economically farmed. Thus it often lay idle. National's 1967 Maori Affairs Amendment Act allowed the government to make available for sale Maori land valued at under £50, or owned by fewer than four people. The Act also allowed for 'improvement inspectors' to decide on the use of Maori land. Both these measures frequently saw the land ending up in Pakeha ownership. Maori were bitterly opposed to what they called the government's 'last land grab'.

Amenities @ 1960	Percentage of Homes	
	Maori	Non-Maori
Bath or shower	58	93
Piped water	51	86
Hot-water service	48	88
Flush toilet	31	80
Refrigerator	20	55
Washing machine	19	58
Rooms per house	3.9	4.7
Occupants per house	5.6	3.6

"An estimated 30% of the Maori people lived in grossly overcrowded conditions, mainly in Northland, Waikato, Bay of Plenty, East Coast and urban Auckland." – *Hunn Report.*

ACTIVITIES

Refer to Source E

1 What is the only statistic in the Table where the figures for Maori are higher than they are for Pakeha?

2 Compare the relationship between 'Occupants per house' and 'Rooms per house' for Maori and Pakeha.

3 Provide suitable evidence from the Table that *could* be used to support the statements given below. *Some statements may not have appropriate evidence.*

- a Pakeha houses were larger than Maori houses.
- b Pakeha houses were more likely than Maori houses to have electricity.
- c Most Pakeha lived in urban areas.
- d Most Maori houses were only single storey.
- e Diseases caused by foodstuffs going off were more likely in Maori households.
- f Diseases caused by poor water supply were more likely in Maori households.
- g Diseases caused by poor hygiene were more likely in Maori households.
- h Most Pakeha households had two children
- i Pakeha households were generally wealthier than Maori.

Refer to Source F

4 According to the Source, why do Pakeha think that Maori do not use their land in the same way as Pakeha?

5 According to the Source, what was the real cause of Maori land not being farmed?

> **SOURCE F**
>
> 'European observers are apt to think that the reason why a good deal of Maori land lies idle is due to indifference or indolence [laziness] of the Maori people. The fact is that much Maori land is practically unusable because of the unsatisfactoriness of its [legal] title. This situation is the result of the application of the system of European individualistic land title to Maori land, the title to which has always been communal and hereditary.'
>
> Response of the Maori section of the Anglican Church to the *Hunn Report*, 1960

Refer to the 'Land Issues' section of text (on this page).

6 Was the government right to deal with the 'problem' of fragmented Maori land by compulsorily buying it? Explain your answer.

SOURCE G

The *Hunn Report* on Maori land, 1960

'Everybody's land is nobody's land. That, in short, is the story of Maori land today. Multiple ownership obstructs utilisation [use], so Maori land quite commonly lies in the rough or grazes a few animals apathetically [lazily], while a multitude of absentee owners rest happily on their proprietary [ownership] rights, small as they are .... Whereas European land is usually in the name of one person, Maori land often has hundreds, even thousands of owners in minute [tiny] fractions. The reason is that even the smallest interest in land will save that owner from being a 'landless' Maori, a person without "turangawaewae" or standing to speak on the tribal marae .... It would be a good thing if the Maori people ... could come to regard the ownership of a modern home in town (or country) as a stronger claim to speak on the marae than ownership of an infinitesimal [tiny] share in some scrub country that one has never seen.'

SOURCE H

Response of the Maori section of the Anglican Church to the *Hunn Report*, 1960

'Land is more than soil.... It must be emphasised again that the Maori is a community person.... His values are community values, his satisfactions come from the community. Not the small individual family, but the tribe, the big family, is the basic unit of his society.... For the Maori his whole history and cultural heritage is enshrined in his tribal land in which he has a share, and of which he feels himself to be a part, and which gives him the right of participation in the community life of his people. The Maori has his roots deep in the past... this treasure of the past is embedded even in the walls of his meeting houses, and enshrined in the rocks and mountains, the rivers and the plains of his home place.'

ACTIVITIES

Refer to Sources F to H

1. In Source G the *Hunn Report* refers to Maori land that 'quite commonly lies in the rough ....' Quote the term used in Source F to describe land that is not being used for farming or other activities.
2. In Source G the *Hunn Report* says that 'Maori land often has hundreds, even thousands of owners in minute [tiny] fractions.' What explanation is given for this situation in Source F?
3. What, in Source G, does Hunn suggest Maori should consider as the modern turangawaewae?
4. Bias is seeing something from only one point of view (often while ignoring other points of view). Refer to Source G. Identify, by providing quotes, two cases where the *Hunn Report* uses biased language.
5. Explain how the last sentence in the *Hunn Report* (Source G) caused the response from the Maori section of the Anglican Church in Source H.
6. How relevant would the response of the Maori section of the Anglican church (Source H) be for urban Maori? Explain your answer.

REVIEW ACTIVITIES

1. In paragraphs of about 100 words for each, describe the perspectives (views) and actions (with an accompanying explanation) for the following:

   a **Urbanisation**
   - A young Maori person living in a rural area
   - Whina Cooper, of the Maori Women's Welfare League
   - The Labour government in the 1940s
   - The *Hunn Report* (for actions, give recommendations for action)

   b **The 'Maori Land problem'**
   - The National government/Hunn Report
   - The Maori section of the Anglican Church.

2. Use the main ideas from this section of the text to create a mind-map OR a structured overview diagram that shows the responses of the following groups to 'Maori issues':
   - The Labour government
   - The National government
   - The Maori Women's Welfare League.

CHAPTER NINE

'ENOUGH IS ENOUGH!' – MAORI ACTIVISM FROM THE 1970S

THE BEGINNINGS OF ACTIVISM

By the 1960s some Maori leaders were beginning to demand greater mana motuhake or self-determination. These demands grew out of concern over the continuing loss of Maori land. This was particularly so after National's 'last land grab' under the 1967 Maori Affairs Amendment Act. These calls for self-determination were part of what some commentators have called a 'Maori Renaissance' (revival of Maori culture). The key figures that emerged to lead the protests of the 1970s were generally from urban centres and many were university-trained. They were frustrated by the inability of the Ratana MPs to make any difference, especially with Labour out of power for much of the post-war period. Furthermore, traditional leadership in the countryside – such as the Ratana and King Movements – was seen as irrelevant and ineffective in terms of urban needs. The activists were well aware of Pakeha methods of protest, and used them to deliver a Maori message of mana motuhake and rangatiratanga.

A common Pakeha response to Maori demands for self-determination was to deny that there was anything wrong with the way things were. On this basis, Pakeha rejected the granting of any degree of mana motuhake to Maori. Self-determination, Pakeha believed, was separatist and would result in division and conflict.

Mana motuhake
Self-determination (control over one's own affairs)
Rangatiratanga
Chiefly authority

ACTIVITIES

Study the graph (Source A) below and answer the following questions.

1 Between what two consecutive years given on the *x-axis* was the loss of Maori land the greatest? (What feature of the *x-axis* on this graph would make the historian cautious in using it?)

2 What might explain the lower rate of land loss in the 20th century? (Refer back to page 26. Also study an atlas which shows the type of land that remained in Maori ownership.)

3 What evidence in the graph supports the claim that it wasn't the *amount* of land taken in the government's 'last land grab' from 1967 that particularly angered Maori?

4 What is the link between the graph and the maps?

Refer to the maps

5 Make comments comparing land alienation in the North and South Islands.

6 Identify TWO areas in New Zealand where Maori held onto their land longest. Why do you think this might be?

7 Explain the ways in which the maps and graph are each useful to the historian.

8 What social and economic effects might the loss of land shown in the graph and maps have on any people/culture?

9 What other information might an historian want to find in order to understand the nature of Maori land loss?

SOURCE A

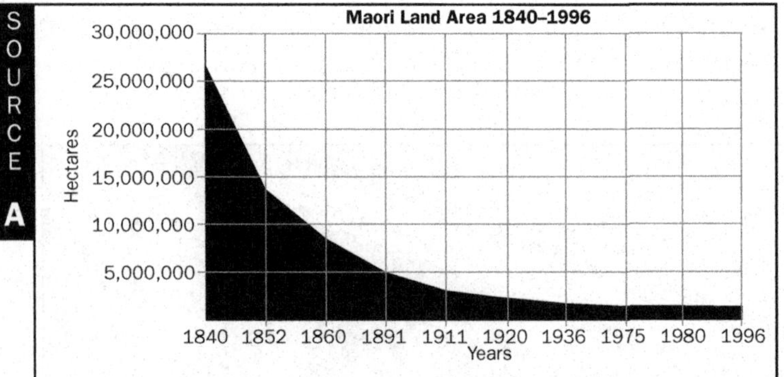

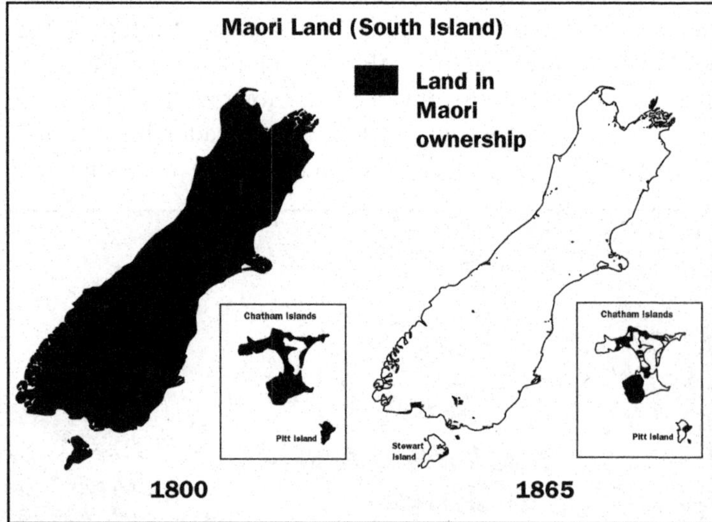

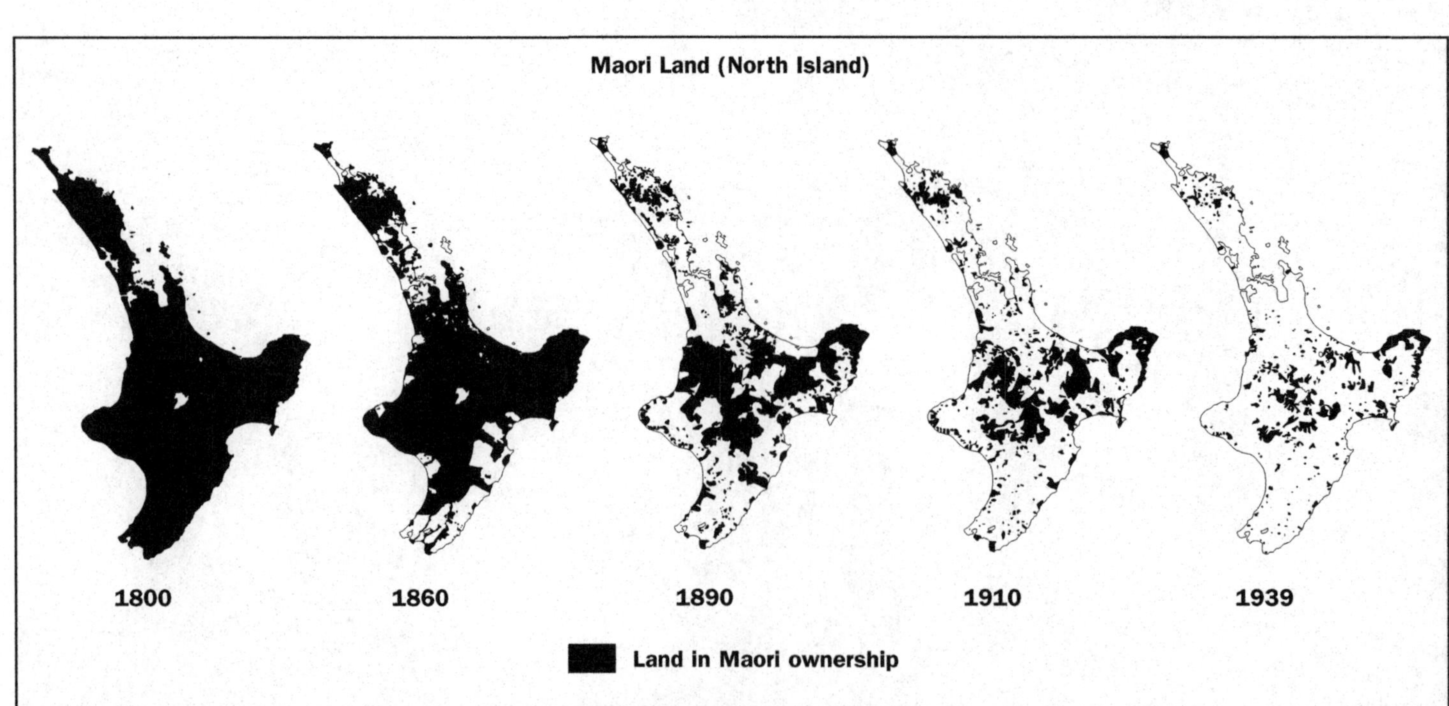

"Very little evidence [of racial discrimination] has come to light either from the [Maori Affairs Department] files or from the knowledge of senior officers. A few instances have been cited [given] but they are isolated and extend over many years."
The *Hunn Report*, 1960

SOURCE C

"I just do not believe that racism or discrimination exists in this country."
Sir Arthur Porritt, Governor-General, 1971

SOURCE D

"In 1844, the Maoris went to war. They had no guns, so they used their bums, in 1844."
A rhyme chanted by schoolchildren in the 1950s, as recalled by historian Michael King.

SOURCE E

"There is a colour-bar in New Zealand. I have been refused accommodation in hotels from Invercargill to Auckland, simply because I am a Maori. I have gone around the corner and rung the same place up and given a Pakeha name and they have said yes. Then when I've gone there they have said: "Oh, I'm sorry, I thought Mr So-and-So was a Pakeha." This has happened to almost everyone who is Maori. And there are still areas in New Zealand where Maori cannot get work. Insurance companies and banks, for example."
John Rangihau, Welfare Officer, early 1960s.

SOURCE F

"Our observation is that regrettable and damaging racial discrimination is being practised by a harmful minority of both Pakehas and Maori, and that the incidence of these attitudes has tended to increase rather than decrease in recent years.... We also feel it our duty to point out that much of the European attitude to Maori land, including those revealed in sections of the *Hunn Report*, cause deep feelings of resentment among members of our race and tend to increase those feelings of racial tension which it is our prayer should be dissolved."
Response of the Maori section of the Anglican Church to the *Hunn Report*, 1960

ACTIVITIES

Refer to Sources B–F

1. In what way do the views expressed in Source B and Source F agree?
2. How does the writer in Source F respond to the claim in Source B that the incidents of racial discrimination are "isolated and extend over many years"?
3. Who does the writer in Source F believe is practising racial discrimination in New Zealand? What does the writer identify as one of the main causes of increasing tension?
4. In what way is Source D useful to the historian as evidence about racial attitudes in the 1950s? For what reason must the historian be careful in using this rhyme as evidence?
5. What is meant by a 'colour-bar' (Source E)? Explain how the attitudes expressed in Source D *could* lead to the experiences of John Rangihau (Source E).
6. If you lived in New Zealand in the 1960s, do you think that you would agree with Sir Arthur Porritt's statement in Source C? Explain your answer.

Nga Tamatoa

Nga Tamatoa (Young Warriors) was a university-based activist organisation. Initially the movement was split between radicals and conservatives. The radicals wanted to use a confrontational approach based on that of the American Black Power movement. However, the conservatives won out and soon offices were established in Auckland, Christchurch and Wellington. Nga Tamatoa wanted the 1967 Maori Affairs Amendment Act overturned in order to stop the further loss of Maori land. It also called for more assistance for urban Maori to cope with the pressures of urban life. Another issue was the continuing celebration of Waitangi Day. Nga Tamatoa wanted the celebrations stopped until the Treaty of Waitangi had been honoured. Nga Tamatoa was also active in its opposition to New Zealand's continued sporting links with South Africa (see page 70–71). The view that tied in most closely with the new mood of activism in the 1970s was the call for increased Maori mana motuhake.

Nga Tamatoa came to be seen by some as the new voice of Maori. Its tactics and aims appealed especially to the young. However, Nga Tamatoa was an urban group that did not necessarily have the same goals as rural, tribally-based groups. In addition, few Maori elders liked the bold new tactics that seemed to show little respect for traditional ways. As has always been the case, no single group has ever been the voice of all Maori. In 1975, both Nga Tamatoa and the Maori Organisation on Human Rights merged with Te Roopu o te Matakite – the Maori Land Rights' Movement.

ACTIVITIES

1. Explain the terms 'Maori renaissance' and mana motuhake. Draw a pictorial representation of both terms.

2. Imagine that you are a Maori activist going on a (Pakeha-style) protest to demand greater *mana motuhake*. In your exercise book, come up with ideas for banners or placards to take with you on the protest. Also, think up some chants that the crowd could say.
   - To be taken seriously you need to state FACTS.
   - Think back on the ideas covered in this course in terms of government policy on assimilation and land.

3. You are now a Pakeha concerned that Maori protests are threatening New Zealand's stability. You believe that New Zealand's race relations are the best in the world.
   - Come up with ideas for banners, placards and chants to oppose Maori *mana motuhake*.
   - Again, base these on the FACTS, as you see them.

THE MAORI LAND RIGHTS MOVEMENT

As well as the high profile actions of groups like Nga Tamatoa, hui were being held in marae around the country during the 1970s to discuss issues affecting Maori. In early 1975 at Te Puea marae in Mangere, Auckland, a number of speakers shared their grievances. One of the most well-known actions to come out of the hui was the 1975 hikoi, from the top of the North Island to Wellington.

1975 Hikoi (Land March)

The issue behind the hikoi was long-standing concern over the loss of Maori land. From 1900 up until the mid-1950s an average of 44,000 hectares per year was shifting out of Maori ownership. The trigger for the action was the 'last land grab' brought on by the 1967 Maori Affairs Amendment Act. An organisation was formed – Te Roopu o te Matakite (those with foresight) – to do the planning.

The 1975 hikoi was the largest ever protest action by Maori. Its scale was especially significant because Maori had traditionally lacked unity, with divisions occurring along tribal lines. The march began on September 14th from Te Hapua in the Far North, with Wellington as the destination. It was a journey of 1100km to be made in 30 days. 80 year-old Whina Cooper was its leader. The fifty core marchers were joined by thousands more as the hikoi progressed. Estimates of the total number involved range between 30,000 and 40,000, making it the single biggest pan-tribal action of the 20th century. On September 23rd the marchers crossed the Auckland Harbour Bridge. Over the rest of their march they stopped at 25 marae. At each marae the reasons behind the march were explained. On October 13th the hikoi made its way into Wellington.

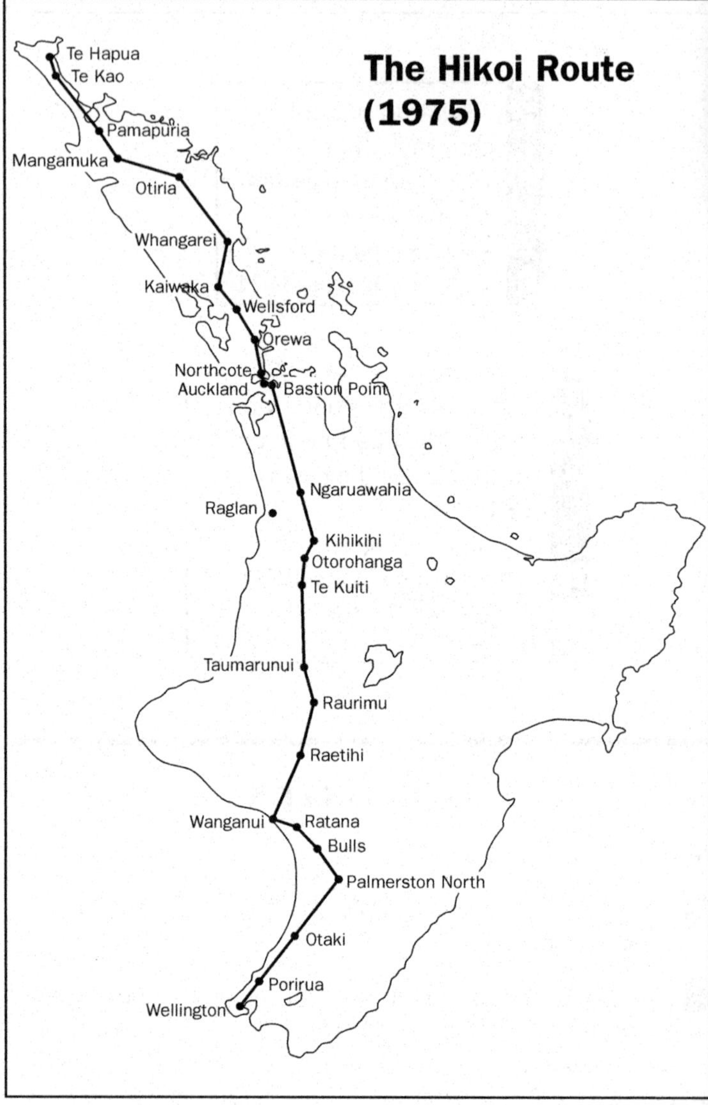

ACTIVITIES

Refer to Source G

1. According to the map, at how many marae did the marchers stop?

2. Provide evidence from the map that would support the claim that the Waikato-based Kingitanga approved of the hikoi.

3. Why did the hikoi occur in the North Island, rather than the South Island?

The 1975 Hikoi.

> "When it eventually happened it began as a very lonely affair. No Maori wanted to host us or join us. We had no encouragement. Far from it – we had been warned against provoking a Pakeha backlash, that we would wake the sleeping giant of the State. But a handful of us started out nonetheless with Whina Cooper at the head. By the time we got to Warkworth the mood was changing; marae started to receive and support us. And then they came in their thousands and then tens of thousands. When we got to the Auckland Harbour Bridge there were so many of us, walking in time, that the bridge began to sway, and I was scared we would bring the whole thing down. As we marched to Wellington no marae was big enough to hold us. We walked for weeks, and the day we walked into Wellington we had a larger crowd than I have ever seen. The country was behind us."
>
> Donna Awatere (daughter of the Maori Battalion's Arapeta Awatere) recalls her part in the 1975 hikoi.

SOURCE I

The hikoi was an action designed to raise awareness amongst both Maori and Pakeha about the loss of Maori land. The marchers' banner – "Not one more acre of Maori land" – summed up their concerns. A Memorial of Rights (a type of petition) was signed by 200 kaumatua (elders) and 60,000 other Maori and Pakeha. The Memorial called for the protection of remaining Maori land and the removal of laws which allowed Maori land to be taken by the government. The media covered what was certainly a newsworthy event. Pakeha journalists failed, however, to understand or communicate the key issues that were raised in the Memorial.

When the hikoi finally arrived in Wellington there were differences over what to do next. The unity of the march broke down. One group of about 60 decided on a sit-in outside parliament. They set up a tent city, against Whina Cooper's wishes. Another group set off on a further march to the East Coast. This division allowed the newly elected Prime Minister, National's Robert Muldoon, to ignore the Memorial of Rights. While Matakite's hikoi had not achieved any of its main goals, it had begun to raise awareness amongst both Maori and Pakeha. Other Maori actions were inspired by the march.

ACTIVITIES

Refer to Source H

1. What are the limitations of this source for a historian studying the 1975 hikoi?

Refer to Source I

2. Give evidence from Source A that suggests that prior to the march the Maori people were not confident in challenging the State (government).
3. Why does Awatere refer to the State as a 'sleeping giant'?
4. Give TWO pieces of evidence from the text that support Awatere's claim that were thousands and then tens of thousands of people on the hikoi.
5. Why was Wellington the destination?
6. Which of Donna Awatere's statements is most likely an exaggeration?

BASTION POINT (TAKAPARAWHAU) OCCUPATION

Between 1977 and 1978 members of Ngati Whatua and its supporters carried out a 506-day occupation of land at Bastion Point at Orakei (Auckland). This action was taken because it seemed that only a bold move would stop the government's plans to sell the land. The origins of this action can be traced as far back as the purchase and settlement of Auckland in 1840. Ngati Whatua had sold land to the government of the time, but had been careful to preserve their tribal homeland at Orakei. Over the following decades the government gradually eroded the laws that protected Ngati Whatua's remaining land. Attempts at using the legal system and petitions to parliament all failed to stop the losses. In 1951 the remaining people at Okahu Bay were evicted from their land by the government under the Public Works Act and put into housing further up the hill.

The Occupation Begins

The trigger for the occupation in 1977 was a move by the National government of the time. It intended to sub-divide and sell the Ngati Whatua land that it had acquired up to the 1950s. There was a lot of pressure from developers who wanted the land – it was by then some of the most valuable in Auckland. To prevent the land being sold, the Orakei Maori Action Group (OMAG), led by Joe Hawke, occupied Bastion Point. The 150 core protesters were soon joined by members of the local community, unions and other concerned groups. The original tent village gradually became more permanent. Some Maori leaders did not support Hawke and OMAG. Whina Cooper, the leader of the 1975 hikoi, initially did, but later changed her mind. Nor would Ngati Whatua kaumatua support the action. It was more radical than they were accustomed to.

Things came to a head in the autumn of 1978. In April, Justice Speight ruled that the land was owned by the government and that the occupiers were trespassing. On May 25th New Zealanders watched on television as the largest ever police operation took place to remove the protesters. Supported by the army, 600 police moved in and arrested 222 protesters. Bulldozers demolished the make-shift buildings. Once the protesters were removed the issue died down in the public mind, but it was not over. The media had again failed to investigate the real reasons behind the occupation. Many New Zealanders thus viewed the action as simply another stunt by radical Maori. The fact that few traditional Maori leaders supported the occupation seemed to prove this view. The issue did not die down for Joe Hawke. He took the Orakei case to the Waitangi Tribunal in 1985. Although the Tribunal criticised the occupation, it recommended the return of Bastion Point and other land, plus compensation of $3million. In July 1988 the Labour government announced that it would fully abide by the Tribunal's recommendations.

ACTIVITIES

1 Place the following statements into the correct order in which the events happened, then write a one paragraph summary.

- **a** The police, backed by the army, remove the protesters.
- **b** Justice Speight rules that Bastion Point is owned by the government.
- **c** The Waitangi Tribunal recommends that Bastion Point be returned and compensation paid.
- **d** Joe Hawke takes the Orakei case to the Waitangi Tribunal.
- **e** Ngati Whatua kaumatua do not support the action.
- **f** The National government announces plans to sell the remaining Ngati Whatua land.
- **g** Over time, the government acquires much of Ngati Whatua's land.
- **h** The Labour government agrees to the Waitangi Tribunal's recommendations.
- **i** Joe Hawke leads the Orakei Maori Action Group onto Bastion Point.
- **j** The people at Okahu Bay are evicted.

2 You have been asked to design a poster supporting the cause of the Orakei Maori Action Group. On a full page in your book draw up a draft for the poster. Use a strong central image and a few key words that capture at least some of the key ideas behind the occupation, such as:

- Ngati Whatua's historical ownership of Bastion Point
- Maori unity in the face of the government
- A new form of direct, non-violent action led by new (non-traditional) leaders.

3 In your view, were the occupiers right to take their action? Give evidence to support your answer.

WHAINGAROA (RAGLAN) GOLF COURSE

Orakei was not the only place where Maori land was taken under the Public Works Act. At Raglan during WWII land was taken in order to build an emergency airfield. The local Tainui Awhiro tribe accepted this, especially when they were told that it was only a temporary measure. However, once the war was over the land was given into the control of the local Council. They then leased it to the local golf club. What made this worse was that Tainui Awhiro were not allowed back onto their land, even though it held burial sites.

Eva Rickard took up the protest that had been begun by her mother in the 1950s. Both women demanded that their land be returned. On behalf of Tainui Awhiro, Rickard petitioned the local Council, the Raglan Golf Club and even the Minister of Maori Affairs. She joined in the 1975 hikoi to Wellington. Afterwards she was supported in her struggle by one of the hikoi's break-away groups. On February 12th 1978, using the same tactic as the Bastion Point protest action, Rickard led over 150 people in an occupation of the golf course. She hoped that such decisive action would force the government or local Council to return the land. Rickard and 17 other protesters were quickly arrested. As hoped, the action received media attention. In 1984 the government agreed to hand the land back. In all it had taken over 30 years to have the grievance set right.

> The Public Works Act was intended to allow the government to compulsarily buy land if it urgently needed to, in the wider public's interest.

AS1.4 REVIEW ACTIVITIES

1 In paragraphs of about 100 words for each, describe the perspectives (views) and actions (with an accompanying explanation) for the following:

a **The place of Maori in New Zealand society**
- Nga Tamatoa

b **Land issues**
- Whina Cooper and/or Te Roopu o te Matakite
- Joe Hawke and/or the Orakei Maori Action Group
- A Pakeha television or newspaper journalist
- Ngati Whatua kaumatua (elders)
- Eva Rickard
- The Raglan County Council.

2 What key issue lay behind the 1975 Hikoi to Wellington, and the occupations at Bastion Point and Raglan?

3 Use the main ideas headings in this section on Maori Activism and the Maori Land Rights' Movement to create a mind-map OR structured overview diagram (see page 5) that shows the main developments.
- 'Maori Renaissance' (rangatiratanga and mana motuhake)
- Nga Tamatoa
- The 1975 hikoi
- Bastion Point Occupation
- Raglan Occupation.

CHAPTER TEN

SPORTING CONTACT WITH SOUTH AFRICA

Sporting contact with South Africa and the Springbok's 1981 tour led to the greatest civil unrest New Zealand had seen, at least since the riots of the Depression in the 1930s. Curiously, many New Zealanders were prepared to risk physical injury in protests against South Africa's treatment of blacks. Many, however, failed to make any link between the concerns of blacks in South Africa and Maori in New Zealand.

There were two clear views on the issue of playing sport with South Africa. Supporters of the Tour were generally dedicated followers of rugby who believed that sport and politics should not mix. Opponents of the Tour believed that it was immoral to allow racially-selected teams to come here. This was, they said, because it sent a message that New Zealand did not mind South Africa's racist policies of apartheid. Other parties that became involved in the issue included the police, Prime Ministers Norman Kirk (Labour) and Robert Muldoon (National), black African nations, the Commonwealth and even the United Nations.

THE 1981 SPRINGBOK TOUR

Background

In 1960, the New Zealand Rugby Union excluded Maori from a tour to South Africa in line with South Africa's wishes. A growing number of people saw this as an extension of South Africa's apartheid policy into New Zealand. Later that same year the 'Sharpeville Massacre' occurred, and international pressure went on South Africa. This included a sporting boycott. In response to this, the All Black tour of South Africa planned for 1968 was stopped by the government. Rugby supporters, including many Maori, were deeply disappointed. Under pressure, South Africa modified its policy and allowed Maori to be included in a tour in 1970. It rather bizarrely classified Maori as 'honorary whites'. This did not satisfy the different protest groups, which had come together to form HART (Halt All Racial Tours). Despite the activism of the anti-Tour protesters, they were still a minority. An opinion poll taken in 1972 showed that 80% of New Zealanders supported the tour scheduled for 1973.

SOUTH AFRICAN APARTHEID

In 1948 South Africa introduced its policy of apartheid. Officially it was a policy of 'separate but equal development' for whites and non-whites. The laws, however, made the majority non-white South Africans into second-class citizens. Inter-racial mixing of any sort was forbidden. This meant separate train carriages, buses, drinking fountains, park benches, toilets, stairways and other public facilities. Non-whites were forcibly moved out of areas designated as white. Non-whites were not allowed to play in national sporting teams with whites – such as the Springboks. South Africa's government also made it clear that it did not want its white-only teams playing against other countries' teams if they contained non-white players. As resistance to all these laws grew within South Africa so did police brutality. Many countries expressed outrage in 1960 when 69 unarmed black protesters were killed in the 'Sharpeville Massacre'. A further 236 were killed in the Soweto Riots of 1976. International pressure on South Africa to end its apartheid policy increased. A number of nations agreed to end all contact – including sporting contact – with South Africa, until its policy changed.

SOURCE A

Rugby and South Africa played a part in the 1975 election, helping Robert Muldoon's National party to win. In line with his party's policy, Muldoon refused to prevent a 1976 tour by the All Blacks to South Africa. International opinion now swung against New Zealand. Concerns were voiced in the Commonwealth and United Nations. Muldoon, however, was prepared to go against world opinion. New Zealand's international reputation hit its lowest point that year. Thirty countries, including twelve black African states, boycotted the 1976 Montreal Olympics. This was because a New Zealand team was attending. Some countries even talked of evicting New Zealand from the Commonwealth. Muldoon now realised that New Zealand was too small to resist international pressure. However, he was still not prepared to give in entirely. This made him popular with the many pro-Tour supporters.

Gleneagles Agreement

In 1977 the Commonwealth Heads of Government meeting was held in Gleneagles, Scotland. Attempts were made there to clarify the Commonwealth position on sporting links with South Africa. Muldoon resisted signing up to a declaration that committed New Zealand to ending such links. He argued that 'bridge-building' was better than boycotting South Africa. According to Muldoon, South Africa would see how a country could have good race relations, and it would then willingly change its ways. The watered-down final version of the 'Gleneagles Agreement' stated that countries would 'vigorously ... combat the evil of apartheid ... each government to determine, *in accordance with its laws*, the methods by which it might best discharge these commitments.' Because New Zealand had no laws forbidding sporting contact with South Africa, the Agreement did not *oblige* the government to do anything.

ACTIVITIES

1 From the information above, select only the key ideas to go onto a timeline that shows the background to the 1981 Springbok Tour. Include at least information from the following dates:

- 1948 (apartheid)
- 1960
- 1968
- 1970
- 1972
- 1975
- 1976
- 1977

2 Explain the difference between 'boycotting' and 'bridge-building'. Which do you think would be the most effective? Explain your answer.

The Tour

When the Rugby Union proposed an eight-week tour by the Springboks, scheduled for July 1981, the Muldoon government merely informed rugby officials that it disapproved. This was all that was required by the Gleneagles Agreement. The public, however, increasingly felt that stronger action was needed. A poll in May 1981 showed that 43% of people opposed the tour, with 41% in favour. (By the end of the tour the figures were 54% against and 42% for.) This reflected the division in New Zealand society over sporting contact with South Africa. In some cases, families were bitterly divided between pro- and anti-tour support. The issue polarised the wider community too, with few people not having a view one way or the other.

Robert Muldoon, Prime Minister 1975–1984.

Protest groups took an organised approach, working out tactics in advance. To counter them, specially trained police were formed into the Riot Squad, the first such force in New Zealand. To counter the Riot Squad's aggressive approach, front-line protesters donned crash helmets and padded clothing. Some carried shields, on occasions with spikes imbedded in them. Dedicated protesters would sometimes travel great distances to be present at demonstrations. At some rugby fields, barricades of barbed wire were erected by the Army. Shipping containers were also brought in to block demonstrators' access to the playing field.

Over the eight weeks of disturbances, nearly 2000 New Zealanders were arrested. The second game (at Hamilton) was cancelled after protesters occupied the field, possibly scattering tacks and glass. A light aircraft buzzed the seating stands, the pilot's intentions unknown. After the protesters had been escorted off the field by the police, rugby supporters attacked them. A game at Timaru was also cancelled for security reasons. At the final test in Auckland a protester dressed as the referee ran onto the field and stole the ball. The game went ahead, with some 10,000 protesters outside the grounds. Also outside the grounds was the Riot Squad. Charge and counter-charge by police and protesters alike saw some of the bloodiest scenes of the tour. A light aircraft again buzzed the field, this time dropping flour bombs and flares onto the pitch below. All these images were relayed on national and international television, showing a nation divided amongst itself. No further official tours to (or by) South Africa occurred until after the collapse of apartheid in 1990.

SOURCE B

'By this time the Wellington game of the Tour was fast approaching. I was by now quite skilled at padding my chest and shoulders, and on the day of the match, I set out wearing Mark's crash helmet ... [*The protesters then entered the playing field before the game, but were moved off by the police.*] We finally hit the road and started back to town. On the way we passed a pub where rugby fans who hadn't been able to get into the park had been watching the match on television. They poured out of the pub and assailed us, threw beer cans, and a young Maori man spat in my face. Someone saw a man he knew behind me and lashed out with a punch. Unfortunately he missed and punched me very hard, catching me below my padding.'

Sonia Davies was 58 when she participated in this anti-Tour protest. The blow she received broke three ribs and cracked two others.

SOURCE C

'After the game was officially called off the police had the job to escort the hard-core protesters from the field. Their selected route was in the corner between our stand and the long, low touchline stand. The police had to cordon off both sides of the path out. As rugby fans' communal anger boiled over there were two distinct crowd rushes toward the departing protesters, and mayhem ensued. Through gaps in the police line the protesters were kicked, punched, cursed and spat at by rugby 'hooligans' – a priest-protester was punched and the nearest line-cop turned around quickly and said to the puncher: "If you do that again, I'll kick your f...ing head in." This fighting carried on spasmodically outside the ground into the evening. All of NZ was shocked at this first 'heavy' confrontation over the 'Tour', with the police trying to be the barrier between two committed factions – showing up real divisions in NZ society.'

A rugby supporter recalls the aftermath of the cancellation of the Hamilton game.

SOURCE D

'All the training, all the planning now came into focus ... this final showdown was the battle that had to be fought. Those opposing us were the protesters that had chosen of their own free will to take the police head on .... We would, in a disciplined, professional and positive manner, maintain the rule of law and defeat those who sought to bring anarchy to the streets .... At first we were pelted with rocks, bottles, cans and several incendiary [fire] devices, two of which had to be extinguished. The [Red] Squad smashed its way through what had seemed an impenetrable wall of shields and was, for a few moments, forced to baton down on those in front to stop the momentum of the mob. But within minutes the superior fortitude [courage] of the few overcame the brute force of the many and the tide began to turn with the relentlessness of our advance ...'

Ross Meurant was second-in-command of a police riot team known as the Red Squad. The events described occurred at the final Springbok match at Auckland.

ACTIVITIES

1 From the list below, select only what you think are the FIVE key ideas from the text on pages 70–71. For each, draw an appropriate pictorial.

- **a** Rugby officials were contacted.
- **b** Muldoon did not stop the 1981 Tour.
- **c** Front-line protesters wore crash helmets and padded clothing.
- **d** New Zealanders were becoming increasingly divided over the Springbok Tour.
- **e** Muldoon did not believe that 43% opposition to the Tour was significant.
- **f** Both protesters and police prepared for serious action.
- **g** There had been public protest during the Vietnam War.
- **h** Shipping containers were sometimes used to stop protesters.
- **i** The level of protest action and violence increased with each game.
- **j** Nearly 2000 protesters were arrested.
- **k** In Auckland and Hamilton, an aircraft buzzed the playing fields.
- **l** There were no more tours to (or by) South Africa.

Refer to the text and Sources A–D in this section

2 Imagine that you are going on a protest against the Springbok Tour. In your exercise book, come up with ideas for banners or placards to take with you on the protest. Also, think up some chants that the crowd could say.

- You need to decide what the key ideas are that you wish to express.
- To be taken seriously, you need to state FACTS.

3 Write a letter to the editor of a newspaper outlining thoughtfully the reasons for your opposition to – OR support for – the 1981 Springbok Tour. Include factual material to back up your point of view.

4 Create a sketch of a 'typical' confrontation between police and protesters.

5 Create a plan for an anti-tour protest action – OR for the police tactics to be used to counter a protest. Include a sketch of the rugby grounds, showing roads and any barriers, and where you and your 'side' will station yourselves.

ACTIVITIES

Refer to Source A (page 70)

1. Why is the crowd protesting? Provide evidence to support your answer.
2. What does the Minister of Police mean when he says "lyin' commy"?
3. What is the cartoonist's attitude towards the Minister of Police?
4. How useful is this Source on its own to the historian trying to understanding the issues surrounding the 1981 Springbok Tour?

Refer to Source E

5. What is it that the protester in the cartoon wants?
6. What organisation is represented by the protester?
7. Is the cartoonist critical OR supportive of this organisation and its goals? Explain your answer.
8. How might the organisation itself respond to this cartoon?

Refer to Source F

9. What aspects of the poster indicate that it has been produced in response to New Zealand playing rugby with South Africa?
10. What immediate action does the poster call for?
11. What organisation produced the poster? What is its attitude towards sporting links with South Africa? Explain your answer.
12. What is the link between the cartoon (Source E) and the poster (Source F)?

SOURCE F

FIGHT APARTHEID !
STOP THE TOUR

MOBILISE - JULY 3RD

ASSEMBLE 6·30 pm MARION STREET

published by Wellington Section PSA

SOURCE E

ACTIVITIES

Refer to Source H

1 In your own words, what is it that the poster wants people to do in order to 'stop the Tour'?

2 What is the *visual* link between this source and Source F?

3 How does this source show that New Zealand is in danger from the Tour?

4 What might be the link between this source and Source A?

Refer to Source G

5 What organisation is referred to in the poster as 'New Zealand's top street gang'?

6 Is this poster likely to have been produced by a pro- OR anti-Tour group? Explain your answer.

7 Explain the common link between this source and Source A.

8 How does the police response as shown in Source G compare to the sort of protester shown in Source E? Which poster do you feel more accurately reflects what actually happened during the Tour? Explain your answer.

AS1.4 REVIEW ACTIVITIES

In paragraphs of about 100 words for each, describe the perspectives (views) and actions (with an accompanying explanation) for the following:

a **Prime Minister Robert Muldoon and sporting contact with South Africa**

b **Black African Commonwealth nations and sporting contact with South Africa**

c **Pro-Tour supporters and the 1981 Springbok Tour**

d **Anti-Tour protesters (Nga Tamatoa, CARE, HART) and the 1981 Springbok Tour**

CHAPTER ELEVEN

THE RETURN OF THE TREATY

In the period covering the activism of the 1980s and beyond, the Treaty of Waitangi was the focus for both protest actions and political actions. These actions grew out of the demands for mana motuhake and rangatiratanga that had developed in the 1970s. Encouraged by the response of Maori to these demands, an attempt was also made to establish a political party that would further promote these aims. This was Matiu Rata's Mana Motuhake party.

WAITANGI ACTION COMMITTEE (WAC)

The Waitangi Action Committee (WAC) put the Treaty, as well as Waitangi Day, firmly in the spotlight. WAC argued that the celebration of Waitangi Day as a day of unity should be stopped. This was, they said, because the government had not done enough to fully settle Maori grievances. WAC operated under the slogans 'The Treaty is a Fraud' and 'The Cheaty of Waitangi'. Activists used various (Pakeha) means of getting their message across. These included publishing newsletters, linking up with other protest organisations, participating in demonstrations and protests, and publicly challenging politicians. WAC's first significant action was at the 1981 Waitangi Day ceremony. Scuffles on the marae resulted in the police arresting eight activists. The media tended to sensationalise the incident, with one newspaper saying that the police had to intervene to prevent a 'full-scale riot'.

Waitangi Day protests took place in the remaining years of the century. These included several hikoi (marches) from Auckland to Waitangi. The largest hikoi was organised by WAC for the 1984 commemorations. Eva Rickard and another prominent activist, Titewhai Harawira, were elected leaders. In a major shift, the conservative Kingitanga added its support to the action. This made it the first action widely supported by different Maori (and Pakeha) groups since the 1975 hikoi. By the time the march reached Waitangi it numbered over 3000 supporters. Protests at other commemorations often became quite vigorous, with Governor-Generals jostled, spat at and, on one occasion, hit by an egg. On another occasion smoke bombs were thrown. During the Queen's visit to Waitangi she was subjected to a whakapohane (bared-bottom). The police reaction to protests, especially after the disruptions of the 1981 Springbok Tour, was not gentle.

ACTIVITIES

1. How did the Waitangi Action Committee (WAC) use the Treaty of Waitangi as the basis for its protest actions?
2. Give evidence from the text that shows that Maori were using Pakeha styles of protest.
3. Give evidence from the text that shows that the actions by radicals were becoming more acceptable to a wider range of Maori organisations.
4. Draw a continuum like that shown below.

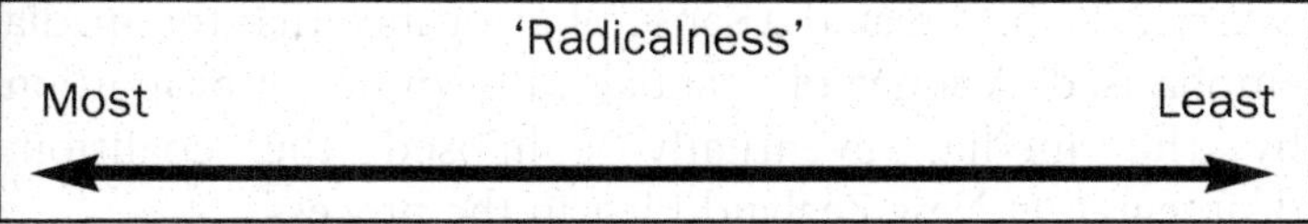

   Identify WAC's protest actions as noted in the text. Place them in the appropriate place on the continuum. Make a brief note on possible positive AND negative effects of each action.

5. What other actions could have been taken? Consider a range and give a positive and negative effect of each.
   - For example, an extreme action could be assassinations or bombings. These would certainly get attention (positive) but would lose support amongst moderate Maori and Pakeha (negative).

A POLITICAL TURNING POINT: THE 'MAORI COUNCIL' CASE

One of the most important political actions that occurred in this time was a successful challenge to the 1986 State Owned Enterprises Act. The background to the Act lay in the Labour government's economic reforms of the mid-1980s. Labour was looking to privatise (sell off) any State activities in which it felt a government should not really be involved (see page 116). As part of this process the government also created what it called State-Owned Enterprises (SOEs). These were independent, profit-making businesses that were *owned*, but not *run*, by the government. Some of the key ones were to be granted enormous amounts of State-owned land. Once set up, these SOEs could be sold off to private buyers at a later date. If this happened, the land that they owned would also pass into private hands. The New Zealand Maori Council was alarmed that a means to settle Maori grievances or claims through the Waitangi Tribunal could be lost (see page 78).

The Maori Council's victory in its legal challenge to the State Owned Enterprises Act had two major outcomes. Firstly, it ensured that Crown land would be available to be used as part of compensation packages for successful Treaty claims. Second, it required the government to consult Maori and take into account the principles of the Treaty of Waitangi in all laws that it made.

ACTIVITY

Draw and label one pictorial to represent the effects of the 1986 State Owned Enterprises Act (before the challenge by the Maori Council). Draw and label a second pictorial that represents the outcome of the Maori Council's successful legal challenge.

ANOTHER TURNING POINT: THE 1996 ELECTION

The 1996 election marked a turning-point in Maori political involvement. Major electoral changes had seen the introduction of the Mixed Member Proportional (MMP) voting system. Under this system, every vote for a political party could actually make a difference. By 1996, an appealing challenge to Labour's hold on the Maori vote had emerged: Winston Peters and his new party, New Zealand First. New Zealand First was able to benefit from both the changes in the voting system and the disillusionment Maori voters felt with Labour. In addition, Maori could vote for Matiu Rata's Mana Motuhake party. The 1996 election was also significant in other ways. It saw the largest number of Maori standing for various political parties in general seats (88), and the highest Maori voter turnout ever (63%).

Winston Peters, leader of New Zealand First.

Once the votes were counted, Maori candidates had won 15 of the 120 seats in parliament, or 12.5%. For the first time, Maori representation in parliament was roughly the same as the percentage of Maori in the population. New Zealand First won all five of the Maori seats, ending the 61-year-old Ratana-Labour political relationship. Yet, Maori voters were still content to stick with mainstream parties under the MMP system. The Maori parties with their policies of mana motuhake/self-determination did not do well.

Nor did the two main parties do as well as they'd hoped, with neither National or Labour winning enough seats to govern outright on their own. New Zealand First, with its solid core of Maori MPs, was the third largest party in parliament. It was in the position of being able to choose which party it would form a government with. In the end, contrary to all expectations, Winston Peters chose to enter into a coalition with National. In the early months of the new National-New Zealand First coalition government the Maori Members of Parliament were watched closely by the media. New Zealand First's Maori MPs were dubbed the 'Tight Five' (the term for the core of a rugby scrum). They were outspoken and encouraged the public to view them as 'warriors'. This created a sense of arrogance that the media emphasised. A series of 'scandals', blown out of proportion by the media, eventually collapsed the coalition, disintegrating New Zealand First in the process.

Maori voters returned to Labour in the 1999 election. The government then began a process of gradually granting more decision-making power to Maori groups. This marked a continuing gradual shift by the government away from the policies of the past. Maori were now being given greater opportunities to control their own futures. An example of this increasing role was the existence by the year 2000 of over 100 different Maori community welfare agencies, and a number of business-oriented organisations. The Treaty settlement process had also given some tribes a sound economic base from which to develop.

ACTIVITIES

Refer to Source A (published by the 'Waitangi Action Committee')

1 What key idea in the 'Waitangi Action Committee' section of the text does this poster provide evidence for?

2 How are both the Maori and Pakeha cultures represented in this poster?

3 Why might an historian be cautious about using this as evidence to show how Maori felt in the early 1980s?

Refer to Source B

4 In what part of New Zealand was this public meeting to take place?

5 What is it that the public are being called upon to oppose?

6 What issues do the publishers of the poster believe need to be addressed?

7 To what event in 1990 do you think this poster is referring?

ACTIVITIES

1 From the text on page 76, find evidence that could be used to back up each of the key ideas below.

- **a** In the 1996 election Maori had a real choice in terms of political parties to vote for.
- **b** Maori participated in the political process more than ever before.
- **c** Maori could feel satisfied with the outcome of the 1996 election.
- **d** Maori were satisfied that mainstream political parties would represent their interests.
- **e** New Zealand First became a significant political force in New Zealand politics in the 1990s.
- **f** New Zealand First's coalition with National was not stable.
- **g** Maori voters were put off by the 'scandals' that involved NZ First MPs.
- **h** By the end of the 20th century Maori were being granted a degree of mana motuhake.

2 **Pictorial timeline (see Official Maori Policy box below)**
Create a pictorial timeline from 1900–2000 showing the changes in government policy. Label each new policy.

AS1.4 REVIEW ACTIVITY

In paragraphs of about 100 words for each, describe the perspectives (views) and actions (with an accompanying explanation) for the following:

- **a** **The Waitangi Action Committee and Waitangi Day celebrations**
- **b** **The New Zealand Maori Council and the State Owned Enterprises Act**
- **c** **Maori voters in the 1996 election**

AS1.5 ESSAY PRACTICE

Follow the steps on the inside back cover to write the following essay.

Describe the background to the 1981 Springbok Tour, and the main events of the Tour itself. What other actions were taken by Maori in the 1980s to resolve injustices?

- South Africa's apartheid policy; pre-1981 Tours; Gleneagles Agreement; protest actions
- Mana Motuhake; Waitangi Action Committee; the 'Maori Council' case; 1996 election.

Official Maori Policy

Assimilation: the creation of 'brown Pakeha' with Maori losing all their culture. This was government policy up until at least the 1960s.

Integration: the interaction of two distinct cultures, which, in theory, could eventually produce a single blended culture with aspects of both. This was government policy from the 1960s to mid-1970s.

Bi-culturalism: two distinct cultures existing together in harmony and equality. This was government policy from the mid-1970s. Some suggested that it should be replaced by multi-culturalism.

Multi-culturalism: a suggested alternative to bi-culturalism, with other cultures such as Pacific Island and Asian also given recognition.

THE WAITANGI TRIBUNAL

The poor showing of radical Maori parties in the 1996 MMP election was an indication that Maori were mostly satisfied with the processes in place for resolving their grievances. Cases of direct protest action had become uncommon. Two exceptions were Mike Smith's 1994 chainsawing of the One Tree Hill pine tree (Auckland), and the 1997 attack on the America's Cup by Benjamin Nathan. Neither of these actions was widely supported by Maori.

The most significant development in having Maori grievances resolved was the establishment of the Waitangi Tribunal, under the 1975 Treaty of Waitangi Act. The Tribunal's job was to inquire into claims based on the Treaty, and then make recommendations for resolving them. It was also required to point out if any new laws that the government made were in conflict with the principles of the Treaty. The 1986 State Owned Enterprises Act (see page 76) was the first major case where a new law was challenged under the Treaty of Waitangi Act.

The Five Principles of the Treaty of Waitangi

Principle	Explanation
1 Kawanatanga (governorship)	The government had the right, and responsibility, to govern and make laws fairly for all New Zealanders.
2 Tino Rangatiratanga (chieftainship)	Maori were to have control of their own possessions and resources, and the right of iwi to manage their own affairs was acknowledged.
3 Partnership	Known as the 'Good Faith Principle', it involved developing a sense of support and fair dealing between the partners.
4 Protection	The government had the responsibility to ensure that Maori taonga (treasures) such as language and customs were preserved.
5 Participation	Maori would have equality with Pakeha, and fair access to resources and educational opportunities.

The Treaty of Waitangi and the Five Principles (5Ps)

One of the fundamental issues to be addressed before the Treaty of Waitangi Act could be effective was determining the exact meaning of the Treaty. The different understandings of 1840 were no longer useful in the 20th century. (Go back and review the '3Ps', page 8.) Eventually, a definition of the principles of the Treaty was developed (see the table above).

The Tribunal in Action

The Tribunal's actual powers and ability to carry out its duties were at first quite limited, and Maori were disappointed. The Tribunal could not investigate claims from issues arising before 1975. This was of little comfort to Maori, as the bulk of their concerns pre-dated 1975. In addition, only parliament could actually decide on the nature of any settlements. As unsatisfactory as this was for Maori, it still marked a major shift in the government's approach to their concerns.

In 1985, a new Labour government allowed the Tribunal to investigate issues arising as far back as 1840. It also increased the number of Tribunal members to seven, with more Maori representation. These moves led to an enormous increase in the number of claims. Each claim required in-depth investigation and the hearing of evidence. This lengthy process in turn led to a huge backlog of claims. In 1989 there were 180 waiting to be processed; ten years on there were around 800, with more to come. Critics felt that this was an indication of a process gone out of control. Supporters pointed out that the backlog had come about because of more than a century of neglect of Maori concerns. They argued that Maori had repeatedly attempted to use the legal system to have grievances resolved, at great expense and with little success.

Waitangi Tribunal Claim Process

1. A claim is submitted to the Tribunal by Maori (the claimants)
2. Research is carried out by trained historians and other specialists, as well as by the claimant group.
3. The Tribunal members begin hearing evidence based on the claim and the research. *The claimant may choose at this stage to negotiate directly with the government by applying to the Office of Treaty Settlements.*
4. The Tribunal produces a report either dismissing the claim, or recommends to the government a way to settle the claim.
5. The government considers the recommendations. It may act on them in full, in part, or not at all.

ACTIVITIES

1 Read the explanations for each of the five principles of the Treaty of Waitangi carefully (Source C), and then draw pictorials for each. Provide a title, and labels for each pictorial.

2 Review the 'Three Ps' (page 8). Explain the similarities and differences between the '5Ps' and '3Ps'.

3 Why were Maori disappointed with the Waitangi Tribunal in 1975? What extensions were later made to its powers?

4 Summarise the two views of the Waitangi Tribunal process, as at the end of the 20th century.

5 For each step in the Claim Process (Source D) draw a pictorial with a few key words for headings.

Members of the Waitangi Tribunal delivering a report on the Chatham Islands.

Direct Negotiation with the Crown

By the late 1980s the government was concerned about the nature and extent of some of the Waitangi Tribunal's recommendations for settling Maori grievances. For this reason, and to speed up the process of settlements, the government invited tribes to negotiate with it directly, bypassing the Waitangi Tribunal. Maori claimants quickly saw the advantages of doing this. It was cheaper, more flexible and quicker. Under the National government an Office of Treaty Settlements was established to handle the negotiations. Doug Graham was the Minister in charge.

The 'Fiscal Cap'

In the early 1990s Doug Graham announced the government's intention to wrap up the claims process within ten years. In addition, the settlements reached were to be 'full and final'. This meant that, by law, later generations of Maori could not try to renegotiate a settlement that had already been agreed upon. A limit of $1billion was placed on the total amount that the government was prepared to set aside for settlements. This became known as the 'fiscal cap'. While a few Maori were prepared to accept the 'fiscal cap', others were angry at the lack of consultation. They also felt that the whole scheme was in conflict with the requirement of both sides to negotiate in good faith.

Doug Graham's proposal caused a mixed reaction. There was an increase in Maori protest activity to a level not seen since the Land March and Bastion Point occupation of the 1970s. One direct action was the 1995 occupation of Moutua Gardens/Pakaitore in Wanganui. Other actions included smaller-scale occupations at Whakarewarewa in Rotorua, a school in Auckland and a university in Hamilton. Protests at the Waitangi Day celebrations in 1995 were the noisiest for some years. Many Pakeha, however, saw the 'fiscal cap' as a necessary means to stop the cost of settlements blowing out. Some even said that $1billion was too high. After the 1996 MMP election, National agreed to drop the 'fiscal cap' as part of the coalition deal with New Zealand First. In reality, however, the idea of a 'cap' remained government policy.

Treaty Settlement Issues

Both Maori and Pakeha were concerned about the Treaty claims' situation. Many Maori felt that the time taken to have claims heard was too lengthy. Many Pakeha were worried about the sheer number of claims and the potential cost to the country. Another concern was that the whole process had become a new industry – a 'grievance industry' – where lawyers got rich and tension between Maori and Pakeha increased. In addition, according to many Pakeha, Maori who had never felt any sense of grievance were suddenly 'finding' issues to present to the Tribunal in the hope of getting big payoffs.

The Tribunal process, however, was designed to sort out the genuine from the false claims. Each claim was investigated, at least partially at the expense of the person or group claiming. The claims that were not considered to be genuine were thrown out. For example, Joe Hawke, the leader of the Bastion Point occupation, had his 1977 claim that Maori be allowed to take shellfish by any means (including scuba gear) disallowed.

ACTIVITY

Sort the following events into the correct order. Each event caused the one that follows (the relationship of 'cause and effect').

Government's desire to wrap up Treaty claims, with 'full and final' settlements.	National-New Zealand First coalition drops 'fiscal cap' proposal.	Claim process is sped up.	Pakeha concerns about the cost of the Treaty process grow.	'Fiscal Cap' policy announced.
Office of Treaty Settlements (OTS) established.	Direct protest action increases.	Government concern about Tribunal recommendations increases.	More claimants opt to use OTS as total number of claims grows.	

Many Pakeha saw the Tribunal's proposed settlements as 'giving Maori something for nothing', or for some vague wrongdoing that was well in the past. This view misunderstood the basis of the whole settlements' process. Firstly, nothing was 'given' to Maori as a handout. Any settlements, whether cash or otherwise, were for losses caused by government actions that were in breach of the agreement between Maori and Pakeha made at Waitangi in 1840. Furthermore, settlements were usually set at a tiny proportion of the value of the original loss. For example, the Tainui settlement of $170million was a fraction of the estimated billions of dollars worth of loss of income and land since the original confiscations (see page 83).

WAITANGI TRIBUNAL CLAIMS

Claims before the Tribunal fell into three broad categories. The first was to do with land that Maori said had passed unlawfully into the Crown's hands. The second category recognised the Treaty's guarantee that Maori could control their own resources such as fisheries and forests. The third was related to the Treaty's guarantee to protect taonga (treasures). The Tribunal interpreted this to include things such as te reo. There are a large number of settlements that could be looked at, but rather than simply list them all, one or two from each category will be examined.

ACTIVITIES

1. Refer to the '5Ps' (Principles of the Treaty of Waitangi). Which one of these did Maori claim the proposed 'Fiscal Cap' was in breach of?
2. Summarise the two views on the government's proposed 'Fiscal Cap'.

Refer to Source E

3. Who is represented by the people standing on the shore? Who do you think is represented by the ship?
4. Explain the cartoonist's viewpoint with regard to Maori grievances. Provide evidence from the cartoon to support your answer.
5. Refer to the text in this section. What group of New Zealanders might be likely to agree with the views expressed in this cartoon?
6. Why might an historian be careful in using this cartoon as evidence of how New Zealanders felt about the whole Treaty process?

SOURCE E

Land-related claims: Tainui/Waikato

One of the most significant land claims settled in the 1990s was that of Tainui/Waikato. The settlement was to compensate for nearly half a million hectares of Waikato land confiscated after the New Zealand Wars. Direct negotiations were entered into with the Office of Treaty Settlements. In 1995 a settlement involving the return of some land, an apology and monetary compensation was finally reached. All up, the whole package was valued at $170million. The money was used to fund scholarships, build a college, renovate marae and some was invested (not always wisely) on behalf of the 33,000 members of the tribe. Robert Mahuta, a Tainui leader and one of the negotiators, expressed some satisfaction with the outcome and a sense that his people could now move forward. This was despite the fact that the package represented no more than 2% of the market value of the confiscated land.

The Tainui/Waikato deal illustrated one of the key problems in the whole settlement process: who had the authority to represent those making a claim? Some Tainui/Waikato Maori criticised the deal reached. Eva Rickard, the veteran protester who forced the government to return land at Raglan, was one. She argued that the negotiating body, the Tainui Trust Board, did not have the authority to make a deal on behalf of everybody else. She said that negotiations should have been with the 33 individual hapu (sub-tribes) rather than the larger iwi. This was not what the government wanted to hear, for it would have made negotiations immensely more complicated.

> 'The Crown acknowledges that the confiscations of land were wrongful, have caused Waikato to the present time to suffer feelings in relation to their lost lands akin to those of orphans, and have had a crippling impact on the welfare, economy and development of Waikato... The Crown recognises that the lands confiscated in the Waikato have made a significant contribution to the wealth and development of NZ, whilst the Waikato tribe has been alienated from its lands and deprived of the benefit of its lands ...'
>
> *– from the text of the Crown apology, which was part of the Tainui settlement package.*

Land-related claims: Ngai Tahu (Kai Tahu)

A second major settlement was for a claim involving huge amounts of land in the South Island. The Tribunal found that the government of the 19th century had not properly purchased the land. In addition to these grievances, the Tribunal found that reserves of three million hectares of land promised by the government were never set aside. Nor had promised hospitals and schools been built. As in Tainui's case, the Ngai Tahu claim was negotiated directly with the government. In 1996 a settlement involving $170million worth of land and compensation was reached. One of the chief Ngai Tahu negotiators, Tipene O'Regan, was not happy with the settlement but accepted that it was the best that could be done. Ngai Tahu is seen as a clear success story in terms of using the settlement package to develop a sound economic base for its members.

ACTIVITIES

1 Read the text on Waitangi Tribunal Claims including the boxed text. The key terms in Column A are in the order found in the text. Match the related term from Column B. For example, Term 1 from Column A matches with Term C from Column B.

2 For each matched term, write a complete sentence. This will produce a summary of this section.

Column A (in same order as the text)	Column B (mixed order)
1 Three categories	A Reserves, hospitals and schools not set aside
2 Half a million hectares confiscated	B Tipene O'Regan unhappy, but...
3 Compensation package	C Land, resources, taonga
4 'Some satisfaction'	D Scholarships, a college, marae and investments
5 Crippling impact on Waikato	E Eva Rickard: 33 hapu
6 Key negotiation problem: who can represent Maori?	F Significant contribution to wealth and development of NZ
7 Land not properly purchased	G But only 2% of the market value
8 Land, apology and compensation	H Direct negotiations entered into

ACTIVITIES

Both the Maori claimants and the Crown agreed that no privately-owned land would be used to settle any claims, thus avoiding creating new (Pakeha) grievances. One exception was in 1995. The government negotiated with a Northland man, Alan Titford, to accept compensation of $3.25million for the return of 38 hectares of land to Maori. This worked out at about $85,500 per hectare. This settlement stands in contrast to those made with Maori.

The chart below shows the settlements that some tribes could have expected if the government used the same formula to compensate them as it used to compensate Titford. The right-hand column shows the value of final settlements agreed to, as a percentage of what might have been expected (at the 'Titford rate').

Tribe seeking a settlement	Land area of claim (hectares)	Compensation (based on the Titford settlement)	Actual compensation	%
Waikato/Tainui	480,000	$41.5billion	$170million	0.4
Ngai Tahu	13.8million	$1192billion	$170million	0.01
Te Maunga (Bay of Plenty)	0.6	$51,800	$129,000	294
Hauai (Northland)	25	$2.1million	$716,000	34

1 Compare the Titford model of compensation with the Actual compensation:
- **a** which tribe has come out worst off?
- **b** which tribe has done best?

2 From the evidence given in the Table, make a generalisation about the relationship between the land area of a claim, and the value of compensation paid by the government.

3 Look at the Ngai Tahu claim. Find a statement in the previous section of the text which could be backed up with evidence from this Table.

4 Do you think it is a valid exercise to compare Alan Titford's compensation package with Maori compensation packages? Explain your answer.

5 Argue for or against the following statement: 'Maori claimants have been ripped off by the Treaty compensation process.'

Resource-related Claims: The 'Sealord Deal'

The most significant resource-related claim came to be known as the 'Sealord Deal'. Along with the government's 'Fiscal Cap' proposal, the 'Sealord Deal' caused an increase in Maori activism and protest. The issue began with a claim lodged with the Waitangi Tribunal. It was based on the Tino Rangatiratanga Principal (see page 79). This confirmed that under Article Two of the Treaty Maori had been guaranteed possession of their resources – specifically fisheries. The claim stated that since the 19th century the Crown had illegally taken possession of the fisheries around the coastline. Evidence was provided of extensive Maori fishing at the time of the signing of the Treaty, particularly around Northland and the South Island. Early suggestions that the claim be for 100% of New Zealand's fisheries were modified to 50%. When the claim became public there was widespread disbelief and outrage. Nonetheless, direct negotiations with the government began and in 1992 a complicated agreement was reached. The settlement package came to a total value of $170million. Maori also retained the right to traditional access to seafood for private use.

Even before the Sealord Deal was settled there were major disputes over how the proceeds should be distributed. Differences arose between tribal Maori and urban non-tribal Maori. Coastal tribes argued that coastline size should form the basis of distribution. However, urban Maori and tribes with small coastlines rejected this. Some said that distribution should be through traditional iwi only. Non-tribal urban Maori also rejected this, arguing for distribution based on population. To complicate matters more, in 1999 an urban Maori organisation – Auckland's Waipereira Trust, headed by John Tamihere – had been given official iwi status by the government. This reflected the fact that many urban Maori had lost touch with their tribal roots. On the face of it, urban Maori would be eligible to receive the same rights to fisheries resources as traditional iwi. The issue, however, had not been fully resolved by the turn of the century. It showed just how difficult it could be to find solutions satisfactory to all, because Maori society had changed dramatically. It also showed that inter-tribal rivalry was still alive and well.

Taonga-related claims: te reo

Under a claim to the Waitangi Tribunal te reo Maori was said to be one of the most important taonga for Maori. Claimants explained that there had been a long history of neglect of the Maori language, as well as active discouragement by the education system. This was part of the policy of assimilation, whereby Maori were to be taught to speak and think in English. In 1986 the Tribunal released its report, and a number of its recommendations were soon put into law. The 1987 Maori Language Act made te reo Maori an official language of New Zealand. Although changes were slow to occur, this Act was a significant acknowledgement of the place of Maori culture in New Zealand society. Steps were also taken to encourage the learning and use of te reo, through the establishment of the Maori Language Commission. In addition, broadcasting policy was changed to include increased Maori control of part of the radio and television network. More broadcasting hours were also to be devoted to Maori language programmes. These changes were also slow to eventuate.

ACTIVITIES

1. What resource was the 'Sealord deal' all about?
2. On what basis *might* Maori have continued to demand 100% of New Zealand's fisheries?
3. Explain the views of the two main sides in the dispute over distribution of the fisheries compensation package.
4. What government policy change in the 1990s was a recognition of the urbanisation and detribalisation that Maori had undergone since World War II?
5. What did Maori claimants say was the main cause of the loss of te reo?
6. Give three actions that were taken to improve the place of te reo in New Zealand. Why might Maori be so concerned about saving te reo?

REVIEW ACTIVITY

You will need a full page for this (and perhaps even a double page). Use the main ideas from this section of the text to create a mind-map OR structured overview (see page 5) that shows the development of the Waitangi Tribunal and the key claims. Include the following:

- The '5Ps'
- The Waitangi Tribunal's role and operation
- The 'fiscal cap' and resulting protest
- The three main types of Waitangi Tribunal claims
- Issues over Maori representation (hapu/iwi, and urban iwi).

MAORI-PAKEHA RELATIONS @ 2000

Over the course of the 20th century the government's policy on issues affecting Maori changed considerably. Up until the 1930s it was characterised by 'benign neglect' (see page 22) and assimilation. From the mid-1930s the Labour government, in partnership with the Ratana MPs, began to take a more active interest in Maori welfare. This approach continued after WWII, as did the assimilationist policy. Changes that began in the 1970s, such as the creation of the Waitangi Tribunal, were a positive step but were not intended to give Maori more decision-making power. Even the new policy of bi-culturalism made little real difference. Both Labour and National did, however, genuinely strive to improve conditions for Maori. This made it difficult for the government, and many Pakeha, to understand why Maori were still unhappy. It was not until the end of the 1990s that the government finally began to grant what Maori had been asking for since the 1970s: some degree of mana motuhake, or self-determination.

By 2000, race relations in general were seen by many to have improved through the process of dealing with past Maori grievances. However, for some Pakeha New Zealanders, the Treaty process in particular was viewed as a new 'grievance' industry that over-focused on the negatives, creating division. Others criticised the Tribunal for too readily accepting Maori claims as fact, without carefully checking them out. In addition, some felt that the value of Pakeha culture was being marginalised by all the focus on Maori culture. Others claimed that Maori were receiving special privileges in the areas of health, education and other government services. (This view tended to ignore the fact that Maori were still over-represented in many of the worst social statistics.) Many were offended by the claim of some Maori that Pakeha were merely tauiwi – outsiders. This view saw Pakeha as having less right to be in New Zealand, and their contribution in the past as being only negative.

A side-effect of the 'Maori Renaissance' of the 1970s, according to former Prime Minister David Lange, was an over-emphasis on cultural activities for Maori schoolchildren. This, he said, was often at the expense of learning time on academic subjects. His concern was echoed by Sir Charles Bennett, former Maori Battalion leader and public servant in Maori Affairs. Bennett warned against young Maori being tempted to reject formal education in favour of focusing solely on traditional Maori culture. From another perspective, South Island artist and social commentator Grahame Sydney pointed out that the impact of the 'Maori Renaissance' was primarily a North Island experience. His view was that while urban centres in the North increasingly embraced a Maori (and Polynesian/Asian) identity, the South Island was getting more in touch with its own identity, based on the wide open spaces and mountains. This position, while acknowledging past injustices, took a more positive view of the relationship of Pakeha with the land.

CHAPTER TWELVE

NEW ZEALAND IN THE WORLD AFTER 1945: NEW DIRECTIONS?

Pakeha New Zealanders in particular still felt a close relationship with Britain in 1945, and they had clearly proved this through previous actions. In the thirty years prior to 1945, many New Zealanders – including Maori – had fought in two of Britain's wars. One of the reasons for this close relationship was the fact that much of the Pakeha population of New Zealand had originated in Britain. A second key element was New Zealand's economic dependence on the 'Mother Country' (see page 11 on refrigerated shipping). Thirdly, New Zealand was geographically isolated and surrounded, as many saw it, by potential enemies, particularly in Asia. Up until World War Two, New Zealand relied for protection on Britain's naval power. This included the development of a British defensive base at Singapore.

Although the bonds with the British Empire still remained strong after 1945, there had been a change away from uncritical enthusiasm. This was due in part to the experiences in the two World Wars. Another factor was a new independence in foreign policy with the election in 1935 of the first Labour government.

THE DEVELOPMENT OF NEW ZEALAND'S FOREIGN POLICY

Foreign policy is the relationship countries have with each other. It usually includes diplomatic links (where officials from each country keep in regular touch), and issues of trade, culture and security.

New Zealand's foreign policy from the beginning of the 20th century was decided by Britain. Up until at least the 1930s, New Zealand resisted the trend of taking more responsibility for itself. In this respect, New Zealand was unlike other former British colonies such as Canada and Australia. With little enthusiasm, New Zealand accepted a degree of independence in 1907, when it was granted 'Dominion' status. In 1931, the British parliament passed the Statute of Westminster, giving its former colonies the option to be fully independent. The New Zealand government refused; it was not until 1947 before this right was at last accepted.

With the election of the first Labour government in 1935, a more independent approach to foreign policy was adopted. As a left-wing government (see page 86), Labour believed in collective security through a world organisation, the League of Nations. Collective security was a policy whereby countries supported each other, agreeing that any aggressive act against one would be treated as a hostile act against all. Where Britain was only lukewarm about the League of Nations, New Zealand was strongly in favour of it.

SOURCE A

Kiwi: "I think I would look better without it."

ACTIVITIES

1. Explain why New Zealand maintained a close relationship with Britain up until at least World War Two.
2. Draw pictorials that show what 'Foreign Policy' is. Include key words only.
3. What was it that the Statute of Westminster gave New Zealand when it was finally adopted in 1947?
4. What policy of the first Labour government prior to the outbreak of WWII differed from Britain's?

Refer to Source A

5. What does the kiwi represent in this cartoon?
6. What is it that the kiwi does *not* want?

SOURCE B

> 'We had all the self-government we wanted. We could choose our fellow citizens [for parliament] and do the other things we wanted to do. We didn't see any need for the Statute of Westminster. We were doing all right without it.'
>
> *– a New Zealand government official.*

ACTIVITIES

Refer to Source B

1. Provide a quote of no more than SIX words that is a fact.
2. Locate the key idea in the main text to which this quote refers. Summarise the sentence in the text that contains this key idea.
3. Why would an historian be cautious about using this quote alone to describe how New Zealanders felt about the Statute of Westminster?
4. Describe the link between Source A and Source B.

A NEW WORLD ORDER: THE COLD WAR

Most New Zealanders became aware after WWII that there was growing tension between two very different world orders. The first was represented by the United States, which called itself the champion of the 'free world'. The countries that rallied – with varying degrees of willingness – to support the United States were often referred to collectively as 'the West'. The economic and political philosophy of the West was (and still is) capitalism. The other major world order was represented by the Soviet Union and, from 1949, China. The Soviet Union's economic and political policy was communism. After WWII, the Soviet Union had extended its control over much of Eastern Europe. The place where the two increasingly hostile systems met was across a divided Germany. West Germany was capitalist and East Germany communist.

Both sides began to compete for dominance militarily, and for influence elsewhere in the world. The resulting power struggle became known as the 'Cold War'. This was a dangerous time. Although no all-out 'Hot War' ever broke out directly between the two powers, each side had soon developed weapons that could destroy the world. A crisis over Cuba in 1962 came very close to escalating into all-out nuclear war. New Zealand, like many other countries, found itself taking sides in the Cold War. The Cold War finally ended in 1989 with the collapse of communism in the Soviet Union and Eastern Europe.

In the early 1960s the US government promoted nuclear fallout shelters.

CAPITALISM VERSUS COMMUNISM

Both capitalism and communism are economic systems that determine how countries as a whole are run.

- Capitalism is about freedom of choice for individuals. Under capitalism everyone (in theory) has the chance to do what they want, such as making a lot of money. Capitalist countries are often democracies, where people also have the freedom to choose their government through elections.
- Communism as an idea was developed in the 19th century. It was a response to the huge inequalities that appeared under capitalism, where the rich got richer and the poor poorer. Those who support communism argue that there is not really any freedom of choice for the poor under capitalism. Communism puts the needs of society as a whole above those of the individual. The government thus decides what types of goods should be produced; this is called a command economy. In theory at least, it also distributes the wealth evenly amongst all people. (In practice, communism in China and the Soviet Union was oppressive.) Those who sympathise more or less with the aims of communism are often called left-wing.

ACTIVITIES

1. Use pictorials and/or diagrams to show the main features of the communist and the capitalist systems.
2. Explain what is meant by the term 'Cold War'.

New Zealand and the Cold War

The Cold War affected New Zealand in several ways. It was a key factor in determining the country's relationship with its allies, and helped define who its enemies were. It also influenced actions inside New Zealand. From the early 1950s fears about communists within New Zealand led the government to take some heavy-handed measures. In 1951 a dispute involving waterfront workers was seen as a test case. In an effort to break the power of the unions, the government passed emergency measures that had not been used even during World War Two. Freedom of speech, the right to an open trial, and even the ordinary running of parliament were all suspended. Sid Holland, the National Prime Minister, claimed that these moves were necessary. He accused the unions of being part of a communist plot to cripple New Zealand. Despite these extraordinary measures, the dispute dragged on for 151 days. Some New Zealanders believed that the unions were getting what they deserved. Others were afraid that New Zealand was becoming more like the Nazi totalitarian state against which they had fought during WWII. National governments through until the late 1980s would continue to use the 'communist threat' for political purposes. They regularly accused Labour of being 'soft on communism'. National's 1975 'Dancing Cossacks' election video is a classic example of this.

ACTIVITIES

1. Write a 100–150 word speech to be delivered by Prime Minister Holland explaining why he needs to take such drastic action against the waterside workers. Include references to the 'communist threat' and the nature of communism.
2. Write a 100–150 word article for a pamphlet to be published on a secret printing press by the waterside workers. Explain why the government's actions are anti-democratic.

Refer to Source C

3. What organisation produced this election poster?
4. What, in general, are the sort of benefits this poster promises?
5. Refer to the explanation of communism on page 86. Explain how the poster links to the key ideas about communism.

SOURCE C

NEW ZEALAND AND THE COMMONWEALTH

New Zealand had close links with Britain for much of the 20th century. This included immigration, cultural and trade ties, as well as shared war experiences. For this reason, New Zealand chose to be part of the Commonwealth. Membership was seen as a way of maintaining a close trading relationship with Britain. It also gave a small country a means of having a voice in world affairs. In addition, it provided a forum in which New Zealand could establish contacts with other member nations. New Zealand also continued to support Britain in military action.

In 1947, the Commonwealth consisted of only seven nations – Britain, Australia, New Zealand, Canada, South Africa, Pakistan and India. The last two mentioned were the only nations governed by non-whites (they had become independent of British rule that year). By the end of the century the Commonwealth extended from Africa to Asia, and from the Pacific to the Caribbean. It included 54 member nations and contained 1.7 billion people, 30% of the world's population.

The most well-known activities of the Commonwealth included the four-yearly Commonwealth Games and the biennial (two-yearly) Heads of Government meeting. The

BRITAIN, NEW ZEALAND STILL LOVES YOU! THE 1953–1954 ROYAL TOUR

One of the clearest indications of how most New Zealanders felt about Britain was the 1953–1954 Royal Tour by Queen Elizabeth II. This was a major event for several reasons. Pakeha New Zealanders – and many Maori – still identified closely with Britain and the Commonwealth. Less than ten years earlier New Zealanders had still been dying as part of Britain's effort to defeat Nazi Germany. Also, about 75% of New Zealand's import and export trade was with Britain. Furthermore, over 65% of the country's immigrants at the time were British. Finally, New Zealand in the 1950s was booming. Wartime restrictions were over, and Edmund Hillary had in May 1953 conquered Mt Everest for the first time. The Royal Tour – the first by a reigning monarch – seemed to cap off a perfect year.

The Queen and her husband toured through 46 towns and attended 110 different functions in five weeks. In some places sheep were dyed red, white and blue in displays of patriotism. In others, instructions were given on how to plant flower gardens in similar patriotic colours. Towns tried to outdo each other in the size and spectacle of their greeting. Children formed an important part of most receptions. This was in order to reinforce in a new generation the traditional ties with Britain. It was also to show off the healthy vibrancy of the country.

All was not entirely well on the tour. The Queen had been in the country less than two days when the Tangiwai rail disaster occurred, in which 151 people died. More problems arose when the government announced that there would be only one Maori reception for the Queen. The Minister of Maori Affairs, E.B. Corbett, showed insensitivity to the Maori desire to demonstrate their loyalty along tribal lines. 'So far as the Queen herself is concerned, they will just be the Maori people. She will not be concerned to know from what tribes they have come.' Initially there were no plans to attend a welcome at Turangawaewae, the base of the Maori King Movement. In the end, the government gave in and scheduled a three-minute visit. The Queen, impressed by the preparations and reception, ended up staying a total of 17 minutes.

Games were successfully held in Christchurch in 1974 and Auckland in 1990. The Heads of Government meeting in 1960 raised the issue of New Zealand's sporting links with South Africa. In the early 1970s, New Zealand's Prime Minister Norman Kirk raised the issue of French nuclear testing in the Pacific. The 1977 meeting produced the Gleneagles Agreement condemning South Africa's policy of apartheid (see page 71). In the 1990s, the Commonwealth expressed grave concerns about undemocratic activities in Fiji, Nigeria, Pakistan and Zimbabwe.

Don McKinnon became Commonwealth Secretary-General in 2000.

ACTIVITIES

1 Summarise the reasons why the 1953–54 Royal Tour was so important for New Zealanders (see page 88).

2 Use the information in the first two paragraphs to devise one or more of the following:
- a placard welcoming the Royal couple to your area
- a poem expressing your patriotism
- an action similar to dyeing sheep, or planting a garden, in red, white and blue colours.

3 Explain why you think it was seen as particularly important for children to be involved in the celebrations.

4 Why would many Maori have found E.B. Corbett's remark insensitive?

5 Draw a star diagram showing SIX reasons why New Zealand decided to join the Commonwealth.

6 Draw and label pictorials to represent the Commonwealth in 1947 and in 2000.

7 Find evidence in the text (a fact, statistic or quote) that supports each of the following key ideas.

a. The Commonwealth had grown into a large, global organisation by the year 2000.

b. The Commonwealth Heads of Government meetings provided an opportunity to deal with international problems that affected the members.

c. New Zealand supported sporting links between Commonwealth countries.

NEW ZEALAND AND THE UNITED NATIONS

After World War Two, the Labour government increased its commitment to collective security by actively supporting the formation of the United Nations (UN). The principles of the UN were set out in 1945 in its founding document, the UN Charter. Important amongst these was the solving of disputes between nations without the use of war. Another was to improve economic and social conditions for all peoples. The UN policy of decolonisation was one promoted strongly by New Zealand's Prime Minster, Peter Fraser. At the end of 1945 there were only 51 UN member nations, but by 2000 there were some 190 members. Most of the new members came from the Africa/Asia regions, as a result of decolonisation.

> **Decolonisation**
> The process whereby European powers, such as Britain and France, handed back government to the peoples that had been under their control.

Prime Minister Fraser devoted much of his energy in the early post-war years to helping build an effective UN structure. He believed that an international organisation should give all nations a chance to be heard, instead of larger nations always dominating world policy. New Zealand thus took a leadership role in representing the interests of smaller nations.

Fraser's view of how a fair and effective UN would be structured was not shared by all nations. As the major power, the focus of the United States was mostly on military security. Fraser argued (unsuccessfully) for a greater focus on social and economic issues. He was disappointed in another area too. The major powers were unwilling to let a world body make decisions that they might not agree with. The most significant debate on the structure of the UN, and thus its power, came down to the role of the Security Council.

In the post-war period the Security Council was the most important UN body. It had 'primary responsibility for the maintenance of international peace and security.' Five powerful countries sat as permanent members (Britain, France, America, pre-communist China and Russia). Ten other member states were elected for two-year terms on a rotating basis. Despite the efforts of politicians like Fraser, the five major powers demanded – and got – the right of veto. This meant that any one of the five could oppose a planned UN action and thus stop it. With the growing Cold War, one side or the other would frequently block actions that it felt affected its own interests. This in turn meant that some countries became disillusioned with the UN's inability to function effectively. (New Zealand, with National's Sid Holland as Prime Minister from 1949, was one of them.)

Despite Fraser's disappointment at losing out on the issues above, New Zealand was at first an active UN participant. Support was given to the UN decolonisation plan and various aid programmes. Troops were committed to UN peacekeeping actions in the Middle East, Africa and Asia. In the 1990s, peacekeepers were also stationed in the Balkans and East Timor. However, the major UN military action in which New Zealand was involved was the Korean War, 1950 to 1953.

The text below is part of the 1945 draft of the United Nations Charter, the rules by which the UN would be governed. The sections that have been ~~crossed out~~ are the changes that New Zealand (unsuccessfully) wished to have made to the draft.

CHAPTER V. – THE GENERAL ASSEMBLY
B. Functions and Powers
The General Assembly shall have the right to consider any matter within the sphere of international relations.

1. In particular the General Assembly should have the right to consider the general principles of co-operation in the maintenance of international peace and security including the principles governing disarmament and the regulation of armaments.... Any such questions on which action is necessary should be referred to the Security Council by the General Assembly either before or after discussion. ~~The General Assembly should not on its own initiative make recommendations on any matter relating to the maintenance of international peace and security which is being dealt with by the Security Council.~~

2. The General Assembly should be empowered to admit new members to the Organization ~~upon the recommendation of the Security Council.~~

Between 1945 and 2000 there were 250 major wars. By the end of the 20th century, an estimated average of 500 people, mostly civilians, were being killed each day through armed conflict. About $2 billion a day was being spent world-wide on weaponry. (The last time there was no major conflict was 1816.)

NZ Herald, 21/9/02

ACTIVITIES

1 Find evidence to support the key idea that the aims of the Commonwealth and the United Nations were similar. (You will need to look back at the previous section on the Commonwealth.)

2 Provide a quote from the text that supports the key idea that the Security Council was where real power lay in the early United Nations.

3 What was the power of veto? Explain how it could affect the ability of the UN to take decisive action.

4 What were the different views of National and Labour governments with regard to the UN?

Refer to Source D

5 In your own words, what was the job of the General Assembly of the United Nations?

6 According to the original draft, which organisation in the UN was responsible for deciding on any action the UN would take?

7 In your own words, what was the intended effect of New Zealand's proposed changes to the UN Charter?

8 Draw a diagram that shows the difference between what the draft of the Charter states, and what New Zealand wanted, in terms of power in the UN.

Refer to Sources E and F

9 What is the 'Arms Industry' (Source F)? How has the cartoonist represented it?

10 What do the graphs on the charts attached to the end of the bed represent? What effect has this had on the Arms Industry?

11 How does the evidence in Source E compare to the cartoonist's view in Source F?

THE KOREAN WAR, 1950–53: NEW ZEALAND, THE UN AND SOUTH EAST ASIA

One of the ways in which New Zealand became more involved in South East Asia in the 1950s was through the sending of troops to fight as part of the United Nations forces in Korea. Immediately after WWII, Korea had been divided into a communist north and non-communist south. This was supposed to be a temporary measure while negotiations were undertaken to reunify the nation. These negotiations failed to produce a solution. On June 25th 1950 North Korean troops, backed by the Russians, invaded South Korea. In response, the UN Security Council passed a resolution calling on North Korea to withdraw its troops. UN member nations were also asked to prepare military forces to intervene. (Russia was absent for the crucial vote, and thus could not use its right of veto.) Eventually sixteen nations, mostly allies of the United States, contributed. Once Britain had indicated that it would be involved, New Zealand and Australia were quick to respond.

There were several reasons why New Zealand responded so quickly. The first was a commitment to the United Nations' notion of collective security. This had been especially true for Fraser's Labour government. The new National government, under Sid Holland, was not quite so enthusiastic. Holland's motive for participating in the UN action was more political. He wanted to put pressure on the United States to sign a separate defence treaty with New Zealand (see ANZUS, page 95). By supporting the US in Korea, Holland believed that the US would in turn feel obliged to support New Zealand. A third reason, perhaps the most important, was that Britain had asked New Zealand to contribute. On this basis, two frigates (naval vessels) were rapidly dispatched. Overall, half of New Zealand's naval force was involved in the Korean War. Ground troops were also promised. Eventually – after many delays in sending them, and pressure from the US – these troops fought as part of the Commonwealth Brigade in a unit called 'Kay Force'. By the time a ceasefire was signed in 1953, 38 of the 3794 men who served had been killed.

Aftermath

The Korean War showed New Zealand's commitment to the UN and collective security. As in earlier wars, New Zealand's contribution was large compared to the country's size. Only the United States and South Korea sent more men into combat, as a proportion of their population. Prime Minister Holland, never a strong supporter of the UN, now felt a greater respect for it. The war also brought New Zealand more directly into South East Asia, and helped persuade the US to sign the ANZUS treaty. This made some New Zealanders uneasy about moving away from Britain and into the influence of the United States. On the other hand, the Korean War also served to maintain the traditional links with Britain – New Zealand's troops had fought as part of the Commonwealth Brigade. It also convinced many that communism *was* a real threat. This was especially so when China entered the war. However, many people also came to believe that war was not the answer to international problems. Nearly two million people had died, and the cease-fire agreement reached in 1953 saw both sides roughly where they had been when the war started.

UN troops on patrol in Korea.

ACTIVITIES

Indicate whether the following statements are TRUE or FALSE. If FALSE, correct them in your book.

The Korean War

- **a** New Zealand became involved in South East Asia in the 1950s through its Commonwealth links.
- **b** On June 25th 1950 South Korean troops, backed by the Russians, invaded North Korea.
- **c** Russia vetoed America's original plan to send in UN troops.
- **d** The new National government in New Zealand, under Sid Holland, did not believe in 'collective security'.
- **e** By agreeing to send troops to Korea, NZ Prime Minister Holland wanted to pressure the United States into signing a defence treaty with New Zealand.
- **f** NZ troops fought as part of the British Commonwealth Brigade in a unit called 'Jay Force'.
- **g** Prime Minister Holland was quick to despatch ground troops to Korea.
- **h** All New Zealanders were uneasy about moving away from Britain and into America's influence through signing the ANZUS Treaty.
- **i** The Korean War convinced many New Zealanders that communism was a real threat to the country's security.
- **j** The Korean War convinced many New Zealanders that conflict was the answer to international problems.

OTHER UN PEACEKEEPING

New Zealand's largest overseas commitment of troops for a UN action since the Korean War was to East Timor. The tiny island north of Australia had been under Indonesian control since 1975. After years of international pressure, Indonesia granted the East Timorese a vote in 1999 on whether or not they wanted independence. Violence erupted as pro-Indonesian militia tried to terrorise the population into voting 'no'. Estimates are of 1000 killed and 250,000 fleeing as refugees, while 80% of buildings and other infrastructure was damaged or destroyed.

Australia led the peacekeeping mission, in which up to half of New Zealand's Army was involved at any one time. This was another instance of the continuing ANZAC relationship. During these operations, Private Leonard Manning became the first New Zealand soldier killed in combat since the Vietnam War. The government explained the reason for New Zealand's involvement, speaking in terms of responsibility to the international community and the Pacific region. Despite this commitment, it rapidly became apparent that New Zealand's military capability was limited. Critics pointed to New Zealand's reliance on Australian assistance as proof of the under-funding of defence, and a willingness to freeload off other nations.

ACTIVITIES

1 Indicate whether the following statements are TRUE or FALSE. If FALSE, correct them in your book.

New Zealand and UN Peacekeeping

- **a** New Zealand's second largest commitment of troops to UN peacekeeping overseas since the Vietnam War was through the UN's peacekeeping mission in East Timor.
- **b** Indonesia willingly granted East Timor a vote on independence.
- **c** Australia led the peacekeeping mission in East Timor, in which up to half of New Zealand's Army were involved at any one time.
- **d** The government explained New Zealand's involvement in East Timor in terms of responsibility to the international community.
- **e** The New Zealand military coped with the requirements of the East Timor peacekeeping mission.

Refer to all of Sources G–I

2 Which are primary sources? Explain your answer.

3 Provide TWO pieces of evidence (from any of the sources) to support the claim that the presence of the New Zealand peacekeepers was welcomed by the East Timorese people.

4 Refer to Sources G and H. Provide TWO pieces of evidence from each source that show that the operation in East Timor is a military one.

5 Refer to Source G. Give one piece of evidence that shows that the New Zealand forces are prepared for casualties.

6 Refer to Source H. What image does this photograph give of the military operation in East Timor?

7 What evidence is there that the APCs are being offloaded from an Australian ship? (Source G.)

8 What key idea from the text on peacekeeping could Source G be used as evidence for?

Armoured Personnel Carriers (APCs) being offloaded from *HMAS Balikpapan*.

Operation Farina: Corporal Fiona Thomas with an East Timorese child, in Suai.

Refer to Source I

9 What country are the two soldiers from? Provide evidence to support your answer.

10 What does this cartoon suggest caused Australian involvement in East Timor?

11 How useful is this Source to an historian? Explain your answer.

Refer to Source J

12 Provide evidence from the cartoon that New Zealand's military became involved in the Gulf War.

13 What, according to the cartoon, was one of the main roles that New Zealand's military played? Provide evidence for your answer.

14 Why do you think the New Zealand deployment is so far behind the others? (You may wish to refer back to the section on New Zealand's commitment of troops to Korea.)

15 In terms of New Zealand foreign policy, what are the similarities between Sources I and J?

SOURCE I

SOURCE J

The Gulf War

AS1.4 REVIEW ACTIVITY

In paragraphs of about 100 words for each, describe the perspectives (views) and actions (with an accompanying explanation) for the following:

a **New Zealand's involvement with the Commonwealth**

b **New Zealanders and the 1953–54 Royal Tour**

c **Prime Minister Fraser and the United Nations**

d **Prime Minister Fraser and the Security Council's veto**

e **Prime Minister Holland and the United Nations**

f **New Zealand and other peacekeeping activities**

CHAPTER THIRTEEN

NEW ZEALAND'S INCREASING INVOLVEMENT IN SOUTH EAST ASIA

New Zealand's first commitment of troops overseas to aid Britain in the South East Asian area was to Malaya. This developed from an informal security agreement between Australia, Malaya and New Zealand (ANZAM). As part of this, in 1955 a rapid reaction force was created that could act as a 'fire brigade' in the case of any emergencies. This was called the Commonwealth Far East Strategic Reserve (CSR), and it was headed by Britain. In 1957, the newly formed Malayan government asked for help in stopping the activities of communist agents during the 'Malayan Emergency'. The CSR did this by stationing troops in 'forward defence' positions. 'Forward Defence' was a military strategy of placing troops near a potential enemy (forward), rather than waiting in a rearward position for any attack. The Commonwealth Strategic Reserve saw occasional action in Malaya up to 1960. Further action came from 1963 on, when New Zealand troops were engaged in the 'Confrontation' with Indonesia.

The 'Far East' is the area now known as South East Asia, covering countries such as Vietnam, Cambodia, Laos, Thailand and Malaysia.

National Prime Ministers – Sid Holland (1949–57) and Keith 'Jacka' Holyoake (1960–72)

The 'Confrontation' came about because Indonesia's leader, Sukarno, rejected what he saw as the re-establishment of British power in the Malay area. He sent in his own soldiers to oppose Britain. The low-scale conflict finally came to an end in 1966. In the ten years of intermittent fighting, over 1300 New Zealand soldiers served. Of these, 66 were killed.

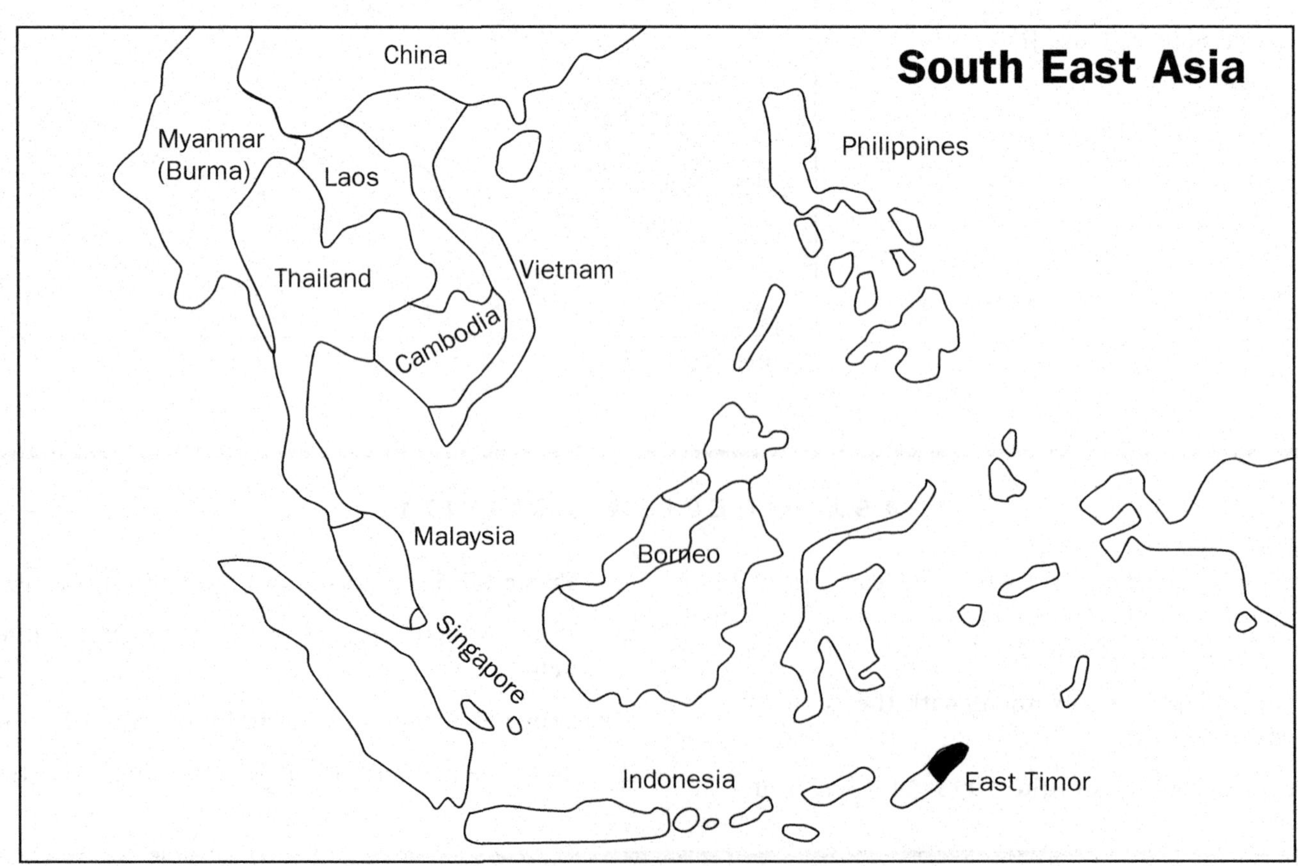

ACTIVITIES

Refer to Source A

1. What does Prime Minister Holland believe is a serious threat to New Zealand (and the world)?
2. What does Holland mean by '[we must be] prepared to pull our weight in the British boat'? What other country does he see as being important to New Zealand's interests?
3. What significant world organisation does Holland *not* mention when considering security issues? How does Holland's view differ from that of Prime Minister Peter Fraser in the 1940s?
4. The last sentence talks about a 'cold war front in Malaya'. What key idea from page 94 is Holland referring to?

Refer to Source B

5. Refer to page 94. Who is most likely to be the figure with the sword?
6. What country is shown in the cartoon as being under threat?
7. What, according to the cartoonist, is the attitude of Prime Minister Holyoake to the threat? How does his attitude compare to that of Prime Minister Holland (Source A)?

SOURCE A

Prime Minister Sid Holland speaks to parliament after his return from a Commonwealth Prime Ministers' Meeting in 1955, which discussed the establishment of a Commonwealth Strategic Reserve.

'Civilisation is today at the crossroads. We must strive to see that the seeds of communism are not sown in other countries that may bring about our downfall .... I say with great seriousness that we as a country can no longer [leave] a great deal of the burden of maintaining peace to our Mother Country .... Not only must we justify help from Britain by being prepared to pull our weight in the British boat, but also we must earn the active support of the United States by demonstrating to her that we are prepared to play our part in our own defence .... We have been invited [by Britain] to undertake a very special duty, and that is to form what you might term a cold war front in Malaya, the idea being to ensure that an enemy that wants to indulge in infiltration and subversion [rebellion] is going to be stopped before he gets here [New Zealand].'

SOURCE B

National's Prime Minister Holyoake to Labour leader Walter Nash: "Better not interfere, old boy – he might lose his temper!" (1964)

ANZUS: AUSTRALIA, NEW ZEALAND AND THE UNITED STATES (BUT NOT BRITAIN)

After WWII, New Zealand and Australia were greatly concerned that Japan would again rise up to be a major power in the Pacific. Neither country liked the generous peace settlement that the United States was looking to make with Japan. When the Korean War broke out in 1950, New Zealand and Australia had already been negotiating a security arrangement with the United States. The rapid promise by both countries of support for the UN forces helped convince the US to enter into an agreement. Thus, on the basis of different security concerns, the ANZUS Treaty was signed in 1951 by Australia, New Zealand and the United States. ANZUS offered New Zealand and Australia a degree of collective security with regard to Japan, and against the growing communist threat. For the US, the Treaty formally extended its influence into the South Pacific. It also gave the US the right to respond to what it saw as any communist threat to its allies.

ANZUS marked an important shift in foreign relations, although New Zealand governments at the time did not want to see it that way. ANZUS was the first major treaty that New Zealand had signed with an 'outside' power. Prime Minister Holland was worried that ANZUS would be seen as disloyalty to Britain. Anticipating public concern, he denied that this was the case. There was also a degree of unease that New Zealand was, almost against its will, moving along a path away from Britain's interests and towards America's.

ACTIVITIES

Refer to Source C

1 What country is represented by the figure holding the blanket? Provide evidence to support your answer.

2 To whom does the figure in the cartoon want to sell the 'new blanket'?

3 What does the 'new blanket' represent? Explain why the idea of a 'blanket' is appropriate in this cartoon.

4 The cartoonist seems to be suggesting that the figure in the cartoon came up with the idea of the 'new blanket' on his own. Explain why this is not true.

Refer to Source D

5 Which section(s) of the Treaty below do you think are represented by the ideas shown in the cartoon (Source C)? Explain your answer.

For each of the following, give the Article number and a short quote from the Article.

6 Which section of the Treaty states that ...

- **a** if there is a threat, then each country's government would discuss amongst itself how to respond?
- **b** the Treaty does not require regular renewal?
- **c** there is not really any other effective means for ensuring security in the Pacific area?
- **d** it is a collective security arrangement?

Selected Articles of the ANZUS Treaty

Introduction

"[Australia, New Zealand and the United States] ... declare publicly and formally their sense of unity, so that no potential aggressor could be under the illusion that any of them stand alone in the Pacific Area."

Article 4

"Each Party recognizes that an armed attack in the Pacific Area on any of the Parties would be dangerous to its own peace and safety and declares that it would act to meet the common danger in accordance with its constitutional processes."

Article 8

"Until ... the development by the United Nations of more effective means to maintain international peace and security, the [ANZUS] Council ... [will work to] contribute to the security of [the Pacific]."

Article 10

"This Treaty shall remain in force indefinitely. Any Party may cease to be a member of the Council ... one year after notice has been given ..."

SEATO: AMERICA'S ANTI-COMMUNIST ALLIANCE

This Treaty was signed after two significant Cold War events. The first of these was the Korean War (1950-53), in which the communist North attacked the non-communist South. The second was the 1954 defeat of the French in Vietnam, also by communist forces. The resulting peace settlement saw Vietnam divided 'temporarily' into a communist North and non-communist South, much as Korea had been. The United States was determined to 'contain' communism in North Vietnam. One means of doing this was to have surrounding countries sign up to an agreement that prevented communist aggression against South Vietnam. The fear was that if the South 'fell', the neighbouring countries would be the next to 'fall' to communism, like a row of dominoes. This was a process that the American Secretary of State, John Foster Dulles, called the 'domino theory'.

The South East Asian Treaty Organisation Treaty (or Manila Treaty) was signed in 1954. One of the aims of SEATO was to improve social and economic conditions in South East Asia. It was also a collective security agreement similar to ANZUS, where an attack on one member was seen as an attack on all. However, the United States informed members that it would only become directly involved if an aggressive action looked likely to aid the spread of communism. From New Zealand's point of view, SEATO seemed to offer little protection over and above what ANZUS already offered. What it did do – ten years later – was put pressure on New Zealand to participate in America's war in Vietnam.

ACTIVITIES

1 Refer to the text where it talks about the 'domino theory'. Draw an appropriate pictorial which shows North Vietnam (backed by Russia and China) as the force which could make the dominoes fall. Represent the following countries: South Vietnam; Laos; Cambodia; Thailand; Malaysia/Singapore; Australia (?); New Zealand (?).

2 **For each of the following, give the Article number and a short quote from the Article. (Source E)**

Which section of the Treaty states that …

- **a** A country that is threatened must ask for military assistance before it will be given?
- **b** It has goals other than just military ones?
- **c** The threat to a nation does not necessarily have to be a military one in order for Treaty members to act?
- **d** The Treaty has not taken over responsibilities that belong to other international organisations?
- **e** The United States is focused mainly on the communist threat?
- **f** Governments will be encouraged to contribute to looking after the well-being of their own peoples themselves?

Selected Articles of the Manila Treaty

Article 3

The Parties undertake to … cooperate with one another in the further development of economic measures, including technical assistance, designed both to promote economic progress and social well-being and to further the individual and collective efforts of governments toward these ends.

Article 4.2

If … any of the Parties … is threatened in any way other than by armed attack or is affected or threatened by any fact or situation which might endanger the peace of the area, the Parties shall consult immediately in order to agree on the measures which should be taken for the common defense.

Article 4.3

It is understood that no action on the territory of any State … shall be taken except at the invitation or with the consent of the government concerned.

Article 6

This Treaty does not affect … in any way the rights and obligations of any of the Parties under the Charter of the United Nations, or the responsibility of the United Nations for the maintenance of international peace and security.

Additional Article

The United States of America in [joining] the present Treaty does so with the understanding that its recognition of the effect of aggression and armed attack … apply only to communist aggression, but affirms that in the event of other aggression or armed attack it will consult….

SEATO and the Vietnam War

New Zealand's involvement in the Vietnam War was significant in several ways. New Zealand's links with the United States made it difficult not to participate, even though this participation was reluctant. The Vietnam War also sparked the first major difference between National and Labour on foreign policy issues. It divided the public and brought people out onto the streets in protest for the first time since the Depression. This was also the first war that New Zealand had fought without Britain.

The US wanted both Australia and New Zealand in Vietnam. One of the main reasons for this was so that the US could more easily justify its own presence there. If New Zealand and Australia said that they were worried about the spread of communism, America could claim that it was supporting its smaller allies. In response to this pressure, New Zealand sent medical and engineering teams, but no combat troops. Prime Minister Holyoake argued that New Zealand's troops were fully committed in the Commonwealth Strategic Reserve in Malaya (see page 94). The Americans were not satisfied with this.

In 1964, the President of South Vietnam requested assistance in the growing conflict, as required under the terms of SEATO. When Australia decided to send troops, New Zealand felt that it had no choice. An artillery battery of 120 men was sent in 1965, eventually totalling 550 men. New Zealand fought under Australian command in the renamed ANZAC Infantry battalion. More pressure went on in the next two years, and additional commitments of troops were made. Two Rifle Companies, Victor and Whiskey, were sent in 1967. These soldiers were all volunteers, and in all 3500 men served. Unlike Australia and the United States, New Zealand did not conscript its soldiers. New Zealand's troop commitment was still not a large one, but it eased US grumblings. By the time the last New Zealand troops were withdrawn in December 1972, 35 had been killed (including one female nurse) and 187 wounded.

Those who did return came back to a hostile reception. They were accused of being war-mongers and 'baby-killers'. The government did not even formally welcome the soldiers home. This indicates the level of division that involvement in the war had caused. It was not until 1998 that an official welcoming ceremony was conducted. Vietnam veterans struggled to get compensation for war-related conditions. One of these was cancers caused by aerial spraying of Agent Orange. This was a chemical designed to kill the forests in which Vietnamese soldiers took cover.

ACTIVITIES

Refer to the text above. Match the sentence starter from Column A with the correct ending from Column B. (Be careful – some are similar, but not the same!)

When you have matched the pairs, use them to write a brief summary of New Zealand's involvement in the Vietnam War.

Column A	**Column B**
1 New Zealand's involvement in Vietnam came about because ...	A ... America applied pressure for a contribution to the war in Vietnam.
2 New Zealand's involvement in Vietnam was significant politically because ...	B ... of New Zealand's commitment to the Commonwealth Strategic Reserve in Malaya.
3 America wanted to contain communism because ...	C ... of obligations under SEATO (and indirectly through a commitment to ANZUS).
4 America wanted both Australia and New Zealand in Vietnam because ...	D ... it could more easily justify its own presence in Vietnam.
5 New Zealand committed medical and engineering teams to Vietnam because ...	E ... it saw the first major division between National and Labour on a foreign policy issue.
6 The Holyoake government argued that New Zealand could not send combat troops to Vietnam because ...	F ... the President of South Vietnam requested assistance, and Australia had made the decision to do so.
7 New Zealand eventually committed combat troops because ...	G ... of a belief in the domino theory.

ACTIVITY

Refer to Source F
Which of the reason(s) given by Prime Minister Holyoake for joining the Vietnam War are most likely linked to the key ideas of:

1 containment.
2 domino theory.
3 forward defence.
4 collective security.

Prime Minister Holyoake outlined in 1965 his seven main reasons for making a military commitment to Vietnam.

a "... the Government must always be concerned with the security of the people of New Zealand, both short-term and *long-term.*"

b "... New Zealand's first line of defence is in South East Asia ...."

c "... the war in Vietnam is not a civil war or a popular rising .... It is a ruthless Communist aggression directed and supplied by Communist North Vietnam ...."

d "... the South Vietnamese are fighting for their freedom and liberty."

e "... events in Vietnam affect New Zealand just as much as events in Malaysia, and indeed at this stage probably more so."

f "... the New Zealand Government has a fervent [strong] wish to bring about a peaceful settlement which will guarantee the territorial integrity [borders] of South Vietnam and of the neighbouring countries in that area."

g "... the independence of the people of South Vietnam must be safeguarded. It cannot be safeguarded with words. At present it can only be done with military means."

THE VIETNAM WAR: NATIONAL AND LABOUR

Holyoake's National government had no real enthusiasm for the Vietnam War, but found itself having to publicly support it. Those in favour of New Zealand participating in the war argued that New Zealand had to support its larger ally, especially in stopping the spread of communism. Publicly, this was the position the National government took. Privately, Holyoake and other key officials wanted to limit involvement. They were not convinced by the 'domino theory', or the supposed threat of communism to New Zealand. In addition, the government was aware that involvement in wars was a costly business, and it felt that New Zealand could ill-afford it.

The Labour Opposition did not feel the same sense of obligation to the US. It argued that the war was morally wrong. Labour urged instead that a non-military solution be found, using the Commonwealth and UN. However, it reluctantly supported sending the first non-combat units in 1964. As the war progressed and the brutal images were played out on television (for the first time), Labour's opposition to the conflict grew. Many now saw the war as an attempt by a bullying United States to impose its views and beliefs on the Vietnamese people. Norman Kirk, the new Labour leader, called for the withdrawal of New Zealand troops. This call was joined by church groups, students and an increasing number of the public. By the late 1960s, protest marches were being held in the main centres. They linked into the mass demonstrations taking place in the US. The largest demonstration in New Zealand took place in 1971, even though the troops were already being brought home. When Labour became the government in 1972, Prime Minister Kirk withdrew the remaining combat units.

Vietnam was the first 'television war'. Night after night the horror of war was broadcast to people's living rooms.

A mass protest in the United States, 1967. Such events inspired similar (but smaller-scale) actions in New Zealand.

Aftermath

The Vietnam War divided New Zealand as no other international issue had before. Although National had regularly accused Labour of being 'soft on communism', National and Labour had in the past mostly agreed on foreign policy. Increasingly, though, Labour looked to take a moral position on issues, even if this meant offending traditional allies. National's view, however, was that a small country like New Zealand had to acknowledge that it depended on its bigger allies, and therefore work closely with them. National's view has been called pragmatic. This means that it was a practical approach that acknowledged New Zealand's vulnerability.

By the end of the Vietnam War in the early 1970s, the links with Britain had loosened considerably. For one thing, New Zealand had fought alongside the United States in the war, not Britain. At the same time, bonds with Australia had tightened through serving together in the ANZAC Infantry Battalion. The new Labour government under Norman Kirk also took a much more internationalist and moral approach to foreign affairs. Kirk believed that New Zealand was going to have to stand more on its own, and he stated this new approach in a speech in 1973: *'From now on, when we have to deal with a new situation, we will not say, what do the British think about it [or] what would the Americans want us to do? Our starting point will be, what do we think about it?'*

Prime Minister Norman Kirk (1972–1974).

ACTIVITIES

1 In what way were the policies of both Labour and National similar with regard to Vietnam?

2 Create two star diagrams. One should show the reasons that persuaded or pressured the Holyoake government into publicly supporting America in the Vietnam War. The second should show why privately Holyoake wanted to limit involvement.

3 In what way did the development of television in New Zealand in the 1960s influence the way some New Zealanders reacted to the Vietnam War? Why do you think this was?

4 What did Holyoake discover was the 'down-side' of being allied to America?

5 What terms are used in the text to describe the foreign policy approach of:

- National governments?
- Labour governments?

6 Which foreign policy approach noted in **5** do you think New Zealand should take? Give reasons.

SEATO Conference in Manila 1966. New Zealand's Prime Minister Holyoake is 5th from left. President Lyndon Johnson is on far right.

> 'Had a three-year old die on me today. She came in with her guts torn apart by a grenade. Her mother, just a girl really, was with the child all the time, helping us to try and save her, and it was not until the child had died that we realised that the mother too had several wounds herself. The terrible sight of the dying child in the arms of the injured mother was most upsetting. It is horrible to think that our own troops will be inflicting the same sort of wounds on the same sort of people.'
>
> *Part of Dr Peter Smith's report in March 1969. Smith was the leader of a voluntary civilian surgical team, based at Qui Nhon hospital in South Vietnam.*

7 Refer to Source G

- **a** In what part of Vietnam did the events described take place?
- **b** Identify TWO facts in this source.
- **c** Identify TWO opinions in this source.
- **d** What is Doctor Smith's view of the war as whole? Provide evidence for your answer.
- **e** Give TWO ways in which civilians from either side in the conflict were affected by the war.
- **f** How might a supporter of the war respond to the incident in Source G?
- **g** Why is this source on its own not enough to get a good understanding of the effects of the war on civilians?

8 How had New Zealand's relationship with Britain changed by the end of the Vietnam war?

> 'The emphasis was on small but persistent action. Guerrilla protest. Pickets, leaflets, posters, parades. We were hounded and persecuted by police and public alike. Three times during the year I was assaulted. One guy spat in my face, another time about six clean-shaven rugby types surrounded me and started taunting.... We used to have marches down Queen Street. Our biggest rallies drew as many as 35 people. On one occasion we had six.... We also picketed American warships.... An Auckland housewife was arrested for singing anti-war songs on an American ship and was charged with offensive behaviour.'
>
> *Tim Shadbolt recalls early anti-Vietnam War protest action in 1968. (Shadbolt went on to become Mayor of Waitemata and then Invercargill.)*

Refer to Source H

9 Identify ONE opinion in the source.

10 Provide TWO separate facts that support the claim that the protest actions in which Shadbolt took part were not well supported.

11 Provide evidence to support the claim that the American military had a presence in New Zealand.

SOURCE I

Refer to Source I

12 How would the sort of events described in Source G and Source H lead to the Conference shown in Source I?

13 **History road**

Create a 'history road' showing the development of the New Zealand response to the Vietnam War.

- a Re-read the text carefully. Begin by identifying the key events on the 'road'. Start with the general agreement on foreign policy prior to the Vietnam War and go through to the election of the Labour government and Kirk's declaration of greater independence.
- b Identify events that are 'crisis points'. These can be sharp 'turns' in the road.
- c Begin your 'history road' in one corner and do a rough sketch laying out the key events. Each event should have a signpost, and pictorials should be added in. Where the government was faced with a decision, you can create crossroads (with appropriate signposts) or even separate 'side roads', in cases where Labour's view differed from the government's actions.
- d Do a good copy.

AS1.4 REVIEW ACTIVITY

1 In paragraphs of about 100 words for each, describe the perspectives (views) and actions (with an accompanying explanation) for the following:

- a **New Zealand and ANZAM**
- b **New Zealand and ANZUS**
- c **New Zealand and SEATO**
- d **Participating in the Vietnam War – National**
- e **Participating in the Vietnam War – Labour**
- f **Foreign policy in general – National** (views only)
- g **Foreign policy in general – Labour** (views only)

2 Refer to the information in this section of the text. Use the main ideas under each to create a mind-map OR structured overview. It should include the key events that saw New Zealand increase its involvement with international organisations, as well as in South East Asia, and with America.

- a Commonwealth (including the 1953–54 Royal Tour)
- b United Nations (veto, Security Council)
- c UN Peacekeeping (including the Korean War)
- d International alliances (ANZAM, ANZUS, SEATO)
- e Vietnam War (including the foreign policy division that developed between National and Labour).

AS1.5 ESSAY PRACTICE

Follow the steps on the inside back cover to write the following essay.

How did New Zealand attempt to achieve collective security between 1945 and 1955? Describe New Zealand's involvement in international organisations during this period.

- ANZAM; ANZUS; SEATO
- United Nations; Commonwealth

OR

For what reasons did New Zealand become involved in military actions between 1945 and 1970? Describe the responses of New Zealand governments to these conflicts.

- United Nations' collective security; ANZAM; SEATO
- general agreement on foreign policy; different views of UN; division over Vietnam.

PART TWO

CHAPTER FOURTEEN

NEW ZEALAND AND THE PACIFIC

Prior to WWII, New Zealand had been somewhat high-handed in its dealings with the Pacific Islands under its authority (see page 13). After WWII, and with Labour in power, New Zealand took its responsibilities more seriously. This was for several reasons. The first was because of a commitment to the United Nations' programme of decolonisation. This meant self-government for all peoples who wanted it. Second, there was a growing belief that improving the living conditions of people was the best defence against communism or revolution. Third, by taking on its share of responsibilities in the region, it would (it was believed) encourage Britain to stay.

New Zealand's process of decolonisation was entirely peaceful. This was different to the French experience, where violent uprisings ended their rule in Africa and Asia. Nonetheless France still clung on to its colonial possessions in the Pacific. This resulted in increasingly violent protest by the Kanaks in New Caledonia in the 1990s. By contrast, some Pacific nations even chose to retain their links to New Zealand. Both the Cook Islands (1965) and Niue (1974) opted for self-government in 'free association' with New Zealand. This meant that New Zealand shared some responsibility for these Island nations' international affairs. Tokelau refused even this form of independence. All three nations retained some citizenship rights in New Zealand.

DECOLONISATION

After WWII, New Zealand had accepted the UN Trusteeship of Western Samoa. The aim was to help that country prepare itself for independence and self-government. In 1962, Western Samoa became independent. By agreement, New Zealand remained responsible for defence and international relations, (other than in the Pacific). Six years later, Nauru became independent. In 1970 Britain withdrew from its responsibilities in the Pacific, with both Tonga and Fiji becoming fully independent.

A NEW PACIFIC ROLE: THE PACIFIC FORUM

New Zealand's relationship with the South Pacific became closer from the 1970s. New Zealand's reluctant involvement in the Vietnam War had made it careful about being caught up in an Asian war again. In addition, despite New Zealand's wishes, Britain continued to reduce its commitments in the Pacific. New Zealand felt obliged to step in and maintain stability in the region. It set out to do this by developing a new role in the Pacific, based on partnership.

An indication of the desire for a more active partnership with Pacific nations was the formation in 1971 of the Pacific Forum. This came about in part due to the frustration of Pacific leaders with the earlier European-dominated South Pacific Commission (SPC). With the establishment of the Pacific Forum, the SPC gradually became less relevant. By the end of the century, the seven founding members of the Forum (New Zealand, Australia, Cook Islands, Fiji, Nauru, Tonga and Western Samoa) had been joined by nine others. Although Australia and New Zealand dominated the Forum in terms of economic power, all member nations met as equals. The informal style of meetings, and decision-making by general agreement, became known as the 'Pacific Way'. An important goal of the Forum was to try to improve the economic situation of Pacific nations. One main step towards this was the formation of the Pacific Forum Shipping Line in 1978. This was set up in order to make the import and export of goods easier throughout the Pacific.

ACTIVITIES

1. Explain the meaning of the term 'decolonisation'. Give examples to back up your answer.
2. Comment on the differences between the decolonisation experiences of France and New Zealand.
3. What was a key aim of the Pacific Forum?
4. What was the 'Pacific Way'?

ACTIVITIES

Refer to Source A

1 How useful is this source to an historian wanting to find out about New Zealand's policy in the Pacific?

2 Under what conditions does the speaker believe that the Soviet Union could become involved in the Pacific?

3 Does the speaker feel Soviet involvement in the Pacific would be a desirable thing or not? Provide evidence to support your answer.

SOURCE A

'It will continue to be of overriding importance for New Zealand that the South Pacific generally should remain Western-oriented ... to avoid the development of conditions of political or economic instability which the Soviet Union or some other unfriendly or opportunistic power could exploit [and] to ensure that the western powers themselves ... are responsive to South Pacific concerns'

An official from New Zealand's Ministry of Foreign Affairs

AID

All New Zealand governments saw the giving of aid as an important part of maintaining stability in various parts of the world. It was accepted that aid would relieve poverty and thus reduce the influence of 'radical' ideas such as communism or revolution. The giving of aid also improved New Zealand's international reputation. In addition, aid had the advantage of helping poorer economies grow so that they could import New Zealand goods. Labour governments in particular also talked about aid in humanitarian and moral terms: it was right to help those who needed it. Despite this, New Zealand never met its United Nations commitment in terms of the amount given. However, much of what it did give was targeted at the Pacific.

SOURCE B

Selected countries receiving official aid from New Zealand

Country / Amount	1988 ($million)	1990 ($million)	1992 ($million)	Aid received *per person* in each country
Cook Islands	14.1	14.1	14.3	$831
Niue	9.3	9.7	9.5	$4,850
Tokelau	4.7	4.7	5.0	$2,280
Tonga	4.1	4.1	4.3	$40
Tuvalu	1.7	1.7	1.8	$168
W. Samoa	5.7	5.7	6.0	$35

SOURCE D

Exports from New Zealand, 1990

Country	Amount ($million)
Cook Islands	3.9
Niue	.035
Tokelau	.003
Tonga	3.7
Tuvalu	.001
W. Samoa	7.2

SOURCE C

Remittances (money sent 'home' by relatives living in New Zealand), 1990

Country	Amount ($million)
Cook Islands	6.0
Niue	2.0
Tokelau	1.0
Tonga	10.0
Tuvalu	No figures
W. Samoa	30.3

SOURCE E

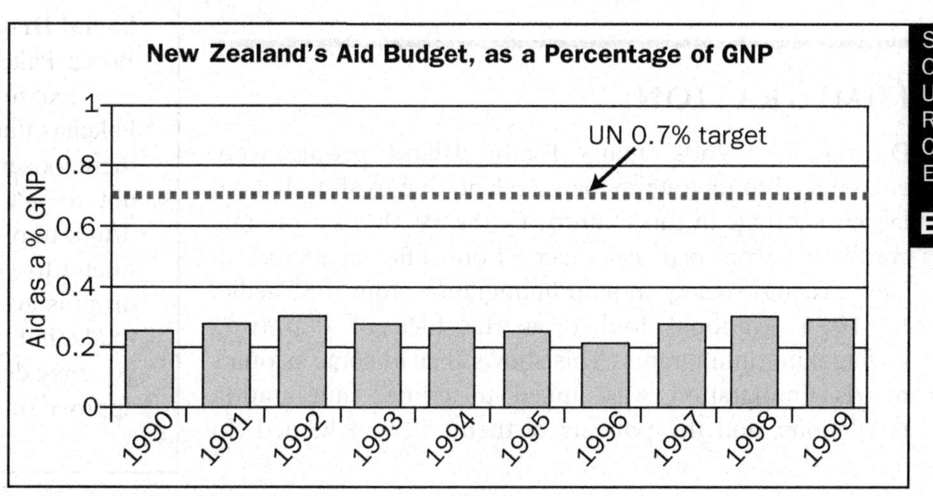

ACTIVITIES

Refer to Source B
Provide evidence to support your answers.

1 Which Pacific nation received the largest total amount of New Zealand aid between 1988 and 1992?

2 Which Pacific nation received the most aid per person?

3 Which Pacific nation received the smallest aid increase between 1988 and 1992?

Refer to Source C
Provide evidence to support your answers.

4 Which group of Pacific Islanders living in New Zealand remitted the most money home?

5 What might explain the difference between this group, and Niueans?

6 How *might* the level of remittances from Niueans living in New Zealand link to the level of aid given to Niue (Source B)?

Refer to Source D
Provide evidence to support your answers.

7 To which Pacific nation did New Zealand send the greatest value of exports?

8 Look at the level of aid given to Niue (Source B) and the value of exports to Niue (Source D). One of the reasons stated for New Zealand's giving of aid is to try to build the economies of poorer nations so that they can then import our goods. Is this likely to be the case with Niue? Explain your answer.

9 To which Pacific nation is it most likely that New Zealand has given aid in the past, in order to develop its economy? Explain your answer.

Refer to Source E

10 What key idea(s) raised in this section of the text does this graph provide evidence for?

IMMIGRATION

During the 1960s, many Pacific Island people were encouraged to migrate to New Zealand due to an industrial labour shortage in this country. By the 1970s, as economic conditions worsened, calls came from different sectors of New Zealand society to stop immigration from the Pacific. In 1975, National looked at the idea of deporting lawbreaking immigrants. This shows that in some people's minds immigration was linked to crime. Immigration regulations, and the policing of them, were tightened. In 1976, the infamous 'Dawn Raids' occurred. Police would call at houses in the early morning, hoping to catch suspected overstayers. This caused an outcry from Pacific Island leaders. Furthermore, the fact that a number of Maori had been caught up in the 'raids' caused accusations of racism. The following year, the Minister responsible for the Pacific made the first-ever comprehensive tour of the Pacific, in an effort to smooth relations.

The following extracts are from *Understanding Pakehas*, published by the Polynesian Advisory Committee in 1978. It was a booklet produced to help recent immigrants from the Pacific Islands adjust to life in New Zealand.

Pakeha Character: Individualistic
Everything in Western society emphasises the individual. In religion, every person has to find his own salvation. In politics, each person is expected to make his views known. With Polynesians, it is the family which gives a person status and position. With Pakehas, each has to make his own way in the world and win status by what he succeeds in doing and owning. In many instances, therefore, Pakehas put the individual before the group, the self before the others.

Pakeha Character: Money-Minded
A Polynesian knows that he can depend on his relatives in time of need because they share what they have with him. Your family is your security, and the more there are, the better. A Pakeha cannot depend on his relatives to the same extent. Usually he alone must be responsible for keeping his wife and children.... He has also been brought up to be proud of his ability to provide for himself and his family without relying on others.

Social Drinks
When Pakehas get together with friends for a chat, they like to have a few drinks. This is because many Pakehas find it hard to relax and a little alcohol helps them loosen up. So they drink in order to be sociable, not to get drunk.... Often, however, Pakehas get drunk in pubs and at parties. Although they may not intend to get drunk, this happens because so much drink is available in these places. If you are not used to alcohol, it is better not to follow their example, as you may do something you would not normally do or approve of.

ACTIVITIES

Refer to Source F

1 According to the pamphlet, what are the main differences between Pakeha and Polynesians with regard to character and money?

2 Identify the facts in these extracts.

3 What, according to this source, *seems* to be the cause of Pakeha finding it 'hard to relax' and thus needing 'a little alcohol' to loosen them up?

4 How useful is this source to the historian in helping understand the problems facing new immigrants from the Pacific? Explain your answer.

5 Refer to the main text. Use the following key ideas to write a one-two paragraph summary of the issue of Pacific immigration. Be sure to add at least one fact or detail for each point given.

- Economic conditions in New Zealand
- Immigration-crime link
- Backlash.

ASIAN IMMIGRATION

New Zealand's links with South East Asia lessened during the 1970s, as the Vietnam War drew to a close. In 1989, the last military link was cut as troops were withdrawn from their base in Singapore. However, as New Zealand's foreign policy began to focus on the Pacific, immigration policy began to widen to include Asia. This was a significant change from earlier times.

Up to WWII discriminatory laws worked to limit the number of Asian people able to enter New Zealand, and restrict the rights of those who were here. An informal 'White New Zealand' policy meant that there were only about 5000 Chinese in New Zealand in the first half of the 20th century. The main changes in immigration policy came about due to economic reasons, rather than a change in racial attitudes. During the 1970s and into the 1980s, New Zealand's economy went into serious decline. Many New Zealanders left to seek better lives overseas, especially in Australia. A large number of these were skilled people, which left New Zealand even worse off. To counter the outward flow, the law was changed in 1987 to make skills, rather than nationality, the basis of immigration policy. Further changes recognised the positive economic impact that immigration could have. By the end of the 20th century, New Zealand was again an 'immigrant nation', with nearly 20% of the population being overseas born.

The number of Asian migrants rapidly increased in the 1990s. By the year 2000 there were 240,000 immigrants from Asia in New Zealand, more than the entire Pacific Island population. Nationally, this represented over 6% of the total population, two-thirds of whom were living in Auckland. The two largest groups of immigrants in 2000 were Chinese (8,700) and Indian (8,400) – well above the third placed United Kingdom (6,600) and fourth placed South Africa (4,300). Asian numbers were further boosted by a policy of promoting New Zealand as an educational destination. By the year 2000, there were 7,000 primary and 11,500 secondary fee-paying students (not permanent) from Asia. They contributed over $500million to the economy, making education the fourth largest export earner.

The number of Asian migrants to New Zealand increased in the 1990s.

Despite this positive impact, some New Zealanders found it difficult to adjust to the 'sea' of new faces. There was a mixed reaction to Prime Minister Bolger's statement that New Zealand must view itself as part of Asia. Nonetheless, the National government helped establish Asia 2000, an organisation responsible for developing cultural and trade links with Asia. These efforts were not enough to calm the fears of those who felt overwhelmed by the suddenness of the changes. Cases of discrimination were not uncommon. One political party – New Zealand First – talked of an 'Asian invasion' and campaigned on an anti-immigration policy. By the end of the 1990s, many New Zealanders were still to come to terms with the fact that New Zealand was shifting 'from Empire to internationalism' – no longer was it the 'Britain of the South Seas'.

ACTIVITIES

1. What policy meant that there were fewer than 5000 Chinese in New Zealand by 1945?
2. What was the basis of immigration law prior to 1987? How did it change after this time?
3. In what New Zealand region was the effect of Asian immigration most noticeable? Provide evidence to support your answer.
4. Explain in your own words the term 'from Empire to internationalism'.

SOURCE G

Asian Immigration (includes Indians)	
Year	**Number**
1945	6500
1966	20,000
1986	54,000
1991	90,000
2000	240,000

Refer to Source G

5. What key idea from the text do the figures from 1986 onwards support?

SOURCE H

Net migration to NZ	
Year	**Net inflow**
1977	-16270
1978	-22156
1979	-26544
1980	-21314
1981	-16209
1982	-4743
1983	15442
1984	10557
1985	217
1986	-18518
1987	4357
1988	-957
1989	-18298
1990	-1633
1991	14576
1992	2938
1993	8080
1994	15793
1995	20401
1996	28626
1997	37779
1998	1923

Refer to Source H
(Note: a negative 'net inflow' means that more people left than arrived in New Zealand during that year.)

6. In what year was there the largest loss of population?
7. Between what two consecutive years was there the single biggest change in net migration?
8. What key idea from the text about economic changes do the figures up to 1982 seem to support?
9. Compare the figures for 1986 in both Source G and Source H. What is the minimum number of people who left New Zealand that year?

THE FIJI COUPS

The most serious Pacific security issue arose in Fiji in 1987, when a military coup toppled the elected government. The background issue was tension between native Fijians and Indo-Fijians. Indians had been brought into Fiji from the late 19th century by the British government to work the sugarcane plantations. Many chose to stay and, due to rapid population growth, by WWII there were slightly more Indo-Fijians than native Fijians. When Fiji became independent from Britain in 1970 there was concern amongst native Fijians. They feared that they would come under the control of an Indo-Fijian dominated government. This did in fact occur in 1987, although the newly-elected government stressed that it would preserve native Fijian interests. This was not good enough for Fijian nationalists, including sections of the Army.

The coup, led by Colonel Sitiveni Rabuka, created great difficulties for New Zealand. What was the appropriate response to a military takeover? The Lange government was quick to defend democratic principles by condemning the coup. Other Pacific leaders – and some Maori in New Zealand – were more cautious. Some even voiced support of the action, claiming that the native Fijians were right to take action to protect their heritage. In the end, neither New Zealand nor Australia did anything more than vigorously protest. Military action had been ruled out early on, partly because the Fijian Army was a well-trained fighting force – thanks to New Zealand. Furthermore, the use of force – even against an illegal military coup – was not considered to be the 'Pacific Way'. Fiji was, however, evicted from the Commonwealth. This affair showed the limitations of the power of New Zealand (and Australia) in the Pacific.

ACTIVITIES

In paragraphs of about 100 words for each, describe the perspectives (views) and actions (with an accompanying explanation) for:

1. New Zealand and decolonisation.
2. New Zealand and political links with Pacific Island nations.
3. New Zealand and the giving of aid.
4. New Zealand and Pacific Island immigration.
5. New Zealand and Asian immigration.

AS1.5 ESSAY PRACTICE

Follow the steps on the inside back cover to write the following essay.

Describe the main ways in which New Zealand has been involved in the Pacific in the 20th century. What issues have strained this relationship?

- Pacific 'Empire' (see pages 13–14); decolonisation; aid; Pacific Forum
- Influenza; Mau (see pages 13–14); immigration; Fiji coup.

CHAPTER FIFTEEN

NUCLEAR ISSUES

The development and testing of nuclear weapons began in WWII and continued in the Cold War era. By the 1970s, the United States, Britain, Russia, France, India and China were confirmed as having 'the bomb'. By the end of the 20th century, Israel and Pakistan were also believed to have secretly developed nuclear weapons. Nuclear testing in the Pacific region began in the 1950s. By the time the United States stopped testing there in 1962, it had exploded 106 bombs on Bikini Atoll and Enewetok. From 1952 to 1962 Britain exploded a total of 21 bombs – in the Australian outback, and on Montebello and Christmas Islands. By the time France stopped testing in the Pacific in early 1996, over 250 nuclear detonations had occurred.

A nuclear explosion on Bikini Atoll, 1946.

FRENCH NUCLEAR TESTING IN THE PACIFIC

Opposition to nuclear weapons and their testing developed throughout the 1950s. During this time New Zealand's government actually provided support for the British testing programme. By 1959, however, a New Zealand branch of the British-based Campaign for Nuclear Disarmament (CND) had been established. It held meetings and marches to raise public awareness. Over 80,000 New Zealanders signed the CND's 1963 petition calling for a nuclear-free Southern Hemisphere – 'No Bombs South of the Line [Equator]'. This sort of public pressure convinced the Labour party to make anti-nuclear issues part of its foreign policy.

When France carried out its first atmospheric test at Mururoa Atoll in 1966, it provided a focus for New Zealand's anti-nuclear campaign. Atmospheric testing – the exploding of a bomb above ground – allowed radiation and contaminated waste to be spread by the wind. This worst form of testing had been banned by international agreement in 1963, but it was now being carried out in the Pacific. By the 1970s, French atmospheric testing was attracting growing criticism. This came particularly from a new global movement, the environmental lobby. One of the organisations at the forefront of this movement was Greenpeace. Many New Zealanders shared their views. In 1971, a poll showed that 82% of New Zealanders were opposed to French testing in the Pacific. When Labour came to power the following year, Prime Minister Norman Kirk pulled together these concerns in his direct challenge to French nuclear testing.

Although previous National governments had been opposed to nuclear weapons and testing, they were not active in condemning them: Labour under Kirk was. In 1973 Kirk, in combination with the Australian Labor government, took France to the World Court over its nuclear testing. This was a bold and confrontational move; two small powers challenging a large power. The Court found against France and ordered it to stop its testing programme. France ignored the order. New Zealand discovered that its allies – particularly the United States and Britain – were unwilling to take any action to force France to comply.

In the face of this lack of support from New Zealand's traditional allies, the nuclear movement began to take on a nationalistic flavour. A new petition against French nuclear testing gathered over 81,000 signatures. Individuals and private peace organisations – including Peace Media and Greenpeace – took matters into their own hands. Some sailed vessels into the test zone, although the French Navy dealt quickly and roughly with them. This caused anti-nuclear (and anti-French) sentiment to increase.

The determination of the French to continue their atmospheric testing in the Pacific, and the lack of any real international pressure forcing them to stop, left New Zealand with a limited number of options. In another bold and even more confrontational move – rare for countries that are 'friendly' – Prime Minister Kirk ordered two Navy frigates to the Mururoa test zone in 1973. The Australian government provided a supply ship, without which the venture could not have taken place. Sending the frigates *Otago* and *Canterbury* was a stunning move. It shocked the French government and earned them instant unfavourable media attention. One effect of this was that the French moved their testing underground. The World Court felt that France had done enough and withdrew its ruling ordering them to stop.

New Zealand's position on nuclear issues depended very much on whether National or Labour was in power. When National became the government in 1975, with Robert Muldoon as Prime Minister, it did not pursue Labour's idea of a South Pacific nuclear-free zone. This was despite a poll showing that over 70% of New Zealanders supported the proposal. National was more concerned about not offending our traditional allies, including France. The government at this time was desperately trying to maintain vital access to European markets for New Zealand's farm produce, against strong opposition from European farmers. National believed that New Zealand had to be realistic about its limited ability to influence major powers, and the potential cost to the country that an anti-nuclear stance could cause.

The *Rainbow Warrior*

On July 10th 1985, French agents blew up and sank the Greenpeace vessel *Rainbow Warrior* while it was anchored at the port of Auckland. The vessel had been preparing for another voyage to protest against French nuclear tests at Mururoa Atoll. Fernando Pereira, a Portuguese photographer on board at the time, was killed. Two of the ten or so French agents involved, Alain Marfart and Dominique Prieur, were soon captured by police. Intelligence reports suggested that French security forces might attempt to free the pair, or even kill them before their trial. They were eventually sentenced in the Court to ten years' imprisonment, even though they did not actually do the bombing. At first, France denied any knowledge of the attack, but eventually it admitted responsibility. France then began to apply pressure to New Zealand to release its agents into French custody. Hints grew stronger that France would block New Zealand's trade into Europe if it did not comply. Prime Minister Lange accused France of 'a sordid act of State-backed international terrorism' but – as with the 1973 World Court ruling – New Zealand received little support from its allies. Only Australia condemned France. Britain and the United States refused to. The *Wall Street Journal* even supported the French action.

The Lange government felt obliged to accept the solution mediated by the Secretary General of the United Nations. Compensation of $13 million was paid by France, and it promised not to interfere with New Zealand's access to European markets. New Zealand released the agents into French custody, for imprisonment on the French atoll of Hao. The public was angry that New Zealand had been bullied by France, and that there had been no international support over what was an act of terrorism. To make matters worse, the French government went back on its word. Within two years the agents were returned to France, complete with an official heroes' welcome. The whole incident thus became a defining moment in the development of an independent New Zealand identity.

After the *Rainbow Warrior*

In 1992 France declared a short-term halt to nuclear testing. New Zealand hoped that this in fact marked the end of its programme. However, in 1995 testing resumed. National Prime Minister Jim Bolger immediately condemned the new blasts. France continued to deny that their testing posed any dangers to the environment, yet it refused to allow an independent scientific study. However, environmental concerns were only part of the issue. Along with other countries in the Pacific and beyond, New Zealand wanted France to sign a Comprehensive Test Ban Treaty. Countries that did so would agree not to test nuclear weapons at all.

Despite increasing pressure, France continued its tests. Prime Minister Bolger reacted angrily. 'France's insistence on continued testing has been outrageous. The overwhelming opposition to their testing programme can only be strengthened by the latest reports of radiation leakages at Mururoa as a result of earlier tests.' A New Zealand Navy vessel was sent to Mururoa and Bolger reopened the case against France in the International Court. In early 1996 France detonated its sixth and last bomb in its series of tests. In March of that year France, Britain and the United States finally all signed the Comprehensive Test Ban Treaty (CTBT). The issue of possible long-term damage at Mururoa had still not been settled by the year 2000.

NUCLEAR SHIP VISITS

The government response to nuclear ship visits changed from the 1960s through to the 1980s, and increasingly depended upon whether National or Labour was in power. Visits by British and American vessels after WWII had been common. Between 1960 and 1984 there were nearly 150 visits by American ships alone. Of these, only about 13 were nuclear-powered. In terms of weaponry, the United States had always had a policy to 'neither confirm nor deny' the presence of nuclear armaments on board its vessels. Muldoon's enthusiasm for visits by American ships caused increasing public concern about the risk of a nuclear accident. In 1976, a 'Peace Squadron' was formed by members of St John's Theological College. It planned to block the entrance of nuclear-powered vessels to Auckland's harbour. Public opinion polls showed a slow but steady increase in support for such actions. Between 1976 and 1982 opposition to the entry of nuclear-powered ships to New Zealand ports grew from 33% to 39%. Yet around 60% of people remained in favour of visits by American vessels, even if they were nuclear-armed. Most New Zealanders felt that it was in the country's best interest to maintain a strong alliance with the United States.

ACTIVITIES

1 Make your own brief notes under the following headings. Use the bullet points as a guide.

French nuclear testing in the Pacific

- 1950s: opposition begins
- 1960s: reaction to French testing in the Pacific
- World Court
- Protesters' actions
- Frigate protest
- National's view

2 Put the following notes into the correct order of events.

The *Rainbow Warrior*

- French agents sentenced to ten years' imprisonment
- New Zealand's allies are unsupportive (except Australia)
- France goes back on its word, angering New Zealanders
- Protest vessel bombed
- UN Secretary General mediates a deal between France and New Zealand
- Compensation of $13 million paid by France
- France pressures NZ, threatening trade access to Europe
- French agents arrested
- Greenpeace vessel *Rainbow Warrior* prepares to protest at Mururoa

3 Again, make your own brief notes under these headings.

After the *Rainbow Warrior*

- French testing resumes
- New Zealand protests
- Comprehensive Test Ban Treaty

Refer to Source A

4 What, according to Prime Minister Kirk, was the role of the *Otago*? Use your own words.

Refer to Source B

5 Provide evidence that supports the claim that the French were prepared for this sort of protest action.

6 How do you think the treatment of the protesters here by the French would have differed from the 'protesters' in Source A?

7 What is Alice Leney's view of the way that the French have treated her? Explain your answer.

8 How effective do you think this sort of protest action would be? Explain your answer.

9 What similarities are there between the actions described in Source A and those in Source B? In what significant way(s) are they different?

SOURCE A

'We are a small nation but we will not abjectly [helplessly] surrender to injustice. We have worked against the development of nuclear weapons. We have opposed their testing anywhere and everywhere .... Today the *Otago* leaves on an honourable mission. She leaves not in anger but as a silent, accusing witness with the power to bring alive the conscience of the world.'

Prime Minister Norman Kirk, farewelling the Navy ship Otago in 1973. Kirk had notified 100 world leaders of his intention, seeking their support.

SOURCE B

As well as government condemnation, private groups such as Greenpeace took action when France resumed its testing programme in 1995. On the tenth anniversary of the bombing of the original Rainbow Warrior, *the* Rainbow Warrior II *was seized by French commandos as it protested at Mururoa. The following report is from Alice Leney, who was part of a small team in an inflatable boat that evaded the French Navy and entered the restricted area of Mururoa Lagoon, in order to chain themselves to equipment used for nuclear testing.*

'We screamed up to this thing, and just as we came real close I realised you could drive a boat right in, right under the drilling rig itself.... Kate jumps up, I sort of slow the boat up, she grabs the walkway and I jump up.... At this point I see French Legionnaires running up the deck, so I quickly ... lock myself to the handrails on the drilling rig and sit down. Well, the French come screaming up ... three or four of them came and then they started wrenching at my arms because they thought I was just hanging on to the pipe .... [*The French soldiers cut through the chain lock.*] They carried me down, because we were non-violent protesters. They put us on a boat, they took us away to the gendarmerie [police] on the atoll.'

Members of CANWAR (Campaign Against Nuclear Warships) in Wellington Harbour 1976.

As the risk of a nuclear confrontation seemed to grow, nuclear war became more of an issue than environmental concerns about a nuclear accident. In 1981, the Auckland suburb of Devonport – the site of New Zealand's major naval base – took the symbolic action of declaring itself to be nuclear-free. Within two years another 37 local authorities had followed suit. In 1982, Christchurch became the first city to declare itself nuclear free. A year later, more than 35,000 people turned out to protest against the arrival of the USS *Truxton* in Auckland. Waterfront unions added their support to the anti-nuclear cause by going on strike. Some 400 different groups, covering a broad range of New Zealand society, were now represented in the anti-nuclear movement. By 1984, polls showed that 70% of people did not want ships capable of carrying nuclear weapons to come to New Zealand. That year, National lost the snap election and Labour swept into power, riding the wave of anti-nuclear feeling. David Lange, the new Labour Prime Minister, would now have to fulfil his party's election promise of making New Zealand nuclear-free.

Prime Minister Lange now found himself caught between a public distaste for nuclear-armed ship visits, and an equally strong desire for the continuation of ANZUS (see page 95). Around 70% of New Zealanders wanted to ban nuclear ship visits, but the same proportion wanted to stay part of ANZUS. Lange was very aware of this contradiction, and the apparent public belief that the US would accept an ANZUS alliance without nuclear ship visits. Lange had very little room for manoeuvring. Earlier, he had tried to convince the Labour party membership to soften its position. The membership had reacted by voting for the complete withdrawal of New Zealand from ANZUS. Lange rejected this, because he knew it would be unpopular with other New Zealand voters. On the other hand, he also knew that he could not compromise the anti-nuclear position without causing a damaging revolt within his own party.

ACTIVITIES

Refer to Source C

1. Which country does Prime Minister Muldoon say 'has the power to realise the ideals we all share'?
2. What does Muldoon suggest could be the consequences of not being a 'reliable ally'?
3. What do you think would be Muldoon's response to the views expressed in Source A (page 109)?

> 'New Zealand can do most to help maintain peace by continuing to act as a reliable ally of the United States... If we, as a community that tries to uphold Western values, have a contribution to make, we can make it most effectively by working with the one country that has the power to realise the ideals we all share.'
>
> *Prime Minister Muldoon, reaffirming in 1981 New Zealand's commitment to ANZUS, and supporting President Reagan's approach to dealing with the Soviet Union*

Refer to the 'Nuclear Ship Visits' text on pages 108 and 110

4 Provide evidence to support each of the key ideas below. Evidence can include facts, statistics, quotes or similar.

a New Zealand had been regularly visited by allied warships, prior to the nuclear ban.

b The American Navy did not want it publicly known whether its vessels were nuclear armed or not.

c From the late 1970s, there was increasing public concern about the visits of nuclear ships.

d Despite opposition to nuclear capable vessels, New Zealanders still wanted to remain part of ANZUS.

e From the 1980s, a broad cross-section of New Zealand society was opposed to nuclear capable ships.

SOURCE D

Refer to Source D

5 Who is the person on the right most likely meant to represent?

6 What is the 'joke' in this cartoon?

7 How might Prime Minister Muldoon (Source C) respond to the ideas shown here?

SOURCE E

'In the sky above Otahuhu the moon turned to blood ... As I walked from the bus stop to my home on a cold winter evening I saw an eerie lightening of the sky. Beams of light radiated from the northern horizon and intersected with each other through the blackness of the night ... the sky pulsated with these brilliant shafts of light. They were red and white. They extended across the night like the ribs of a fan. They were spinning, they were inter-mingling. The sky was diffused with a ghastly brush of red. It was an unnerving spectacle.'

David Lange recalls seeing the effects of an American atmospheric nuclear test above Johnston Island in the Pacific in 1962, the same year as the Cuban Missile Crisis.

Refer to Source E

8 In a quote of no more than five words, identify ONE opinion.

9 What caused the sights described in this source?

10 How might this experience have influenced David Lange in his role as Prime Minister?

11 How reliable is this as an historian's source? Explain your answer.

SOURCE F

'One day when New Zealand and the United States were still on speaking terms he [Gerald Hensley, head of the External Intelligence Bureau] padded into my office to bring me sombre news. He had just been informed, he said, that the American early-warning system had picked up Soviet missiles heading for the continental United States. It looked, he continued, as if nuclear war had finally happened. In twenty minutes we'd know for certain. There wasn't anything I could do about it and, not wishing to start a panic among the staff, I sat signing letters while the minutes dragged past. Hensley came back. False alarm. It must have been a fault in the electronics, or a close formation of Canadian geese....'

Prime Minister Lange in 1984, during the period when President Reagan pursued an aggressive policy towards Russia.

Refer to Source F

12 How did the event described in Source E lead to the situation in Source F?

The End of ANZUS

Lange knew that the whole issue of nuclear ship visits would come to a head when the Americans next requested permission for a ship to visit New Zealand. He tried to convince US officials to send only vessels that could not possibly carry nuclear weapons. The Americans virtually complied, by announcing in late 1984 that they would like to send the USS *Buchanan*. This ship was not nuclear-powered and nor was it of a type that usually carried nuclear weapons. It seems likely that the US believed that the *Buchanan* would be acceptable to the Lange government. The US Navy, however, would still 'neither confirm nor deny' whether there was any nuclear weaponry on board. This was not good enough to satisfy the Labour party membership. Nor did it satisfy the 10,000 protesters who turned out at a march to express their opposition. Lange knew he could not be seen to be making any deals. In early 1985 he announced that permission for the *Buchanan* visit had been refused.

The Americans reacted angrily, although the importance to the US of such a small South Pacific nation should not be overstated. (US Secretary of State Kissinger dismissed New Zealand as a 'dagger pointed at the heart of Antarctica.' Another critic called New Zealand 'a piss-ant little country south of nowheresville.') Nonetheless, the US felt that it could not be seen to be backing down. It did not like a small country like New Zealand attempting to dictate US policy. This was despite the fact that there had never been a requirement under the terms of the ANZUS Treaty to accept visits by the American military, whether nuclear or not. Lange felt that the Americans' unwillingness to compromise was unreasonable.

In terms of retaliatory actions taken by the US, all military and intelligence links with New Zealand were immediately cut. There were threats of other actions, including cutting off New Zealand's trade access to US markets, but these did not eventuate. This time, not even Australia would support New Zealand's position. Although Lange continued to negotiate with the Americans into 1986, neither side would budge. ANZUS was officially declared to be 'inoperative' and New Zealand was downgraded from being an 'ally' to a 'friend'. Secretary of State George Schultz summed up the new situation: 'We part company as friends, but we part company.'

Although Labour's policy came under intense pressure from the US and other countries, it was immensely popular in New Zealand. In June 1987 New Zealand's anti-nuclear legislation finally finished its journey through parliament and became law. Support for the nuclear ban remained high at around 70%. Support for remaining part of ANZUS – *if* the US accepted New Zealand's anti-nuclear position – was as high as 80%. Proof of the extent to which the anti-nuclear position had become part of New Zealand's identity came in 1990. National Prime Minister Jim Bolger announced that his government would not change the anti-nuclear law. This was despite earlier claims by National that Labour was opening the way for communist Russia to enter the South Pacific.

ACTIVITIES

Refer to Source G

1. What has apparently been the effect of New Zealand 'shoving a potato up the exhaust pipe' of America's nuclear policy?
2. What, in reality, is the 'potato' referring to?
3. This cartoonist is using irony. What is the point that he is making about America's nuclear capability, and the *actual* effect of New Zealand's action?

4 Some of the statements below contain errors. Correct them, and then provide evidence from the text on page 112 to support the corrected statements.

a The request by the Americans in 1980 to send the *USS Bucketan* on a visit to New Zealand was acceptable to many, because of the unlikelihood of it carrying nuclear weapons.

b Despite the severe actions taken against New Zealand by Britain, relations with America remained unreasonably friendly.

c By the late 1970s Labour's nuclear policy had become a feature of New Zealand's identity as a nation.

SOURCE H

Exports from NZ to the US, as a percentage of total NZ exports, 1950–2000	
1950	10%
1960	13%
1970	16%
1980	14%
1990	13%
2000	14%

Refer to Source H

5 In what period were exports to the United States highest (as a percentage of all exports)?

6 "New Zealand's exports to the US did not suffer because of its anti-nuclear policy." Use evidence from Source H to back this key idea.

SOURCE I

The following is an editorial from the Christchurch Star, responding to comments made by the British Foreign Secretary, Geoffrey Howe, that were critical of the Labour government's anti-nuclear legislation.

'At best Sir Geoffrey's remarks were thinly veiled threats that New Zealand could suffer in trade terms .... At worst, a remarkably unsophisticated attempt to sway New Zealand voters away from the Government.... This country is no longer the blindly patriotic South Sea outpost that it once was. There is now an independence and a sense of nationality that make his clumsy attempt at influencing New Zealand's affairs deeply offensive.'
McKinnon, p.299

Refer to Source I

7 What idea in the first sentence is also reflected in Source H?

8 In your own words, what 'at worst' was Sir Geoffrey trying to do?

9 What is meant by the term 'blindly patriotic South Sea outpost'? Do you think that the editor of the *Christchurch Star* has made a fair analysis of New Zealand by the mid-1980s? Explain your answer.

SOURCE J

Refer to Source J

10 Why, according to the cartoon, is Prime Minister Lange being thrown out of the café? What does this mean in relation to the ANZUS situation?

11 What appears to be Lange's reaction to being thrown out? Explain your answer.

12 Identify a key idea from the text in this section that shows that Lange did not want New Zealand to be seen as a 'free-loader'.

A NUCLEAR-FREE SOUTH PACIFIC

It was French nuclear testing, beginning in 1966, which led to the first call for a nuclear-free South Pacific. When Labour's Norman Kirk came to power in 1972, he was active in this campaign. He included a plan for a nuclear-free South Pacific at the same time as he took the French to the World Court and sent the Navy frigates to Mururoa. However, it was not until the height of Lange's Labour government in 1985, and its anti-nuclear policies, that a South Pacific Nuclear Free Zone was established.

The Treaty of Rarotonga, as it was called, was signed on August 6th 1985, forty years to the day after the first atomic bomb was dropped on Hiroshima during WWII. Most of the members of the Pacific Forum signed. In doing so they agreed not to produce, store, test, dump or use nuclear materials in the South Pacific. The main purpose of the South Pacific Nuclear Free Zone was to send a message to larger powers to respect the wishes of the nations of the South Pacific. By signing, both Australia and New Zealand showed their solidarity with their smaller neighbours. The Treaty was offered to France, Britain and the United States to sign, but all three refused. The Soviet Union did sign. The Pacific Forum thus found its proposal rejected by its allies and accepted by its one main potential 'enemy'.

AS1.5 ESSAY PRACTICE

Follow the steps outlined on the inside back cover to write the following essay.

What nuclear issues faced New Zealand in the period 1973–1985? Describe New Zealand governments' reactions to these issues during this period.

- Nuclear testing; ship visits; ANZUS relationship
- International Court of Justice (World Court); protests; Muldoon; anti-nuclear laws.

ACTIVITIES

Refer to Source K

1 When and where was the first Nuclear Weapons Free Zone established?

2 What five nations are shown with nuclear capability? What characteristic(s) do they all have in common?

3 Look back to the 'French Nuclear Testing in the Pacific' section (page 107). Quote the slogan of the anti-nuclear organisation *Campaign for Nuclear Disarmament* which had, by 1996, become a reality.

SOURCE K

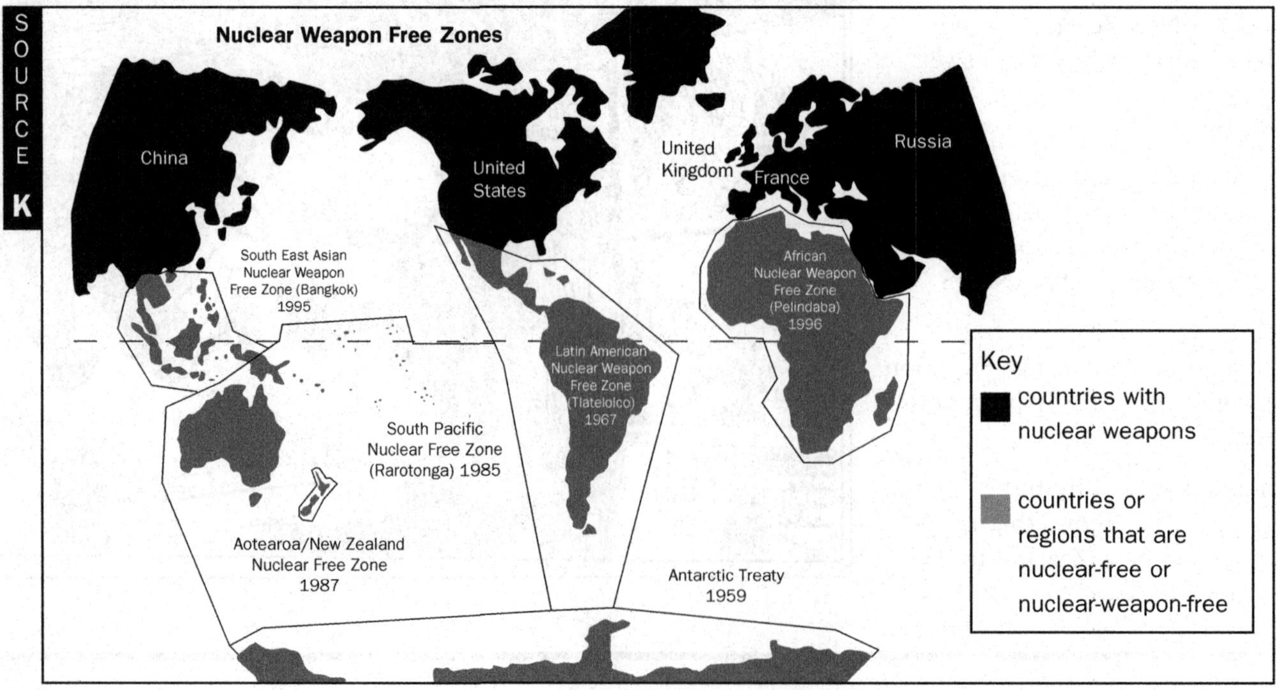

NEW ZEALAND'S INTERNATIONAL RELATIONS BY THE END OF THE 20TH CENTURY

In the 55 years after the end of World War II, New Zealand's view of itself and its place in the world had changed dramatically. The links with Britain that were so important up to the early 1970s were almost entirely gone. Those that did remain were the Commonwealth Games and Heads of Government meetings. Many young New Zealanders still continued to do their 'OE' to England. Britain, however, was no longer important in terms of trade or defence; even visits here by the Queen passed almost unnoticed. Britain, in turn, had few remaining commitments in this area of the world.

The United Nations, by contrast, was an even more important part of New Zealand's foreign policy at the end of the century. This was because the security situation had changed. South East Asia was no longer New Zealand's line of 'forward defence'. Communism there was no longer seen as a threat. Furthermore, by 1989 the 'Cold War' had ended. The need for defensive treaties such as ANZAM, SEATO and ANZUS had disappeared. New Zealand thus looked to a greater peacekeeping role, especially in the Pacific region. Australia was seen as an important partner in this policy.

The nuclear issue in the South Pacific – indeed, the Southern Hemisphere – was resolved to New Zealand's satisfaction. It did have a cost, in terms of a falling out with a significant ally, but the threatened trade reprisals did not eventuate. This issue, more than any other, gave New Zealanders a strong sense that their country was at last asserting its right to an independent foreign policy. As part of this policy, the Pacific had become more important. Immigration had made Auckland the largest Polynesian city in the world, and this was starting to be reflected in aspects of New Zealand's wider culture. The increasing number of Asian migrants was also altering the face and culture of Auckland, in particular. In another area, New Zealand was still not meeting its international obligation in terms of aid. New Zealand's continuing economic vulnerability was often given as the reason for this. Of the aid that it did give, the biggest part by far went to the Pacific.

AS1.4 REVIEW ACTIVITIES

In paragraphs of about 100 words for each, describe the perspectives (views) and actions (with an accompanying explanation) for the following issues:

1 French nuclear testing in the Pacific.
- Labour Prime Minister Norman Kirk
- Greenpeace, the Peace Squadron and/or other protest movements
- New Zealand's traditional allies (Britain and America)
- National Prime Minister Jim Bolger

2 The bombing of the *Rainbow Warrior* and/or the arrest of the French agents
- Labour Prime Minister David Lange
- French Prime Ministers (Laurent Fabius/Jacques Chirac)

3 Visits by nuclear armed/powered vessels
- Labour Prime Minister David Lange
- Greenpeace, the Peace Squadron and/or other protest movements
- National Prime Minister Robert Muldoon

4 South Pacific Nuclear Free Zone
- Labour Prime Ministers Norman Kirk and David Lange

Mind-map

Refer to the headings and key ideas in the text to create a mind-map OR structured overview that shows the development of New Zealand's anti-nuclear policy.

PART TWO

CHAPTER SIXTEEN

TWO REVOLUTIONS? ROGERNOMICS AND THE CHANGING ROLE OF WOMEN

In the 1980s nuclear issues helped define New Zealand's international relations, and the 1981 Springbok Tour shaped New Zealand identity, both internally and externally. There was another equally dramatic development occurring within New Zealand in this decade. This was the major changes made to the welfare state and New Zealand economy as a whole, brought about (again) by a Labour government.

ROGERNOMICS

The economic policies introduced from 1984 were unusual for a supposedly left-wing government (see page 86). They were far more in line with policies of governments leading up to the Depression. The economic policies of the Fourth Labour government came to be known as 'Rogernomics' after Roger Douglas, the Minister of Finance. More generally, they were part of the international programme of the 'New Right'. Douglas set out to reverse the situation of the past fifty years, by removing much of the 'safety net' that had been built up. He believed in a 'free market' with minimal involvement in the economy by the government.

When Labour came to power in 1984, it inherited a financial crisis that had been developing for some time under the previous Muldoon government. New Zealand's overseas debt had blown out dangerously. Douglas took radical measures to deal with this problem, and at the same time began pushing through his free-market ideas. Prime Minister David Lange imposed little restraint on Douglas, as he was occupied with nuclear issues (see page 108).

In the space of a decade, New Zealand went from one of the most protected and regulated economies in the world to one of the least. According to Roger Douglas, this would allow New Zealand businesses to compete internationally. Large government-owned companies such as Air New Zealand, Telecom, the Post Office, the Bank of New Zealand and the Railways were put up for sale to private buyers. In just over a decade, $15 billion worth of State assets were sold (privatised). The remaining 'inefficient' State-owned industries were restructured. All these changes contributed to the unemployment figure rising to over 100,000.

In this new open economic environment, overseas investment poured in. Import restrictions were lifted, and New Zealanders were able to cheaply buy a whole new range of goods that hadn't been available before. However, inflation – the destabilising cycle of increasing prices and wages – had climbed to over 20% by 1987 (by 2000 it had been brought down nearer to 2%). That same year the sharemarket crashed, eventually losing over 70% of its pre-1987 value. Many New Zealand businesses were hit hard. This showed just how exposed the New Zealand economy had become. It also revealed some unscrupulous financial practices amongst some businesses that had invested – and lost – other people's money. Over 900,000 New Zealand investors are estimated to have been affected by the collapse.

Prime Minister David Lange (1984–1989)

Roger Douglas, Minister of Finance in the Labour government.

National in Power

Although Labour was thrown out of power in 1990, National continued Labour's right wing economic policies. 'Rogernomics' turned into 'Ruthenasia', as Finance Minister Ruth Richardson cut welfare benefits by a total of $1.6billion. She claimed that the country could not afford to continue paying benefits, and that too many people had become reliant on them. This was another blow for those who had become unemployed due to the lay-offs of the 1980s. Small businesses suffered also, as the spending power of beneficiaries fell. The ability of workers to negotiate pay and conditions was also weakened by the passing of the Employment Contracts Act in 1991. Unemployment continued to climb, passing 200,000, or 12% of the workforce. Crime rates shot up. By the middle of the 1990s, health, housing, accident compensation, education and welfare had undergone the most dramatic changes since the 1930s.

Despite the claims made by supporters of the 'New Right' policies, New Zealand's economy was not improving. By the end of the 1990s, overseas debt had steadily increased to top $100 billion. Furthermore, New Zealand's standard of living – ranked third in the late 1930s – had fallen to 20th. In large measure this was due to forces beyond the government's control. New Zealand still had a small economy which was at the mercy of larger, international forces. In this light, some wondered why the country had gone through so much pain for so little gain. This was especially so for the regions beyond the main urban centres. Even State spending, one of the main 'evils' that the supporters of the New Right had set out to curb, had not declined greatly. Before 'Rogernomics', the State was spending 42% of the country's wealth, on education, health, welfare and other government functions. By 1999, after all of the reforms and restructuring, this had only dropped to 36%. Critics again asked: was it all worth it? Furthermore, the myth of New Zealand as an egalitarian (equal) society was well and truly dead. The gap between rich and poor was growing. By the end of the decade, the top 20% of the population held over 80% of the nation's wealth. On the positive side, by 2000 a latte could be had anywhere …

ACTIVITIES

Refer to Sources A and B

1. What New Zealand feature is 'endangered' in Source A?
2. What visual evidence shows that this feature is 'endangered'?
3. In reality, what is the threat to this feature (refer to the main text)?
4. What was the name given to the economic policy of the Labour Government at the time the 'stamp' in Source A was issued?
5. What image is used to represent the New Zealand economy in Source B?
6. Which Finance Minister is shown here?
7. What point is the Finance Minister making about the New Zealand economy in the first two frames?
8. What point about the New Zealand economy is the third frame making?
9. The same point is made in the main text. Quote the sentence that contains this key idea.

SOURCE A

SOURCE B

ACTIVITIES

1 From the list below, select only what you think are the EIGHT key ideas from the text on pages 116–117. Most of the other pieces of information given can be used as evidence to support the key ideas.

- Roger Douglas was Minister of Finance in the fourth Labour government.
- Rogernomics: cutting back the welfare 'safety net', and a 'free market'.
- An economic crisis meant radical measures were rapidly taken.
- Air New Zealand, Telecom and the Post Office were sold.
- State assets were privatised.
- Unemployment rose to over 100,000 in the 1980s.
- Inflation rose to over 20% by the late 1980s.
- Overseas investment increased, but economic instability remained.
- The sharemarket crashed, affecting thousands of New Zealanders.
- The value of the sharemarket fell by 70%.
- Unemployment topped 200,000 (12%) by the 1990s.
- 20% of the population owned 80% of the wealth by the end of the 1990s.
- 'Ruthenasia': welfare cuts.
- Unemployment continued to grow, with few signs of real economic improvement.
- Overseas debt climbed to $100billion.
- The end of the egalitarian society.

2 Use the selected ideas and the remaining pieces of evidence to write a paragraph summary of the economic and social changes made since 1984.

THE CHANGING ROLE OF WOMEN

Traditional histories tell us that after women got the vote in 1893, there were few changes in their position in society until the late 1960s. This view tells us that the government wanted women to be only wives and mothers. This is only partially true. There *did* develop from the early 20th century a 'cult of domesticity'. This 'cult' glorified women as wives and mothers in the domestic setting (the home). But, over much of the 20th century, government policies often recognised women as an important part of the workforce. The advances that occurred from the 1960s are thus more of a speeding up of an ongoing process of change, rather than a whole new direction.

Elizabeth McCombs – first woman Member of Parliament.

Mabel Howard – first woman cabinet minister.

First Wave Feminism

The advances made in the late 19th century for women were part of what has been called 'first wave feminism'. What this means is that a number of concerned women worked together to make changes. In doing so they were part of, and helped shape, a social movement. The gains made for women saw them being treated as individuals in the eyes of the law, rather than as daughters or wives. For example, any property women owned upon entering marriage after 1884 remained their own, not their husbands'. Most notably, in 1893 women gained the vote. Beyond this, however, changes were slow to come. Women got the right to stand for parliament in 1919, but it took until 1933 before Elizabeth McCombs was actually elected. The first woman to become a Minister in the government was Mabel Howard, Minister of Social Welfare, in 1947. By the early 21st century things had changed considerably. Four of the top political positions were held by women – Prime Minister, Governor-General, Chief Justice and Attorney General.

The State and Women's Roles

From the late 19th century, the State (government) was influential in determining women's roles. This was done through four main ways. First was through the promotion of high birth-rates for Pakeha. By 1900 the average birth-rate had dropped to 3.5 children per family, from seven in 1876. There was great concern that Pakeha were committing 'race suicide' by not breeding enough. Women were thus

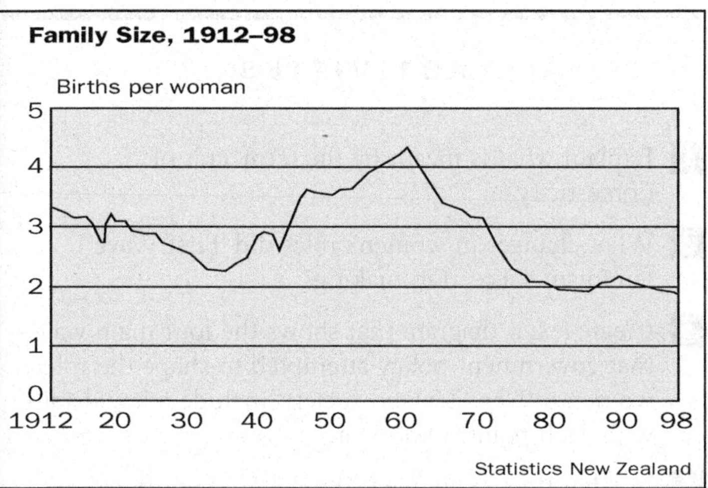

A group of students with their tutor during an engineering class at Wanganui Technical College.

encouraged to be mothers. However, this policy was ineffective, and birth rates continued to fall. It would take the trauma of World War II before they rose dramatically. Soldiers returning from the conflict were looking for the stability and normality that a family could provide.

Wage laws were the second means by which women were 'guided' out of the workforce and into the home. Restrictions were placed on the hours and type of work that women could do. For example, they could not do heavy lifting or night shifts. (At night, women were meant to be tending to the needs of husband and children.) While most women were indeed mothers, up to the 1930s about 18% of women were in the workforce. A significant number worked as domestic (household) servants, or in factories or office jobs, while a few were professionals such as librarians, teachers and nurses. In all cases, they were paid less than men. A man's role as head of the family and main income earner was put into law in 1936. The minimum wage for male workers was set at a level where a man could provide for a wife and three children. This was called the 'family wage' and remained in place until the 1960s. The welfare benefits introduced by the Labour government were also based on the man of the house being able to provide for his family.

The third area of State intervention was in education. Girls in the first half of the 20th century were supposed to learn how to be wives and mothers. Compulsory domestic education was thus introduced in 1917. In their courses, girls learned about cooking, cleaning and child-care. In reality, however, most girls preferred to do more academic courses. This was despite the warnings of people like Truby King, the founder of Plunket. He claimed that studying hard would affect the ability of girls to have healthy children.

Truby King was responsible for the final way in which the State tried to determine the role of women. In 1907 he founded the Plunket society. Its mission was to introduce a scientific approach to motherhood. This was to be achieved by promoting breast feeding, training nurses in maternal and infant welfare, and educating parents in domestic hygiene. By 1930, Plunket was attending to 65% of Pakeha babies. By 1947 this had grown to 85%, along with an increasing number of Maori babies. Although the Plunket Society began as a private organisation, in the 1910s the government began supporting its efforts.

Cooking class at the Christchurch Technical College.

Lady Plunket, wife of the Governor General and patron of Truby King's Plunket Society.

Frederic Truby King, founder of the Plunket Society.

Contradictions in Government Policy

While the government's policies seemed to clearly define a woman's role as wife and mother, other actions contradicted this. First, the education system, whether intentionally or not, trained women to enter the workforce. Between 1890 and the outbreak of war in 1939, the proportion of women in office work jumped from 2% to 40%. Similarly, the proportion of girls going on to secondary school by 1930 had increased to just over half. In terms of work, fewer women were taking up the limited 'career option' of domestic service (housework). This was despite a focus on this type of work in the school curriculum, and an increasing demand for household workers. Second, during both wars (but more especially WWII), women were actively encouraged into the workforce. Not only this, but they took on jobs that men normally did, such as driving buses, trucks and taxis, as well as farm and factory work. By 1945 there was a peak of 236,000 women in employment, making up 30% of the total workforce. (Most did not stay in such work after the men returned from the war.) Finally, in 1960 women working for the government were granted equal pay with men. Thus, while the 'domestic woman' was the ideal, the government was not whole-hearted in its efforts to maintain this situation. This is perhaps best shown by the fact that at the beginning of the 20th century, a quarter of women were in paid work; by the end half were.

SOURCE H

Women repairing Wellington tram lines during WWII.

ACTIVITIES

1. Explain what is meant by the term 'cult of domesticity'.
2. What changes in women's roles did 'First Wave' feminism succeed in making?
3. Create a star diagram that shows the four main ways that government policy attempted to shape the role of women in New Zealand society. Include a few details with each point of the 'star'.
4. In what three main ways did government policy contradict the ideal of women as wives and mothers?

Refer to Source C

5. What government concern is shown in the graph up to 1940?
6. What event caused the sharp increase in birth rates after the 1940s?
7. In what year did the birth rate peak?
8. In what years was the birth rate exactly three children per family?

Refer to Sources D and E

9. Explain the gender roles shown in Sources D and E.
10. How reliable are these sources to the historian studying women's roles in society? Explain your answer.
11. What would be the likely view of Truby King (Source G) on the scenes shown in Sources D and E?
12. In what way does Lady Plunket (Source F) make a good role model for the Plunket Society?

Refer to Source H

13. Explain how World War Two led to the scene shown in this source.

Second Wave Feminism

So-called 'second wave' feminism was a movement beginning in the 1960s. The movement in New Zealand tapped into the women's liberation, civil rights and anti-war movements in America at that time. Like 'first wave' feminism in the late 19th century, there was some confusion about the goals. Some women wanted total equality with men. For them, being male or female would be entirely irrelevant in terms of employment, opportunities and treatment. Others argued that women *were* different, and that these differences should be recognised and valued by law. Things were further complicated when the movement turned upon itself. Conflict arose between gay and straight, and Maori and Pakeha groups. Maori women within the activist organisation Nga Tamatoa also argued that women were discriminated against by Maori men. Donna Awatere and Ngahuia Te Awekotuku were at the forefront of this section of the feminist movement.

Despite the division within the feminist movement, there were some generally agreed goals. These included gaining equality with men in terms of pay, education, and household responsibilities. Equal pay laws came in the 1970s, but by the late 1990s there were still differences. In another area, women were participating more than men in higher education. By the end of the 1990s, nearly 60% (34,000) of university graduates were female. Almost half of those graduating in law in 1992 were female, compared to 2% in 1975. However, a 1999 survey showed that while women as a whole did about 75% of the paid work of men, they did twice as much unpaid housework, and three times as much of the childcare in the home. Even though these figures show full equality had not been achieved by 2000, a United Nations report noted New Zealand's high overall ranking with regard to gender equality.

A pamphlet put out by the Council for Equal Pay and Opportunity, 1961.

Women's Health

Other areas that the feminist movement focused on were women's health and reproduction, and domestic violence. In the first case, abortion was a key issue. Feminists argued that it was a woman's right to choose whether or not to have a baby. Restrictive laws were still in place in New Zealand. In the 1960s, a feminist network helped women travel to Australia for abortions. In 1974, the first private abortion clinic opened. This led to the formation of an anti-abortion organisation, the Society for the Protection of the Unborn Child (SPUC). Vigorous and angry debate between SPUC and feminists followed. In 1976 an unknown person carried out an arson attack on an abortion clinic. In 1979 abortion laws were relaxed, despite strong opposition from SPUC and other concerned groups. The rate of abortion increased dramatically. In 1965 there had been only 63 recorded abortions (and an unknown number of 'backstreet' abortions done illegally); in 1991 there were 15,000. This was despite the introduction of the contraceptive pill from the 1970s, and the Domestic Purposes Benefit (DPB) in 1973. The DPB paid solo parents (usually mothers) an allowance, making it easier to keep and raise a baby on their own.

Domestic Violence

Up until the 1970s, domestic violence by a husband against a wife was generally acceptable. The tone had been set in a 1949 court judgement in a case involving a man using an iron bar to beat his wife. The judge had advised him to use a stick instead: 'While it might be proper for a man to beat his wife at times, he must beat her properly ... the Bible subscribes to and supports the statement, but the beating must be done as a service of love and not in temper.' The issue of domestic violence was brought into the open with the establishment of the first women's refuge in the early 1970s. By 1987 there were 48 refuges. In 1996 the Domestic Violence Act saw police take a more pro-active role. Previously, they had been cautious about involving themselves in private matters, as it was not seen as proper that the State interfere.

ACTIVITIES

1. What overseas influences helped lead to 'Second Wave' feminism in New Zealand?
2. What issues caused division within the movement?
3. Create a timeline from 1960 to 2000, showing the developments affecting women's health.

SELECT BIBLIOGRAPHY

Belich, J. *Paradise Reforged: A History of the New Zealanders from the 1880s to the Year 2000*, Penguin, Auckland, 2001
Brockie, B (ed), *I Was There: Dramatic First-Hand Accounts From New Zealand's History*, Penguin, Auckland, 1998
Brooking, T and P. Enright. *Milestones: Turning Points in New Zealand History*, Dunmore Press, Palmerston North, 1988
Durie, M. *Te mana, Te Kawanatanga: The Politics of Maori Self-Determination*, OUP, Auckland, 1998
Hoadley, S. *The New Zealand Foreign Affairs Handbook*, OUP, Auckland, 1992
King, M. *The Penguin History of New Zealand*, Auckland, 2003
McKinnon, M. *Independence and Foreign Policy: New Zealand in the World Since 1935*, AUP, 1993
Ministry of Defence, *New Zealand Defence Quarterly*, Issues 21, 25, 27–29
Office of Treaty Settlements, *Healing the Past, Building A Future*, 1999
Sinclair, K (ed). *The Oxford Illustrated History of New Zealand*, OUP, Auckland, 1996
Walker, R. Ka *Whawhai Tonu Matou: Struggle Without End*, Penguin, Auckland, 1990
Ward, A. An *Unsettled History: Treaty Claims in New Zealand Today*, Wellington, 1999
Watt, L. *Mates and Mayhem: World War II – Frontline Kiwis Remember*, Harper Collins, Auckland, 1996

PHOTOGRAPH ACKNOWLEDGEMENTS

The Alexander Turnbull Library, National Library of New Zealand, Te Puna Matauranga o Aotearoa for page 7 James Cook (Nathaniel Holland) A-217-001; page 8, Reconstruction of the Signing of the Treaty of Waitangi (Leonard Mitchell) A-242-002; page 9, The Warrior Chieftains of NZ (Joseph Merrett) C-012-019; War in NZ PUBL-0033-1863-212; Okaihau (John Williams) A-079-029; page 10, Te Rangi Topeora (Edward Richards) F-58452-1/2; page 11, Cohorn Motor Gun, near Ladysmith, South Africa F-27597-1/2; Display of frozen export carcasses outside the British New Zealand Meat Company, Christchurch 1/1-009113; page 12, Queen Victoria 094015; page 13, New Zealand Ministry of Defence: Military training. Dominion of New Zealand. 10 April, 1911, Eph-D-ARMY-1911-01; page 14, New Zealand marines transporting Mau prisoners, PA1-0-795-12-1; page 16, WW1 Departures, F-61074-1/2; Landing at Anzac Cove, Gallipoli, PAColl-0063-03; page 17, Evacuation of the wounded from ANZAC Cove in Gallipoli by boat, 1/4-008784; Soldiers in a trench, Gallipoli, Turkey, 1/2-103903; page 18, NZ 2nd Field Ambulance hospital interior, (Solesmes, France) 1/1-002085; page 19, Camel convoy loading frozen mutton, PA1-q-605-31-1; page 20, Ettie Rout with her Volunteer Sisterhood, 1/1-014727; page 32, page 41 Maori family outside Whare (James Bragge) PA1-f-021-043-1; page 24, James Carroll 35mm-00100-d; Sir Peter Henry Buck, 1/1-019099; Maui Wiremu Pomare 1/1-012109; page 26, Apirana Ngata 1/1-014489; Joseph Gordon Coates 1/1-018353; St Mary's Church, Tikitiki 1/2-045105; page 29, Maori group at a farm in Winiata, 1/2-032309; Sheep for transportation at Waipiro Bay beach,1/1-023296; Raukawa meeting house at Otaki, PAColl-0239-1; page 30, Members of the World War I Maori Pioneer Battalion taking a break from trench improvement work, near Gommecourt, France, 1/2-013414; page 31, Rua Kenana Hepetipa's wooden circular courthouse and meeting house at Maungapohatu, 1/2-002915; Rua Kenana, 1/2-C-008873; page 32, Rua Kenana Hepetipa and his son Whatu, handcuffed, 1/2-028072; Prisoners, including Rua Kenana Hepetipa, being led from Maungapohatu,1/2-028066; Rua Kenana Hepetipa, with some of his household and visitors, at Maai, Maungapohatu, PAColl-6001-41; Reverend John George Laughton, his assistant John Currie, and their class of Maori children, outside Maungapohotu School, 1/2-030857; page 34, Te Kirihaehae Te Puea Herangi, 1/2-001920; page 34, Angas, George French 1822–1886: Te Werowero, or Potatau the principal chief of all Waikato, PUBL-0014-4; Photograph of an engraving depicting Tukaroto Matutaera Potatau Te Wherowhero Tawhiao, 1/1-003878; Beattie & Sanderson: Richard Seddon with Maori leaders at Huntly, PA7-28-21-1; Te Rata Mahuta, Tupu Taingakawa, Mita Karaka and Geo G Paul, PAColl-0545-1-045; King Koroki Te Rata Mahuta Tawhiao Potatau Te Wherowhero and others, PAColl-0671-01; page 36, Mate Rewharewha Uruta (influenza), MS-Papers-0151-17-1; page 37, Robson, Edward Thomas, fl 1920s–1940s: Ngati Porou group, including Apirana Ngata, at the opening of Mahina-a-rangi meeting house, Turangawaewae Marae, Ngaruawhahia, PAColl-6208-07; page 38, Tahupotiki Wiremu Ratana publicising the Ratana Movement in Taupo, 1/2-089569; page 39, Ratana youth band, Wanganui, 1/1-017025; Ratana temple, 1/2-018648; page 40, Akatarawa relief work, F-22602-1/2; George William Forbes, 1/2-004974; page 41, Cuba Street riot, Wellington, G-101110-1/2; page 42, [New Zealand Labour Party]: Labour is making them the nation's pride. Safeguard their future! Vote Labour, Eph-B-NZ-LABOUR-1938-01; Michael Joseph Savage on the campaign trail, 1/2-051739; F; page 43, Old age pensioners collecting social security at a Post Office, 1/4-000456; F; [N.Z. Fruitgrowers' Federation]: [Third annual] national patriotic apple show. [Catalogue cover] 1918, Eph-A-FRUIT-1918-01-cover; page 45, If you are 18, join the R.N.Z.A.F. today! Fly with the Victory squadrons. Eph-B-VARIETY-1944-01-p2; page 46, Maori members of the Women's Army Auxiliary Corp, Wellington wharf, 1/4-001636; F; Bernard Cyril Freyberg and Howard Karl Kippenberger in Egypt, DA-03719; F; Members of the Maori Battalion in front of a German Messerschmitt fighter plane, DA-02998; F; Kaye, George 1914–: Arapeta Awatere, DA-08379; Te Moananui-a-Kiwa Ngarimu, DA-03166; F; N.Z.E.F., Middle East, PA1-q-286-400; page 48, Member of NZEF on desert manoeuvres in Egypt 1941, F-1459-1/4-DA; page 49, Cassino. A damned hard nut, just the right job for our New Zealand pals. Eph-A-WAR-WII-German-propaganda-1944-01, Wounded soldiers, F-6849-1/4; page 50, Nursing staff and wounded soldiers of the 2nd New Zealand Expeditionary Force in the Pacific at the 4th General Hospital in New Caledonia, WH-0392; NZEF burial, Vella Lavella Island, F-255-1/2-WH; page 51, Speed the Victory,

EPH-F-ODEA-1940/60-04; How About You Victory Loan, EPH-F-ODEA-1940/60-15; Aid for Britain National Committee: Every worker who plays his part ... helps food production ... helps Britain!" [1947–1949], Eph-D-INTERNATIONAL-1947-01; page 52, Prisoners of war working on Somes Island, 1/2-091241; F; Lantern lecture, "The ghastly horrors of war" will be delivered by Mr Robert Semple at Municipal Concert Hall, Christchurch on Sunday May 13, 7.30 p.m. Come in your thousands. [1934], Eph-C-PEACE-1934-01; Men of the New Zealand Home Guard, Christchurch South Battalion, marching; DA-00478; page 53, Carol Sladden and June Matthews, of the Women's Land Service, helping farmer Bob McKenzie to saw manuka firewood; 1/4-000736; F; Women! over 17 years of age. For a healthy, vital war job, join the Women's Land Service; Eph-C-WOMEN-1942-01; Ford Motor Company of New Zealand Limited :Wanted; 200 more women and girls for Munitions work. This is your opportunity to back up New Zealand's gallant fighting men. 1944; Eph-B-WAR-WII-19; War Work, PAColl-0783-2-0435; page 54, Apirana Turupa Ngata leading a haka at the 1940 centennial celebrations, Waitangi, MNZ-2746-1/2; F; page 55, The fun of the fair, Eph-E-EXHIBITION-1939-01; page 57, Return of the Maori Battalion, 1/4-001663; F; page 59, New Zealand. Department of Health :Clean your teeth for dental health. [1950s], Eph-C-DENTAL-HEALTH-1950s-01; New Zealand. Department of Health: Chew these foods for clean teeth. [1950s]. Eph-C-DENTAL-HEALTH-1950s-02; page 70, Ball, Murray :Okay, step forward any lyin' commy who says that the fact that I support the South African apartheid system and am also minister of police has anything to do with the present situation in this country. [1981]; A-323-060; page 73, Scott, Thomas 1947–:Halt the tour! The tour must be stopped!! Or... aah... or... um... because... otherwise... aah... um... gosh... because... well... aah... um... gulp... people like me will become utterly irrelevant... 30 July 1992; H-110-022; New Zealand Public Service Association: Fight apartheid! Stop the tour. Their sport ... our politics. Mobilise – July 3rd. Assemble 6.30 pm Marion Street / published by Wellington Sections PSA [1981], Eph-C-RACIAL-1981-03; page 81, Tremain, Garrick 1941–:At last!... Somebody to blame! *Otago Daily Times*, 31 August 2000, H-619-023; page 85, Lloyd, Trevor 1863-1937 :Kiwi; I think I would look better without it. *Dominion.* [1907?], C-109-023; page 87, Vote Communist; more community centres, more gas, more transit housing, improved parking facilities, more playing fields, better transport facilities. [ca 1944], Eph-D-ROTH-Communist-1944-02; page 90, Clark, Laurence, 1949–: I'm afraid the reports are not looking good. Arms Industry – Kampuchea; Afghanistan; The Gulf. New Zealand Herald, 16 August 1988, A-289-059; page 93, Evans, Malcolm 1947–:I'm concerned at the difference between what we and the Aussies get for being here! *New Zealand Herald*, 2 August 2000, H-643-007; Clark, Laurence, 1949–:Hang on! Wait for me! *New Zealand Herald*, 4 December 1990, H-189-001; page 94, Sid Holland and Keith Holyoake, August 1957, 1/2-177291; page 95, F; Minhinnick, Gordon (Sir), 1902–1992 :Better not interfere, old boy – he might lose his temper! Malaysia. 7 January 1964, E-549-q-13-004; page 96, Bromhead, Peter, 1933–:ANZUS Security Blanket. 9 November 1982. Everywhere I see Russians! Millions of them! Pouring into the Pacific! Armed to the teeth! I think I'm going to have to sell you a new security blanket to cope. 9 November 1982, A-305-165; page 102, The Queen of Tonga inspecting her soldiers, Tonga; 1/2-082384; F; page 111, Heath, Eric Walmsley, 1923–:You certain all this can prevent a nuclear war? DEAD CERTAIN! [9 May 1983], B-144-020; page 112, Brockie, Bob, 1932–:U.S. Nuclear policy. Fizzz. Those asshole New Zealanders have shoved a potato up our exhaust pipe. [*National Business Review*, 1984], A-317-004; page 113, Scott, Tom:Cafe ANZUS. Get outa here ya free-loader!! Todays special. Fission chips. I wasn't hungry anyway... 5 July 1986, A-312-4-001; page 117, Heath, Eric Walmsley, 1923–:New Zealand 1985. Endangered species stamps to be issued in April. $1. 1985, H-309-001; Brockie, Bob: Market forces and the art of bicycle maintenance. *National Business Review* 29 January 1993, A-296-009; page 118, Elizabeth Reid McCombs, 1/2-150372; F; Mabel Bowden Howard, 1/2-065969; F; page 119, Cooking class at the Christchurch Technical College, 1/1-004105; G; A group of students, all boys, with their tutor during an engineering class at Wanganui Technical College, 1/1-016012; Lady Plunket, 1/1-014571; Frederic Truby King, 1/2-C-005754; page 120, Women tramways employees working in Wellington, F-115784-1/2; page 121, Council for Equal Pay and Opportunity: Equal pay for equal work. A lower rate for the same or similar work is ... a threat for men workers ... an injustice for women workers ... a boon for employers. 1961, Eph-A-WOMEN-1961-0

Archives New Zealand for page 60, NZ Maori Women's Welfare League Conference. Mrs W. Cooper, Dominion President M.W.W.L, photographer T. Ransfield, 1953 (ATL reference – 1/2-040176-F), Communicate New Zealand, Series 6401.

The Dominion Post Collection, Alexander Turnbull Library, Wellington for page 34, Te Arikinui Dame Te Atairangikaahu, EP/1974/0627/26; page 58, Black Power members at gang's convention in Wellington (photographer Ross Giblin), EP/1991/0881/18; page 63, Maori land marchers leaving Parliament grounds for the East Cape, EP/1975/4573/17; page 67, Maori land march passing through Awapuni, EP/1975/4202/8a; page 68, Bastion Point protesters at Parliament, Wellington, EP/1977/2494/7A; page 71, Robert David Muldoon, F-22486-1/4; page 75, Waitangi day protesters, EP-Ethics-Waitangi Day and Treaty of Watangi; page 76, Winstone Peters (photographer John Nicholson), EP/1989/1300/11a; page 110, Members of Campaign Against Nuclear Warships in Wellington Harbour, EP/1976/2841/26a; page 116, Prime Minister David Lange hosting Radio Windy breakfast show, EP/1985/4912/9.

United States National Archives and Records Administration for the photographs on pages 18 (battlefield), 45 (Nazis), 47 (Rommel), 86, 89, 91, 99, 100 (SEATO), 107.

The Hocken Library, University of Otago, Dunedin for the posters on page 74, 'Is this the life for you?' (8998855); 'Mobilise to stop the tour' (8909928); page 77, 'Protest Waitangi' (8607741); '1990 – Who's Country, Who's Year?' (8998855).

The Waitangi Tribunal for the photograph on page 80.

New Zealand Defence Force for the photographs on page 92, Armoured Personnel Carriers and Operation Farina.

GLOSSARY

Alienation (of land) The loss of land, whether willingly through sales, or by government action such as confiscation.
Aliens People from foreign countries. For most of the 20th century this meant from other than the British Empire.
Apartheid See page 70
Assimilation See page 7

Boycott To refuse to trade, play sport or associate with someone, or a country. It is a means of applying pressure.
Bridge-building Prime Minister Muldoon's policy of continuing links with a country to try to encourage it to change their policies (see page 71).

Capitalism See page 86
Cold War See page 86
Collective security Where countries band together to support each other. An attack on one is regarded as an attack on all members.
Colony A country that is governed by another, more powerful country, as part of an empire (see also 'Decolonisation').
Communalism "Where people work together for the benefit of the whole group, rather than for themselves (see 'Individualism').
Communism See page 86
Confiscation To take something away from someone. In this topic, land was taken from some Maori after the NZ Wars of the 1860s.
Confrontation See page 7
Conscientious objectors Those who refuse to go to war on moral grounds (often, but not always, religious) (see also 'passive resistance').
Conscription The compulsory call-up of men to join the Army.
Consolidation See page 27
Containment The United States believed that to stop the spread of communism they needed to boost military forces in neighbouring non-communist countries, thus 'boxing in' or containing communism (see also 'Domino Theory').
Co-operatives See page 27

Decolonisation See page 89 (see also 'Colony').
Depression In this book it refers to a world-wide economic collapse.
Detribalisation The policy of breaking down tribal bonds so that Maori would live a more individualist, Pakeha lifestyle.
Domino Theory The United States believed that if South Vietnam fell to communist forces, neighbouring countries would be next. They compared this to a row of dominoes being knocked over.

Foreign policy See page 85
Forward defence A military strategy of placing troops in a forward position to deter enemy attacks, rather than waiting in a rearward defensive position.

Home Guard An organisation set up in wartime to help defend the country against possible invasion, usually made up of men too young or old to go to war.

Individualism Where people work to benefit themselves or their immediate family (see 'Communalism').
Integration See page 7

Kingitanga A movement begun in 1858 by Maori from the Waikato region in order to rule themselves and prevent further loss of land.

Left-wing See page 86

Mana motuhake The right to determine one's own future (see page 63). Mana Motuhake was also a political party in the 1990s.
Mangai Mouthpiece [of God] – the name given to the prophet-leader Wiremu Ratana.
Man-powered Like conscription, 'man-powering' compulsorily called up people to serve in industries considered essential to the war effort.
Maori Renaissance A term used to describe the revival of Maori culture and self-confidence from the late 1960s.
Marginalised To be left outside of the normal way of life, unable to share in the benefits that others receive.
Mau A Samoan resistance group that was opposed to New Zealand's style of rule after WWI.
Military coup An illegal seizure of power by the Army or other Armed Forces.
Morehu A 'survivor' or 'ordinary person'.

New Right An American economic policy that aimed to limit the role of government in society, by selling off state-owned property and reducing welfare.

Passive resistance Refusing to obey the law, but doing so in a non-violent way.

Rangatiratanga Traditional chiefly authority (see page 63).
Rogernomics An economic policy introduced by Finance Minister Roger Douglas from 1984 (see 'Social Security/Welfare' and 'New Right').

Segregation See page 7
Social Security/Welfare Economic assistance given to people as part of government policy, particularly in the areas of health, housing and education.
Sovereignty The right of a government to make the laws and enforce them.
State-owned Enterprises See page 76

Urbanisation The movement of people from rural areas (the countryside) into urban areas (cities).

Welfare State See 'Social Security/Welfare'